DERBY PORCELAIN

The Golden Years 1750–1770

DERBY PORCELAIN

The Golden Years 1750–1770

Dennis G. Rice

David & Charles
Newton Abbot   London

Hippocrene Books Inc
New York

British Library Cataloguing in Publication Data

Rice, Dennis G.
  Derby porcelain.
  1. Derby porcelain
  I. Title
  738.2′7   NK4399.D4

  ISBN 0-7153-8249-7 (Great Britain)
  ISBN 0-88254-754-2 (United States)

Filmset and printed in Great Britain
by BAS Printers Limited, Over Wallop, Hampshire
for David & Charles (Publishers) Limited
Brunel House   Newton Abbot   Devon

CONTENTS

PREFACE

The history of the Derby factory is a success story. It lasted for almost a century, outliving every other English factory save Worcester. But its very success has served to prevent its products being given the intensive study that they deserve. For every monograph on the factory has attempted to encompass the entire range of what was made at Derby from the factory's beginning to its demise. The result has necessarily been a somewhat sketchy and superficial treatment of all the many facets of this remarkable concern. The factory's output naturally divides itself into three periods—1750–70, 1771–99 and 1800–48—and some might say that each of these periods could be usefully subdivided still further. It is the purpose of this book to discuss the first period alone, the period which in my view represents the golden years of the factory, when its creative impulse was at its highest and when some of the items it turned out made the rare transition from mere craft to art and were never to be surpassed by anything produced at any other English factory.

The opportunity has been taken to make a preliminary study of what is perhaps the most intriguing unsolved problem in English ceramics, namely the provenance of a remarkable group of figures—they can be conveniently called the 'Girl-on-a-horse' factory figures—traditionally attributed to Derby but whose place of origin in all probability lies elsewhere.

It is a sad thing that, notwithstanding the researches over the years of many scholars, collectors and enthusiasts, so much of the history and everyday working of the factory still remains a mystery to us. Even conclusions which are generally accepted are often established solely on the balance of probability, not beyond all reasonable doubt. They would satisfy only a civil, not a criminal, court. In this book I have gone further and postulated views which are merely speculative. The justification of this perhaps questionable course is that solutions, not inherently improbable, can at least be suggested which, it is hoped, the subsequent researches of others may with concrete evidence either confirm or reject.

I
THE ORIGIN AND EARLY HISTORY
OF THE FACTORY

The Derby china factory and the name of the first William Duesbury are and ever will be linked together. However, it was not William Duesbury who commenced the manufacture of porcelain in the town of Derby. That distinction falls to another, who on the evidence available to us was probably Andrew Planché. Duesbury did not enter the field until 1756. Not a great deal is known of his activities before then, but it is fitting that this book should start with a brief reference to the early career of one who was to bring porcelain production at Derby to such a dominant position.

William Duesbury's early life

William Duesbury was born on 7 September 1725,[1] presumably in Longton, Staffordshire. By the age of seventeen he was in London. For his *London Account Book* contains fifteen entries for the year 1742. These entries relate to cash received (ranging from 14s 6d to £2 2s 0d) normally separated by seven days, suggesting the receipt of wages,[2] and it may be that at this time Duesbury was learning the trade of enameller, possibly under the tuition of Thomas Hughes of Clerkenwell.[3] The wages earned by Duesbury, if that was what the entries relate to, seem very high. William Billingsley, under the terms of his five-year apprenticeship entered into on 26 September 1774, when he was probably sixteen, was only paid 5s (25p) a week. The unknown author of *A Short Tour in the Midland Counties of England Performed in the Summer of 1772* (published in 1775) refers to several painters at Derby earning 'a guinea and a half per week'. It would seem that at the early age of seventeen Duesbury displayed an extra-ordinary talent, harbinger of future distinction.

Be that as it may, by late 1750 it is clear from this same *London Account Book* (covering the period from 22 November 1750 to August 1753[4]) that Duesbury had established himself in London as an independent porcelain enameller. At some date unknown he married Sarah James of Shrewsbury, who was a year older than himself. According to Jewitt,[5] their eldest son was 'born in London in 1752 and died there in infancy'. More important, according to this same source, their second child, Mary, was 'born in London in 1753, but baptised at St. Alkmund's, Derby'. The inference to be drawn from this must be that Duesbury left London in 1753 and proceeded immediately to Derby. His departure—confirmed by the absence of any entry in the *London Account Book* after August 1753—may have been encouraged by a growing reluctance on the part of the major manufacturers to make available porcelain in the white for decoration. They were beginning to concentrate on training their own artists. Thus, in *Aris's Birmingham Gazette* for 5 November 1753 there appears the following advertisement:

This is to give Notice to all Painters in the Blue and White Potting Way and Enamellers on China-ware, that by applying at the Counting House at the China-Works near Bow, they may meet with Employment and proper Encouragement, according to their Merit; Likewise Painters brought up in the Snuff-Box Way, Japanning, Fan-painting etc, may have Opportunities of Trial; wherein, if they succeed, they shall have due Encouragement.

N.B.—At the same House, a Person is wanted who can model small Figures in Clay neatly.

Duesbury may have taken the view that for the independent decorator time was running out.

However, it would seem that, with reference to his daughter Mary's christening, Jewitt did not consult the actual baptismal records of St Alkmund's, but relied instead on a family Bible—he referred in connection with William Duesbury to 'entries in the family Bible'[6]—which on this point was inaccurate. For there are no entries in the baptismal register of St Alkmund's for the name Duesbury during the period from August 1753 to October 1754. Far more important, the researches of Major W. H. Tapp[7] have shown that Mary Duesbury (born on 6 February 1753) was baptised on 18 February 1753 at St James's, Westminster (ie St James's, Piccadilly), incidentally the most fashionable church in London in the early eighteenth century. (His researches also show that the first child, William, was in fact born on 18 December 1751, and likewise baptised at St James's, Westminster, on 5 January 1752.) Manifestly, then, there is no case for Duesbury's ever having gone to Derby in 1753.

In any event, even if he had gone to Derby in late 1753, he could not have remained there after October 1754, for William and Sarah's third child Anne was, according to Jewitt,[8] 'born at Longton October 3 1754'. Exactly when he arrived at Longton is unknown, but he was certainly still there in September 1755, for he is described as being of Longton Hall in a deed dated 27 September 1755, by which his father (a currier by trade who lived at Cannock in Staffordshire), also called William, assigned to him his entire estate in return for an undertaking to maintain him for the rest of his life, an undertaking which the son faithfully honoured until the father's death in 1768. Bemrose[9] quotes a letter dated August 1870 that he had received from Miss Sarah Duesbury (the granddaughter of the first William Duesbury) which refers to this deed. It reads as follows:

Amongst the old papers was a deed of gift from a *former* Wm. Duesbury, a worthy leather seller of Cannock (called Cank) in Staffordshire of all he possessed, on condition of being kept in all things by his son the remainder of his days. Which was done [manifestly this refers, not to the place where the deed was executed, but to where the undertaking was carried out] in the cottage which stood on the ground before the building of the big house. An old friend of mine Mr Horrocks, a lawyer remembered being taken to eat cake and drink wine the day of King George IIIrd's coronation at the cottage. This is an undoubted fact, and further my grandfather lived some time at Longton Hall, Staffordshire before settling in Derby.

Bemrose points out that the 'big house' was the place adjacent to the Nottingham Road factory where Duesbury himself lived. It would seem that this house could not have been built until after 22 September 1761, and possibly not until after Duesbury the elder's death.

Traditionally it has been assumed that whilst at Longton Duesbury worked at or for the porcelain factory there and in the process discovered a great deal about the technical difficulties involved in the manufacture of porcelain. This is now confirmed by an item 'Mr Duesbury for work' appearing in a schedule of debts due to workmen and others appended to an agreement dated 1 September 1755 made between the proprietors.[10]

It would seem from the existence of an unexecuted partnership agreement (referred to later) bearing the date 1 January 1756, where admittedly Duesbury is still described as being of 'Longton', that Duesbury in fact came to Derby sometime in 1756, and this conclusion is according to Jewitt[11] confirmed by 'entries in the family Bible'. Further, in a recital contained in a deed dated 1 August 1780 (mentioned by Bemrose in his *Bow, Chelsea and Derby Porcelain* at p. 109) there is a reference to five tenements having been conveyed to the banker John Heath on 19 April 1756 and these tenements are described as having been 'converted into and then continued to be Workshops used and employed by the Sd W. Duesbury & Co. as such in making of China'. The implication is that Duesbury was working in Derby in 1756 and that sometime after 19 April 1756 Duesbury was responsible for a considerable enlargement of the factory. There is a confirmatory hint of this (albeit the date is clearly wrong) in the statement attributed to Locker:[12] 'Mr Duesbury commenced building a manufactory over St. Mary's Bridge, which was finished in 1751, and he made porcelain there in the same year.'

It was from 1756 onwards that Duesbury undertook the manufacture of porcelain in Derby. But for several years before his arrival porcelain had been produced in Derby, including some of the finest pieces ever to be manufactured in that town.

Date of the factory's origin

The origin of the factory taken over by Duesbury in 1756 (commonly known as 'the old Nottingham Road Factory' close to St Mary's Bridge) is to a large extent wrapped in obscurity. The exact date on which porcelain manufacture commenced there is not known. Certainly production had somewhere at least in Derby commenced by 1750, and it may be that it in fact started as early as 1748. The early history of porcelain manufacture in Derby or more particularly the history of Duesbury's factory can conveniently be considered under specific years.

1748–50

Pilkington in his *View of the Present State of Derbyshire* published in 1789 says, 'About forty years ago the manufacture of porcelain was begun by the late Mr Duesbury. . .' According to him, then, the commencement date of the factory's activities was about 1749. His reference to Duesbury as the founder is manifestly untrue, but it does not follow from this that Pilkington was also inaccurate about the date of the factory's origin. It must in particular be remembered that, at the time he was writing, William Duesbury's son, also called William, was running the business and the name Duesbury and the Derby factory were in the public mind virtually indissolubly linked. It is an understandable frailty of human nature for someone whose father has acquired a small existing business and has developed and expan-

ded it to the status of a national institution to do nothing to publicise the contribution of his father's predecessor. Doubtless at the time Pilkington was writing, the name of Duesbury's predecessor had long since been forgotten by persons unconnected with the factory, and William Duesbury the second would have done nothing to draw it to Pilkington's attention. Had it not been for the researches of Jewitt and his discovery of the unexecuted partnership agreement referred to at page 17 it is doubtful whether the name of the person to whom the evidence points as founder would ever have been known to us.

The factory's commencement date is confirmed by William Hutton, who in his *History of Derby* published in 1791 says, 'Porcelain began about the year 1750. . .' and, for what it is worth, by entries in Lysons' *Derbyshire* of 1817 and the Manchester *Commercial Directory* for 1818, 1819 and 1820.

More specific identification with the year 1750 is, however, to be found in the existence in the Victoria and Albert Museum of a white cream jug 89mm ($3\frac{1}{2}$in) high with strawberries and leaves around the base (*Pl. 36*). For the mark on the base comprises a 'D' and the date 1750. Two other such cream jugs are known. One is in the British Museum and has the initial 'D' alone incised on it, whilst the other, now believed to be at Colonial Williamsburgh, USA, has the word 'Derby' incised under its base. Manifestly the 'D' on the example in the Victoria and Albert Museum must stand for 'Derby' and the addition of the date 1750 establishes that china manufacture was being undertaken at least by that early date. Arthur Lane has pointed out in his *English Porcelain Figures of the Eighteenth Century*[13] that flowers in relief on the cream jugs are similar to those on the larger Derby version of the actress Kitty Clive.[14]

Of course, the mere fact that a Derby cream jug has been discovered bearing the date 1750 does not in itself mean that manufacture did not begin *before* that date. Moreover, the three white cream jugs, whilst still having their origin in Derby, could conceivably have emanated from some source other than the factory eventually taken over by Duesbury.[15] The case for suggesting that the true commencement date was prior to 1750 is really dependent on a letter from Josiah Wedgwood to Bentley written on New Year's Day 1775 and now preserved at Keele University. Wedgwood states that in the course of his writing he was interrupted,

by a man from the Derby China works, who wants to be hired—he is a Derby man, has a wife and family there and has worked at the factory 28 years. His name is Holmes—I rather suspect he is sent to learn something from us—However I have learnt from him that they have been making "h^{ds}" for Smith, and have many more to make, I must break off here to save the post—Shall finish my L^t tomorrow & am ever yours.

J. WEDGWOOD

Many happy returns of the Season attend you.

Now, if Wedgwood correctly records what he was told and if Holmes—he is generally assumed to have been George Holmes—was accurate in his claim to have worked at Derby for twenty-eight years, the necessary inference must be that manufacture commenced during the course of 1747. There would appear to be no reason for Holmes's exaggerating the length of his employment. Sometimes there is a temptation to round an odd figure upwards—eg someone who has worked for an employer for (say) twenty-three years might be tempted to claim, for greater effect, to have seen twenty-five years' service—but if anything in the present case the selection of twenty-eight years rather than (say) thirty years suggests a scrupulous regard for accuracy. It is perhaps not without significance that George Holmes was a modeller or repairer; there is a figure formerly in the Leverhulme Collection inscribed on the base 'George Holmes did this figer [sic] 1765'.[16] A craftsman of this kind, as distinct from a decorator (although, according to the Clerkenwell rate-books,[17] Holmes was also an enameller), would be required at the very commencement of a factory's life.

Further support for the view that the factory was founded in late 1747 or early 1748 rather than 1750 can be derived from the following analysis. If Andrew Planché was in fact the originator of

china manufacture at Derby, a point which will be discussed later,[18] his career, such as we know of it, is consistent with his having been in Derby in late 1747 or early 1748. His apprenticeship to a jeweller, presumably completed, ended in July 1747, and he married Sarah Stone at St Pancras Church on 28 September 1747. His son Paul was baptised at St Alkmund's Church, Derby, on 21 September 1751, so that he arrived in Derby sometime between 28 September 1747 and 21 September 1751. As a further son William was baptised at the same church on 3 July 1756 he can safely be regarded as still being at Derby at that time. (There are other entries in 1754 in the register relating to his children.) Now, Jewitt says in his *Ceramic Art in Great Britain*[19] that Planché remained in Derby for at least eight years. As will be shown later, it is unlikely that Planché remained in Derby much after July 1756, and if Jewitt is right—unfortunately he gives no reasons for his supposition, so that we are in no position to test its plausibility—then Planché arrived at Derby in 1748. We would expect him to start work at once, and accordingly it may be that, strictly speaking, production began in 1748 rather than 1750. However, even if this is so, it is difficult to see how the first year or two could have been other than largely experimental. It is difficult to envisage any significant production before about 1750, and this is perhaps the more realistic date to attribute to the proper commencement of porcelain production at Derby. The somewhat primitive cream jugs fit in well with this date.

1751–2

Proof that the china factory taken over by Duesbury existed at Christmas Eve 1752, giving rise to a natural inference that it had by that date been established for some while and therefore had an origin around 1750, can be found in a report contained in the *Derby Mercury* of 26 January 1753, which reads as follows:

We hear that yesterday morning the body of a man who appeared to have lain a considerable time in the water, was taken out of the river near Borrowash [about three miles below Derby on the River Derwent]. 'Tis said he was one of the workmen belonging to the China Works near Mary Bridge, and he had been missing since Christmas Eve, at which time the Waters being much out 'tis thought he fell in accidentally near the said Bridge and was drowned.

It is to be noted that the location of the factory 'near Mary Bridge' accords with the known site of the Duesbury factory. It is, incidentally, nowhere near the Cockpit Hill pottery.

1753

Proof of the continuance of the factory in 1753 is to be found in William Duesbury's *London Account Book* (22 November 1750 to August 1753). For on certain pages he makes specific references to Derby pieces sent to him in the white for decoration. Duesbury does not specifically identify them with the factory 'near Mary Bridge', but unless porcelain was produced elsewhere in Derby[20] the connection is inevitable.

[*page 47*] Mr Morgan

Joun 6 [1753]	1 Darbeyshire seson	1–0
August	3 pr of Darbishire sesons	
		0–6–0
21	2 pr of Dansers Darby figars	
		0–6–0

[*page 71*] Mr Proctor

August 18	1 pr of Dansars Darbey figars	
		0–3–0
[?1753] 20	1 pr of Large Darbey figars	
		0–4–6
	7 pr of Small Single Dº	0–10–6
	1 pr of Small Dº	0–1–6
	1 Dº for a woch [watch]	0–1–6

[*page 78*] Mr Foy

May 5 [1753]	1 pr of Darbey figars large	
	(to enamell)	0–8–0

With reference to the last item no sum is stated in the monograph of the English Porcelain Circle, presumably because in the opinion of the editor the relevant manuscript entry was illegible. However, Bemrose, to whom the account book originally belonged, states in his *Bow, Chelsea and Derby Porcelain*[21] that the cost was eight shillings.

It should also be mentioned that there are references to 'Staggs' and 'Boors' which may be Derby products. Certainly it is very likely to be so in the case of the 'Boors'.

1754

That the factory continued in 1754 is borne out by the registers of St Werbergh's Church, Derby. For they record the marriage on 3 June 1754 of William Whitehall 'labourer in the China House'.

1755
Sale notices

In June 1756 a sale took place at 54 Richmond Wells in Surrey. It was first cited by Edward Hyam in his *The Early Period of Derby Porcelain* (1926) and the relevant part of the notice reads as follows:

the greatest variety of the Derby Porcelain, in Figures, Jars, Candlesticks, Sauceboats, Lettices, Leaves, Roses and several curious Pieces for Desserts, finely enamelled in Dresden flowers, reckoned by Judges who have been purchasers to excel, if not exceed, anything of the Kind in England.

Now, it is inconceivable that a factory which had been in existence for less than six months would have reached the degree of sophistication revealed by the above sale particulars. The factory responsible must have been operative at least for some eighteen months or so. In other words, porcelain must have been produced throughout 1755, and the place of manufacture must have been the premises taken over by Duesbury. Incidentally, sales of Derby items similar to those enumerated above took place in December 1756 and in 1757.[22]

Property advertisement

In the *Derby Mercury* for 30 July 1756 there appeared the following advertisement:

TO BE SOLD, a freehold estate consisting of seven houses and a barn, situated all together near St. Mary's Bridge, which are now occupied by Mr Heath and Company in the China

Manufactory and let at £10 per annum exclusive of all taxes. For further particulars enquire of Charles Shepherdson at Kings Newton, or of Mr Mills at the Green Dragon, Derby.

Apparently the property did not sell because it was advertised again for sale on 25 October 1756, this time by public auction. It is clear from the recitals in a deed dated 1 August 1780 that the property in question was conveyed on 19 November 1756 to John Heath. The vendors were Charles Shepherdson and others. Clearly Heath purchased the property as a sitting tenant. With the reference to its location near 'St Mary's Bridge', this must be the same china works mentioned in the drowning accident of 26 January 1753. If the property was still being used as a china factory in mid 1756, it is difficult to imagine it had had any other use since Christmas Eve 1752. The implication must be that porcelain had been made there during the intervening years, including, of course, 1755. Probably also Heath and Company had been the tenant throughout, in which event John Heath, the banker, might be expected to have financed the venture during the period before 1756.

Accordingly, it follows from what has been said above that porcelain was manufactured at Derby before the arrival of Duesbury in 1756 and that the commencement at least on a commercial scale was around 1750. Moreover, it was made at the factory 'near St Mary's Bridge'.

Andrew Planché

Granted that porcelain manufacture was carried on near St Mary's Bridge during the period from 1750 to 1755, the next question to suggest itself is who was responsible for such manufacture. A clue is to be found in certain observations made by Samuel Keys senior, who was apprenticed to William Duesbury the first in 1785, and William Locker, who started at the factory in 1809. Samuel Keys appears at the request of different people to have written several different accounts of the early history of porcelain production at Derby. Furthermore, some of the accounts he seems to have copied. Thus, Jewitt in his *Ceramic Art in Great Britain*[23] speaks of Samuel Keys having drawn up 'a M.S. account of the old

Derby China Works, from memory, in 1837, of which he seems to have made two or three copies; one of these is in my own possession'. Two versions are known. One is reproduced in Appendix X of F. Brayshaw Gilhespie's *Derby Porcelain* and the other dated 21 June 1837 in Alfred Wallis and Wm Bemrose's monograph on *The Pottery and Porcelain of Derbyshire* (and more recently in John Twitchett's *Derby Porcelain*). They are completely different in form, but as regards the origin of porcelain production at Derby, they are in respect of all material matters substantially the same. The relevant passage from the statement dated 21 June 1837 reads as follows:

China was first made in Derby I believe by a man in a very humble way (but his name I cannot recollect). He resided in Lodge Lane in some old premises up a yard by the (now Brown Bear) public house. When he first began, he fired his articles in a small pipe kiln very near, till he had constructed a small kiln in a fireplace in the old premises he lived in. He had only small animals and birds, laying-down lambs, etc. Mr William Duesbury the first, got his knowledge firstly from that man and improved on it. I never knew much of Mr Duesbury's origin, but believe he came from Walsall, or the neighbourhood.

Mr Duesbury was on friendly terms with Mr Heath, the banker and the proprietor of Pot Works on Cockpit-Hill, and which I well remember.

Mr Duesbury had improved on his small experience with small china toy making, and Mr Heath assisted him in the most liberal and friendly manner, with money and other means to carry on, which he did with credit to himself and benefit to others.

The other version mentions that Keys believed the man who lived in Lodge Lane to be a foreigner and states that the pipe-kiln belonged to a man named Woodward. In neither account does Keys give a specific date for the commencement of porcelain production. Jewitt, however, presumably basing his conclusion on a manuscript account in his possession drawn up in 1837 by Keys from memory, asserts[24] a commencement date of '1750, perhaps a little earlier', 'about a year or so before the works at Worcester were established'.

A further account of the origin of porcelain manufacture in Derby is contained in Chaffers' *Marks and Monograms on Pottery and Porcelain*,[25] but it is attributed not to Keys, but to Locker, who first went to work at the Derby factory in 1809 as a clerk and warehouseman. (Locker, 1797–1859, remained at the factory as clerk until its close in 1848, and thereafter was one of the founders of the new factory in King Street.) It reads as follows:

About 1745, a man, said to be a foreigner, in very poor circumstances, living in Lodge Lane, made small articles in china, such as birds, cats, dogs, sheep and other small ornamental toys, which he fired at a kiln in the neighbourhood belonging to a pipe-maker named Woodward. Mr Duesbury frequently visited this image maker and took great interest in his small manufactory, and becoming desirous of improving the art, he engaged his services on his own account, and with the assistance of Mr Heath, at that time considered a man of large property, he soon added considerably to his stock of useful and ornamental articles.

Apart from giving a commencement date of 'about 1745' the account does not materially differ from the combined effect of the two versions given by Samuel Keys. Indeed, the possibility suggests itself that the last passage cited was wrongly attributed by Chaffers to Locker, and that it was really part of the further statement written by Keys in the possession of Chaffers. The two statements from Keys and Locker respectively are said by Chaffers to have been made about 1855—but Keys died in 1850. In any event, none of the accounts attempts to identify the 'man . . . in very poor circumstances living in Lodge Lane' who was said to be a foreigner.

In his *Bow, Chelsea and Derby Porcelain* William

Bemrose claimed[26] to have discovered the oven-kiln in Lodge Lane belonging to Woodward. However, in an article in *The Connoisseur*[27] F. Williamson demonstrated beyond doubt that that particular oven was made of nineteenth-century bricks and that the eighteenth-century building in which it was located had been erected shortly after 1795 when the land whereon it was built had been sold by the Corporation of Derby. However, the failure of Bemrose to identify the oven belonging to Woodward does not necessarily mean that there never was such an oven. It is to be noted that in various leases and in the poll books from 1748 to 1775 there appears the name of another pipe manufacturer, Benjamin Strong, of Golden Ball Yard, Willow Row (Willow Row connects with Lodge Lane).

As regards the 'small kiln in a fireplace in the old premises ['the man . . . in very poor circumstances'] lived in', this Bemrose did not in his book attempt to identify. He contented himself with saying:[28] 'The late John Keys, a descendent of Samuel Keys . . . informed us that he remembered seeing Planché's kiln, some years ago, in an out-building in Lodge Lane, and that the building was only demolished about 1890.' Clearly Bemrose was unable to attempt an identification because by the time the information came to him the premises in question had been demolished. Whether John Keys was correct in what he said will now never be known.

It must be conceded that the written statements of Keys and, for that matter, that of Locker, were made about a century after the events to which they relate, and were dependent on hearsay. For, as stated above, Keys did not come to the Derby factory as an apprentice until 1785 and Locker did not start working there till 1809. Admittedly, Locker seems to have had in his custody whatever old records the factory possessed and it might be thought from this that he had access to reliable information. However, as appears from the following statement attributed to him by Chaffers,[29] to a large extent this was not the case.

It was a remarkable thing, that the old hands could never furnish any precise data, about the Derby factory, prior to 1751; not even Keys who was an apprentice to the first Mr Duesbury, as far back as 1785; I have had many conversations with Miss Duesbury, who is the daughter of the second Mr Duesbury, and used to sell china at the warehouse over St. Mary's Bridge, about the time Isaac Farnsworth was the leading man for her father, in the figure trade; but I could glean nothing, for she and other branches of the family, when they were at fault for data, always applied to me, as I was the person employed to look over all the old documents, when the Derby factory unfortunately got into Chancery, and everything relating to the figure trade was required by the Chancellor, in order to ascertain the value of the models, for that was the bone of contention between the second Mr Duesbury and Mr Kean, so that the historical part was destroyed, but I have no doubt in my own mind that china was made at Derby some 5 or 6 years before Worcester; I however did not take any particular notice of dates, for I did not like the job of looking over books and papers above one hundred years old; they were very dirty and injured my clothes very much.

It has to be conceded that in view of the essentially hearsay nature of their evidence, what Keys and Locker record with reference to the origin of porcelain manufacture in Derby may be nothing more than myth.

However, there is an inherent plausibility in what they do say. The 'man . . . in very poor circumstances', who would be without financial backing, would initially be dependent on the good offices of someone who was prepared to make available to him facilities for the conduct of his original experiments. Moreover, when he acquired sufficient resources, he would be expected to have built for himself some form of primitive oven. It is also reasonable to suppose that he would have limited his ambition to the production of such modest items as small dogs, cats and other animals. He would not have been in a position to call on the facilities of a well-established undertaking such as the Cockpit Hill pottery, which doubtless wanted all its kilns for current commercial production, and would not welcome the unremunerative intrusions of a total stranger.

Now, it could be the case that the 'man . . . in very poor circumstances' was sufficiently successful in his modest beginnings to attract after a while the financial support of John Heath, the banker. It is known that the latter was the tenant of the original St Mary's Bridge factory from before 1756. He could well have made this accommodation available to the 'man . . . in very poor circumstances' and in addition have given him financial backing.

As will be shown later,[30] the products turned out in the period from about 1750 to 1755 were of outstanding quality, often quite large in size—nothing like the small animals and toys referred to by Keys and Locker. It may be the case, then, that the accounts given by Keys and Locker are basically correct as to the earliest origin of porcelain production in Derby, and that they are deficient only in as much as they fail to record the subsequent period from about 1750 to 1755 when ironically the porcelain produced at Derby reached its high water mark of artistic excellence. The omission is, of course, serious but, in view of the dominant position of the Duesbury family at the time the relevant statements were made, understandable.

But who was the 'man . . . in very poor circumstances'? It was not until January 1862 that Jewitt in the *Art Journal* conjectured that the person referred to was Andrew Planché. The basis for this conjecture is the existence of a draft or copy partnership agreement which Jewitt discovered. It is one of the few documents in the possession of that indefatigable researcher to have survived his death—presumably his executors swept away all the papers he had accumulated throughout his working life and the only surviving documents are those which got secreted in hidden recesses of his desk—and it now reposes in the library of the Victoria and Albert Museum. The commencement of the agreement, which is the relevant part for our purposes, reads as follows:

ARTICLES OF AGREEMENT between John Heath of Derby in the County of Derby Gentleman Andrew Planché of ye same place China Maker and Wm Duesberry of Longton in ye county of Stafford, Enamellor. Made and enter'd into in the 1st Jany 1756.

Now, whether or not the agreement was ever engrossed and signed, there is no reason to doubt the statements contained therein. John Heath, who was a banker, a partner in the Cockpit Hill pottery business and later Mayor of Derby, and William Duesberry (normally spelt Duesbury), who was apparently still at Longton throughout 1755, undoubtedly existed. So too did Andrew Planché and just as it cannot be disputed that at the relevant time John Heath and William Duesbury could properly be styled 'gentleman' and 'enamellor' respectively, so too there is no reason to doubt the accuracy of the description applied to Andrew Planché of 'China Maker'. If, then, Andrew Planché had been manufacturing porcelain prior to 1 January 1756, it is difficult to avoid the conclusion that it was Andrew Planché who was responsible for the porcelain production carried out at the factory near St Mary's Bridge during the period from 1750 to 1755. Moreover, if the early ventures into porcelain manufacture in Lodge Lane recited by Keys and Locker did in fact take place, it is likewise difficult to avoid concluding that the man responsible was also Andrew Planché. Conceivably the founder of the factory near St Mary's Bridge and the 'man . . . in very poor circumstances living in Lodge Lane' could be different persons, but on balance it seems highly unlikely.

Indeed, the only alternative candidate ever suggested for the position of the 'man . . . in very poor circumstances' is Thomas Briand, who in February 1743 demonstrated to the Royal Society[31] 'a fine white ware made here by himself from native materials of our own country, which appeared in all respects as good as any of the finest porcelane or china ware. . .' Major W. H. Tapp argued[32] that Thomas Briand, like Planché a Frenchman of Huguenot origin, could have gone to Derby sometime after 1743 and commenced the manufacture of

porcelain in that town. He could have been joined by Planché in late 1747 or early 1748.

However, as Major Tapp himself concedes, the case for Thomas Briand's ever having any connection with Derby is really dependent upon a statement by Hugh Owen in his *Two Centuries of Ceramic Art in Bristol* (1873)[33] that there was inscribed on a label attached to the back of a biscuit plaque made at Champion's Bristol factory and bearing the initials 'GG' the following: 'Specimen of Bristol china modeled [*sic*] by Thomas Briand of Derby 1777'. But, granted that this particular inscription was more or less contemporary with the plaque, manifestly the reference cannot be to the Thomas Briand who gave the demonstration to the Royal Society. For the Stoke-on-Trent parish registers on 26 February 1747 record his burial as a pauper in Lane Delph.

Thomas Briand's activities in the preceding year are known to us. For a document unearthed by Arnold Mountford and reproduced in an article by him[34] shows that a twenty-one-year partnership was entered into on 5 February 1746 between Thomas Briand 'of Lane Delph etc. Painter' and Joseph Farmer—who, as is clear from other documents, was a pottery manufacturer. That the Thomas Briand there referred to was the Thomas Briand who appeared before the Royal Society is put beyond any doubt by the first covenant of that document. For it recites that 'T.B. had found out ye art of making a beautiful Earthenware little inferior to Porcelain or China Ware. . . . And the Sd T.B. Covenants to lay open and discover all by art method secret and invention to ye Sd J. Ff etc. before 25 March then next.'

Now, it so happened that the above document contained a further provision that in the event of the death of either partner the deceased's wife should be taken into the partnership. Owing to the premature death of Thomas Briand this provision was brought into operation and led to conflict. John Wedgwood and Thomas Heath attempted to reconcile the partners and in the course of their endeavours an interesting letter dated 24 September 1748 was written to John Wedgwood by John Weatherby and John Crowther, the proprietors of the Bow factory, which contains the following passage:

If you remember we told you in few words that we had nothing good to say of the deceased Briand (nor of his wife) that we had been greatly deceived by them, that they have from time to time made great promise to us of what they could do; and Mr Briand showed us several patterns of good china which he protested was of his making and yt he could convince us he could make the like but upon trial all his promises ended in words he never performed any one thing he proposed and it's our Opinion they knew nothing of what he pretended to know and we firmly believe the design of the deceased was only to make an advantage to himself of those he was concerned with.

Of course, we do not have Thomas Briand's side of the story, but it significant that the document of 5 February 1746 contains 'A Covt to indemnify T.B. ags any accon or suit to be commenced ags him by John Weatherby and John Crowther or either or them'. This provision in itself suggests that Thomas Briand was anticipating trouble from John Weatherby and John Crowther and was apprehensive of its outcome.

Accordingly, if the evidence is looked at as a whole, it is doubtful whether Thomas Briand ever succeeded in producing porcelain. It is also particularly significant that the document of 5 February 1746 does not refer to his formula as producing porcelain, but only 'a beautiful Earthenware little inferior to Porcelain or China Ware'.

If Thomas Briand ever went to Derby at all, there was certainly a gap between his departure and the arrival of Andrew Planché. But there is really no evidence for his having gone to Derby in the first place. An attempt was made by Major Tapp to bolster the case for Thomas Briand's presence in Derby by reference to an entry in the baptismal register of All Saints Church recording the baptism on 20 May 1745 of 'Eleanor daughter of Thomas Bryand'. However, the reading of the name Bryand is doubtful in the extreme. It would seem most probably to be Byard, which, even allowing for the spelling

eccentricities of the eighteenth century, is a long way from Briand.

Hugh Owen's reference to 'Thomas Briand of Derby' can with reasonable assurance be explained. The Thomas Briand mentioned is almost certainly the Thomas Briand who on 1 April 1771 was married to Ruth North at All Saints Church, Derby, and is described in the marriage register as 'chinaman', ie a trader in china. Presumably his skills were not limited to the sale of porcelain, but he was in his own right a flower-modeller. Now, it may be—there is no positive or direct evidence—that this Thomas Briand was the son of the Thomas Briand who appeared before the Royal Society in 1743. It is also possible that not only did he marry in Derby, but that he was also born and brought up there, in which event it is conceivable that Thomas Briand senior, assuming that paternity can be attributed to him, did stay at Derby for a period. However, there are too many hypotheses for any connection between Thomas Briand and Derby to be made out. Moreover, even if he was there sometime between 1743 and 1745, the evidence of the document of 5 February 1746 (corroborated by the letter of Weatherby and Crowther) throws great doubt on his ability to produce porcelain. He is unlikely in the extreme to have been the man in very humble circumstances living in Lodge Lane.

Proof positive that Andrew Planché actually existed can be found in the following entries in the registers of St Alkmund's Church, Derby, to which Jewitt draws attention in his *Ceramic Art in Great Britain*.[35]

1751 Sept 21	Baptized Paul Edmund, the son of Andrew Planché and Sarah his wife
1754 12 Oct	Bap. James the son of Andrew Planché and Sarah his wife
1754 Dec 10	Buried James, the son of Andrew Planché and Sarah his wife
1756 March 4	Bap. James, the bastard son of Andrew Planché and Margaret Burroughs

1756 July 3   Bap. William, the son of
Andrew Planché and
Sarah his wife

Research this century into the life of Andrew Planché carried out by Major W. H. Tapp and Mrs Donald MacAlister and published respectively in 1933[36] and 1929[37] has elaborated on what Jewitt tells us, and it is perhaps unlikely that we will learn anything more of substance about Planché. The essential features of his life are as follows.

He was born on 14 March 1728 (and baptised at Ryders Court Chapel, St Anne's, Westminster), one of five sons of Paul Planché, coffeeman, and his wife Marie Anne Fournier, both French refugees (presumably Huguenots). Although Jewitt speaks of his having gone 'into Saxony, and there learned the art of making porcelain at Dresden', he gives no evidence in support of this belief and it is in the highest degree improbable. In the first half of the eighteenth century it was far from easy to gain admission to the porcelain works at Meissen and even more difficult to return therefrom once admission had been obtained. In any event, the Meissen factory was concerned with real or hard paste and the formula for its composition could have had little relevance to the manufacture of artificial or soft paste, which was the material produced at Derby. Furthermore, there would appear to have been little time in which Andrew Planché could have made his journey to and from Meissen, in that it is documented that he was from 3 July 1740 to 3 July 1747 apprenticed to Edward Mounteney, a manufacturing jeweller of Foster's Lane, London. It is not known for certain that he completed his apprenticeship, the relevant records now being missing, but there is no reason to suppose that he did not. It is interesting to note in the entry relating to his apprenticeship he is described as being of 'the Parish of St. Anns Westminster'. In June 1752 James Marchant of the same parish married at St Alkmund's, Derby, Mary Oldfield. He is described in the marriage register as a potter, and one immediately wonders whether there was any connection between him and Andrew Planché. On 28 September 1747 Planché married Sarah Stone at St Pancras Church, London. Undoubtedly he was at Derby in 1751, but precisely when after 28 September 1747 he reached that town is uncertain. For the reasons given earlier, he may well have arrived late 1747 or early 1748.

Likewise the exact date of his departure is unknown. Presumably he was still there on 3 July 1756, but as his name never appears in any document connected with the factory apart from the copy or draft partnership agreement dated 1 January 1756, it is reasonable to expect him to have left shortly after July 1756. Whether or not he ever entered into the partnership contemplated by the document discovered by Jewitt must remain uncertain. It may be that he did, but after he had divulged the formula for the manufacture of porcelain he was edged out by his more commercially minded partners. Alternatively, he may never have been a partner, but may have sold his business outright to Heath and Duesbury, possibly remaining a while to ensure the smooth transition of the undertaking to the new owners.

However, it does seem clear, whether or not Planché ever was a partner with Heath and Duesbury, that he ceased to have any connection with them very early on in the life of the factory under Duesbury. Whether or not his affair with Margaret Burroughs (resulting in the birth of a natural son—tactlessly given the name of his deceased legitimate son James—some four months before the birth of his legitimate son William), and the matrimonial complications to which it must have given rise, were the real cause of his departure must again be a matter of pure speculation. In any event, this possibility would seem a better explanation for his departure than the one sometimes put forward that his blatant immorality offended the delicate susceptibilities of his partners. Jewitt tells us that in 1804 Andrew Planché was living at Bath. Further researches on the part of Mrs Donald MacAlister reveal that he died there in 1809 and was buried under the name of Andrew Planché-Floor. Seemingly he had, following the frequent practice of exiled Huguenots, translated his French name into English and added it to his surname. At the time of his death he appears to have been assisting his family in the dyeing trade.

If Andrew Planché was the founder of the

Derby factory—and the evidence undoubtedly points in that direction—it is interesting to contemplate the source from which he derived his knowledge of porcelain manufacture. Jewitt's suggestion[38] that he acquired it from Dresden cannot stand up to scrutiny. More likely he became acquainted, whilst in London, with some of the workmen from the Chelsea or Bow factories. There is evidence that the Chelsea factory employed Frenchmen, and it may be that Planché through his Huguenot connections got to know some of them. Moreover, Nicolas Sprimont himself, the founder of the Chelsea factory, lived in St Anne's parish, Soho, the same parish from which Planché emanated. It is just conceivable that Planché was acquainted with Nicholas Crisp, who, though by profession a jeweller like Planché, seems to have owned a porcelain factory in Lambeth or Vauxhall—more will be said about him later[39]—and that he learnt from him enough to produce artificial porcelain. Another possibility is that he made the acqaintance in London of Thomas Briand referred to earlier, a fellow Frenchman from Huguenot stock, and learnt something from him. Perhaps it was a combination of two or more of these sources which served to equip him with the necessary knowledge.

It should be mentioned at this point that, although the production of real or hard paste had throughout the period with which we are concerned posed insuperable difficulties—the problem was not solved in England until Cookworthy discovered in Cornwall in the late 1760s the requisite raw materials, kaolin and petunse—soft or artificial paste could be produced from a variety of formulas and the discovery of a technically satisfactory combination of ingredients did not create too great a problem. The real difficulty was how to give commerciality to the technical know-how, ie to turn out from the formula products which, whilst satisfactory in quality, were saleable at an economic price.

Support for the view that Andrew Planché was responsible for the pre-1756 porcelain manufactured at Derby can be found in the attitude of Miss Sarah Duesbury, the daughter of William Duesbury the second and the granddaughter of William Duesbury the first. (A full-length portrait of her, 1270mm × 1015mm (50in × 40in), when she was about eight years old was executed by Wright of Derby for thirty guineas. In 1883 the painting was owned by George Dean and in 1910 by Cade Bemrose. Its present ownership is unknown, but it is thought to be somewhere in the USA.) Sarah Duesbury died in London on 24 January 1876 in her eighty-eighth year, so that, although she could and presumably did have knowledge of what went on at the factory from early on in the nineteenth century, any remarks made by her with reference to the concern in the preceding century must depend on hearsay. The best that can be said of her evidence is that, although she had no personal knowledge of the early period, she was acquainted in her young days with people who had, and there is no reason to suppose that in her declining years she failed to record faithfully and accurately what had been told her by those who had lived through the events in question or at least had been well acquainted with others who had so lived. Accordingly, although too much reliance cannot be placed on what Miss Duesbury is recorded as having said, her evidence is worth something.

Now, it appears that in her old age, when the early history of the factory had become a subject of widespread interest, questions were put to Miss Duesbury as to the part played by Andrew Planché. Perhaps not surprisingly Miss Duesbury was reluctant to give credit to him. All the honour and glory belonged exclusively to her grandfather. Thus, Bemrose in his *Bow, Chelsea and Derby Porcelain* states[40] that after Miss Duesbury had read Wallis and Bemrose's *The Pottery and Porcelain of Derbyshire* published in 1870, she wrote (presumably to Bemrose himself) as follows:

Messrs Wallis and Bemrose have done my
grandfather justice—while this fellow
Jewitt tries to take the credit out of his
hands and give it to the man Planché,
'Master Planchey', as Betty Shipley called
him.

Betty Shipley was presumably the wife or relative of Joseph Shipley, described by Jewitt[41] as a thrower 'in 1774–6'. The name 'Shipley' appears in the Derby list of 23 November 1787 also referred to by Jewitt.[42]

Again in his *Longton Hall Porcelain* Bemrose observes:[43]

There was undoubtedly such a man as Planché, but from remarks made by the late Miss Duesbury to the writer to his disparagement, it is unlikely that he had much to do with the Derby works started by Duesbury and Heath. Planché appears to have dropped out of sight altogether, as his name never occurs amongst the Derby factory papers after 1756.

As regards the last statement, no exception can be taken to it, in that it is not in doubt that Andrew Planché played little, if any, part in the factory's activities after it came under the control of Duesbury and Heath. However, this fact has no bearing on the totally different question whether it was Andrew Planché who was responsible for the pre-1756 porcelain produced at Derby. In her disparaging remarks about Andrew Planché Miss Duesbury does not deny his connection with early Derby porcelain production; indeed she seems to confirm it, albeit she minimises its significance. What she says is still consistent with Planché having founded the factory, but having severed all connection with it on or shortly after its being taken over by Duesbury.

It is also interesting to note the pejorative title 'Master Planchey' apparently used by Betty Shipley. The impression that this conveys is of someone lacking a dominant or overpowering personality. Andrew Planché appears to have been but a shadow of the business tycoon William Duesbury the first, whose energy and commercial astuteness eventually resulted in his eclipsing for a time all real competition in this country with the exception of that from Worcester. There is nothing to suggest that Andrew Planché ever distinguished himself after leaving Derby. He would seem to have been a man of ingenuity and artistic ability, perhaps rather like Nicholas Crisp (of whom more will be said hereafter[44]), but suited for small-scale operations only. He may well have been a man basically of weak character.

Although the evidence points to Andrew

Planché's being the founder of the factory near St Mary's Bridge and responsible for all porcelain production in Derby before 1756, there is always the possibility that some porcelain manufacture was undertaken at Derby by another person or firm. The only alternative source of manufacture ever suggested is the Cockpit Hill pottery, and it is appropriate that we should at this point consider this particular manufactory.

The date of origin of this pottery (often called the 'Derby Pot-Works') is unknown, but in 1751 the manufactory was being run by three partners—William Butts, Thomas Rivett and John Heath. There is some documentary evidence for Ralph Steane's also being an original partner, but little is known of him, and he appears to have dropped out early on. Butts was a practical potter familiar with the trade and doubtless responsible for the running of the works, Rivett was MP for Derby from 1747 to 1754, and Heath was a banker. Certain creamware items have been identified as having come from this pottery, and it may also have turned out white and brown saltglaze and tortoiseshell and other coloured glaze ware. However, the important question for our present purpose is whether the pottery ever manufactured porcelain and, if so, during what period.

Writers in the past (eg William Bemrose in his *Bow, Chelsea and Derby Porcelain*[45] and George Savage in his *18th-Century English Porcelain*[46]) have ascribed to the Cockpit Hill pottery all the pre-1756 porcelain produced at Derby. George Savage suggests that Andrew Planché was a workman there.[47] However, this view does not grapple with the incontrovertible fact that porcelain was being made in the period 1751 to 1755 at the china works near St Mary's Bridge, and the site of that factory is nowhere near that of the Cockpit Hill pottery. Moreover, there is no need to assume any connection between the two enterprises save that John Heath was a partner in the pottery and at the same time tenant of the china works near St Mary's Bridge, and that he may well have given the latter concern independent financial backing.

However, on the closure of the pottery in 1780 because of the bankruptcy of John Heath, who seems to have become, alone or with his brother Christopher (made bankrupt at the same time), owner of the works from 1770, an auction notice appeared,[48] the material part of which reads as follows:

To be Sold without Reserve (and considerably under the usual wholesale prices) at the Derby Pot Manufactory a large quantity of Earthenware, being the whole stock in trade of that great and extensive Factory commonly known by the name of the Derby Pot Works, consisting of an assortment of *Enamelled, and Blue and White useful China*, [my italics] a large quantity of Enamelled Creamware and plain Cream Tea-table-ware, a great quantity of White Stone and Brown ware.

Whether the advertiser by the use of the word 'China' really meant 'porcelain', particularly as the words following 'consisting of' purport to be a description of the *earthenware* being offered for sale, is perhaps problematical. 'China' is a somewhat ambiguous term. However, Jewitt refers[49] to another sale in the same year of 'a large quantity of earthern [*sic*] and china ware from the Pot Works on Cock-pit Hill, in Derby, being the stock-in-trade of Messrs John and Christopher Heath, of Derby, bankrupts', to take place by auction at the King's Head Inn, Derby. This time there is a clear dichotomy between earthenware on the one hand and china ware on the other. It is difficult to avoid the inference that the pottery included in its stock a quantity of porcelain. However, it does not necessarily follow that the porcelain was made at Cockpit Hill. The pottery could simply have been dealing as a wholesaler in porcelain purchased from elsewhere. This was not an unknown practice of potters of the time. Moreover, even if the pottery was making porcelain in the 1770s, it does not follow from this that it necessarily produced it in the period prior to 1756.

The plain fact is that there is not a scrap of concrete evidence to suggest that Cockpit Hill ever manufactured any porcelain before 1756. There is, on the other hand, positive evidence that porcelain was being manufactured at that time at the 'China Works near Mary Bridge'. Accordingly, on the balance of probability it is more reasonable to suppose that *all* the pre-1756 porcelain produced at Derby must be attributed to the latter undertaking. There is one tentative qualification to this conclusion that might be made, and this will be discussed in Chapter 3.

2

'DRY-EDGE'
PORCELAIN 1750–55

So far we have considered only whether porcelain was manufactured at Derby before the arrival there in 1756 of William Duesbury and, if so, where such manufacture took place and who was responsible for it. The evidence establishes beyond all reasonable doubt that porcelain was in fact produced at this time and that almost certainly it was made (at least on a commercial scale) exclusively at the china works near St Mary's Bridge. Further, the evidence shows on the balance of probability that the person responsible was Andrew Planché. It does not necessarily follow that he was the modeller; but if someone else was responsible for the modelling he seems to have left at about the same time as Planché. But what of the porcelain itself? How can it be identified? This question really merges into the wider question of how any of the products of the Derby factory fabricated before 1770 can be identified. For the fact is that Duesbury (with an important exception mentioned below) never marked his products prior to 1770 save from time to time to add a fraudulent red or gold anchor in an endeavour to pass them off as emanating from the more fashionable Chelsea factory. (Perhaps, as he was holding out his factory as the 'second Dresden', he considered the use of a distinctive mark of his own as counter-productive.) It was not until about 1926 that the pre-1770 Derby porcelain came to be identified.

Exactly who was responsible for the discovery is obscure. Bernard Rackham, then the Keeper of the Ceramics Department of the Victoria and Albert Museum, strongly hinted in *The Cheyne Book of Chelsea China and Pottery*[1] (edited by Reginald Blunt) published in 1924

that he had solved the mystery. Certainly two years later he published together with W. B. Honey and Herbert Read an article in the *Burlington Magazine*[2] setting out his reasons for believing that a great quantity of figures hitherto thought to be of Chelsea origin were in fact attributable to Derby. However, Frank Stonor in his *Chelsea, Bow and Derby Porcelain Figures* (1957) claims[3] that it was he jointly with Alfred E. Hutton who discovered the identity of pre-1770 Derby figures. To complicate the picture further William King in his *English Porcelain Figures of the XVIII Century*, published in 1925, correctly (subject to one error) ascribes to Derby a selection of figures hitherto assigned to Chelsea and in his introduction gives the credit to Rackham, citing the latter's comment in *The Connoisseur*, Vol. LXXII, p. 134. It should also be mentioned that Edward Hyam, the Brompton Road dealer, expressed his own independent views on the identification of early Derby in his booklet *The Early Period of Derby Porcelain* (1750–70) published in 1926.

In the light of the foregoing it is difficult to state categorically who was responsible for identifying the pre-1770 Derby porcelain. It may be that from about 1924 onwards there was a free exchange of tentative ideas and theories among those interested in the subject, and that drawing on this communal knowledge different persons or groups of persons more or less reached the same conclusions by about 1926. However, the important point is that around the mid 1920s it was observed that there existed a large group of figures hitherto generally classified as of Chelsea manufacture, though on less frequent occasions attributed to Bow, which, though not possessing the characteristics of items indisputably originating at the Chelsea or Bow factories, nevertheless had peculiarities of their own.

The distinctive features of these figures can be described as follows. The porcelain is non-phosphatic but with a large lead content, the glaze and enamel colours are thin, giving a sharpness to the modelling, the applied flowers are of a kind quite distinct from those used at Chelsea and Bow, and the decoration has frequent recourse to a turquoise colour, often muddied in appearance, to puce and pink, and in the case of the iris of the eye to a particular shade of reddish-brown. Sometimes, eg where figures of the 'pale-coloured family' are concerned, resort is had to crimson, primrose-yellow and yellowish-green colours, often used to pick out rococo scrollwork bases. As a general rule, the modelling, decoration and quality are inferior to those of Chelsea. However, the most noticeable and consistent characteristic is that on the underside (invariably left unglazed) of the bases of these figures there often appear three or four dark patch marks (*Pl. 150(c)*), which sometimes also appear on the bases of useful or ornamental ware. These patch marks were made by the small pads of clay on which the figure was stood when placed in the saggar during the firing of the glaze. (Admittedly, patch marks do occasionally appear on gold anchor Chelsea pieces, but confusion will not arise because of the absence of the other characteristics referred to above.)

It should also be stated that all examples are made by the slip-casting process, ie the slip or liquid clay was poured into the various plaster moulds assembled together to form the separate parts of the figure, eg the head, the limbs, the torso, and the slip was allowed to remain there for a while. Part of the water in the slip would be absorbed into the plaster mould, so that there formed a thin lining of clay within the mould. The clay lining would become thicker the longer the slip was allowed to remain in the mould, and this accounts for the difference in weight between two apparently similar models. In due course the rest of the slip was thrown away. The importance of the fact that the figures now under discussion were made by the slip-casting

process is that it serves to distinguish them from the products of the Bow factory, where the technique used was that of hand-pressing, ie the clay was pressed by hand into the moulds. Finger-marks or tool-marks appear on the rough inner surface of the figure, which is irregular in thickness.

Reference was made above to an important exception to the rule that Duesbury never (save with the false Chelsea mark) marked or otherwise identified his products before 1770. That exception, which apparently started Frank Stonor on the road to identification of pre-1770 Derby figures, is a large figure, now in the British Museum and illustrated in G. Savage's *English Pottery and Porcelain* (Pl. 140), in the form of a shepherd playing a pipe whilst a dog sits at his feet (a smaller example of the model is illustrated in *Colour Pl. J(a)*), on the base of which is faintly incised the notation 'WDCo'. There can be little doubt that this stands for 'William Duesbury and Company', and the figure has the characteristics attributable to the type of figures now under consideration.

However, the case for a Derby attribution can be put beyond doubt when it is seen that many of the models in question—eg St Thomas (or as he is sometimes known 'King Lear' or the 'Roman soldier'), St Philip, many of the gods and goddesses including Mars, Venus, and Father Time clipping the wings of Cupid, Shakespeare, Milton, Falstaff, the sailor and his lass and the 'Tithe pig group'—appear again in later Derby porcelain, this time bearing an incised number (corresponding to that in the factory price-list of numbered models[4]) or the recognised Duesbury mark (or occasionally both). The later examples are indisputably Derby; it follows that the earlier figures must also be Derby. A further pointer to the authenticity of the figures in question is that their most distinctive feature, namely the patch marks under the base, continues on the bases of later numbered or marked Derby examples.

Final confirmation of what has been said above can be derived from Frank Stonor's examination in 1923 of the models and moulds which once belonged to the Derby factory. These, together with the rest of the contents of the old Derby works, were sold on the factory's closure to Samuel Boyle, a manufacturer at Fenton, and he resold them in 1849 to Alderman William Taylor Copeland, earlier on Lord Mayor of London. By 1923 certain of these moulds—he refers in the article to models which Copeland factory, and Frank Stonor was accorded the facility of examining them. He gave an account of his discoveries in an article in *The Connoisseur* of May 1924.[5] Although at this stage Frank Stonor does not appear to have properly distinguished between the Derby and Chelsea moulds—he refers in the article to models which are undoubtedly Derby as being Chelsea—nevertheless it is clear from what he says in his *Chelsea, Bow and Derby Porcelain Figures*, written some thirty years later, that the Chelsea moulds were entirely different from the Derby and that in due course he was able, by identifying particular models with moulds which were undoubtedly of Derby origin, to give to them an incontestable Derby provenance. In particular, he discovered clay squeezes produced from moulds that had been made to turn out the pair of models shown in *Col. Pl. J(a)* and *(c)*, and various squeezes of heads, one of which is identifiable with the head of the Chinese woman in the pre-1756 Chinoiserie group of 'Hearing' *(Pl. 3)* and the head of the Chinese woman musician playing a double drum to be seen in the Indianapolis Museum of Art. The discovery of this head squeeze is particularly important as it serves to link two pre-1756 models with the later Derby factory. Frank Stonor was also able to identify Chelsea models with Chelsea moulds. Accordingly, the survival of certain of the Derby and Chelsea moulds has served to confirm the identification of the pre-1770 Derby products.

Now, the pre-1770 Derby figures admit of sub-classification. For there is a section falling within the general group (eg the base of each figure is solid, the underneath being unglazed), but distinguishable therefrom by certain features which figures of this section share in common. These features are as follows, although, of course, they are not necessarily all present in any one case.

1 The paste is rather creamier than that of the other Derby products, and could readily be mistaken for French porcelain.

2 The glaze around the lower sides of the base has shrunk so as to expose, as it were, a dry-edge. This is a particularly distinctive feature of the group under consideration and it has given rise to their generic description as 'dry-edge' figures.

It would seem that the reason why the glaze was allowed to shrink in the way described was to prevent what has happened in the case of certain surviving examples, namely the over-running of the glaze beyond the edge of the base so as to require the underside to be ground smooth.

3 Many of the pieces have a funnel-shape 'screw-hole' instead of the clear-cut round vertical hole more generally found. The hole is shaped as though it were to take the shank of a counter-sunk screw *(Pl. 150(b))*. Apparently the hole was formed by means of a special tool, tapering in shape.

The purpose of the hole was to release occluded gases into the atmosphere. Sometimes the screw-hole has been combined with a further hole at the top of the base.

The existence of a screw-hole is a less constant feature of the group of figures under consideration than the 'dry-edge' characteristic described above.

4 The modelling of the figure is sharp and clean, particularly as regards the folds of clothing or the body texture of animals.

5 In the best examples the glaze is white and brilliant. However, on occasion it may be speckled or discoloured or dull with a 'candle-grease' appearance.

6 The bases are generally of the 'bun' type, though there are some which assume slightly rococo features.

7 Patch marks never appear on the bases.

8 The mouths of the human figures are usually over-large, a feature which is emphasised in coloured examples.

9 Round holes—the equivalent of the Bow square holes—sometimes appear at the back of the figure in order to hold metal branches carrying porcelain flowers or candle nozzles. Modelled porcelain flowers do not appear on items from any other English factory prior to 1756.

10 The figures in question frequently appear

in the white. Some of them may have been decorated with unfired pigments and in the course of time the paintwork has simply worn off.

It should also be said generally that the group of figures now under consideration are of fine quality, and some are outstanding. Certain of them, eg the Chinoiserie version of the Senses, can be said to be among the finest English figures ever to be produced. Those which are enamelled are normally decorated with plain washes of pale yellow, pink, mauve, a yellowish green and iron-red. The best examples display a degree of charm, imagination and vigour of movement never attained again at Derby and rarely surpassed or even equalled at any other English factory.

The dry-edge figures are early and can on stylistic grounds be assigned to the first five or six years of the Derby factory's life. This is clear from the form of the bases used (normally 'bun' shape, but on later examples the beginnings of the rococo style can be seen), and in some cases from the general primitiveness of the porcelain. That these 'dry-edge' figures are genuine Derby products is demonstrable beyond all doubt by the fact that instances occur where the same model appears in both dry-edge and non dry-edge porcelain (and their authenticity is further demonstrated by the survival of the head squeeze referred to earlier[6]). For example, the figure known as 'St Thomas' or 'King Lear' or the 'Roman soldier' (*Pl. 23*) appears in both types of porcelain and in fact continues into the nineteenth century; so too does the companion figure, generally known as 'St Philip'. Certain of the gods and goddesses, eg Pluto and Cerberus (*Pl. 15*), Venus and Cupid (*Pl. 17(a)*), Mars in Roman armour and Apollo with the emblems of the arts (*Pl. 18*), are to be found in both the early pre-Duesbury paste and the later porcelain. The same is true of the candlestick figure with two Chinese boys either side of it, of 'Taste' as a seated lady with a basket of fruit (*Pl. 6*), of the mapseller, and of a figure of a man playing a flute (*Pl. 8(b)*). The celebrated early boars (*Pl 27*) are found later in a smaller version with patch marks, and a dry-edge model in the form of a shepherdess with dog and sheep appears in patch-marked porcelain and also *c.* 1760–5 as a

fruit seller with sheep only. Furthermore, an instance occurs[7] where a Chinoiserie group representing 'Taste', originally left in the biscuit state during the dry-edge period, was subsequently glazed and decorated in Duesbury's time and is patch-marked by way of confirmation. An example of the 'Flying Chinaman' (*Pl. 16* for the pre-Duesbury version) without the boy is to be seen with patch marks in the British Museum.

So far we have only mentioned dry-edge models with reference to establishing their Derby provenance. It is appropriate that we should go on to consider them more generally. Moreover, although it is customary to refer to figures only when discussing the dry-edge period, this is purely and simply because nearly all the surviving dry-edge pieces are in fact figures. However, useful ware from this period does exist, although it is exceedingly rare. Doubtless it was originally produced in a quantity more proportionate to the number of surviving figures. Presumably when useful ware became damaged it was thrown away. Figures were repaired and preserved. Dry-edge pieces can be conveniently classified under the following heads: (1) human figures, (2) animals and (3) useful ware.

Human figures

Under this head are the celebrated Senses, Elements and Seasons. The Senses are found in two different versions, ie as Chinoiserie and European figures. The former are quite outstanding for the vigour of their modelling. 'Feeling' appears as a Chinaman with large hat, long cloak over an ample robe and very long moustaches about to chastise a small boy (*Pl. 1*), 'Taste' as a Chinaman with phial of medicines accompanied by a small boy leaning over a basket of medicines, a bottle in his right hand (*Pl. 2*). The latter group is sometimes known as the 'Quack Doctor and Assistant'. An interesting example in the Untermyer Collection (Col. Pl. 100, Fig. 270)[8] has both a dry-edge and patch marks. The style of decoration suggests that it was enamelled around 1760, in which event the group was left in the biscuit state around the factory for some years and then subsequently glazed and decorated. Doubtless this accounts for the patch marks, which are characteristic of post-1756 Derby production. 'Hearing' consists of a Chinese woman holding out her left hand and clasping a trumpet in her right, whilst an old man sits listening beside her (*Pl. 3*). In the past this model has been universally identified with 'Sight'. Manifestly, it represents 'Hearing'. 'Smell' comprises a Chinese lady with flowing robe and pointed hat holding flowers to her nose, accompanied by a Chinese boy on a seat leaning backwards in an endeavour to grasp the flowers (*Pl. 4(b)*). 'Sight' is represented by a standing Chinese woman looking into a mirror held in her right hand. She is accompanied by a seated boy in long trousers. It has been suggested that the Chinoiserie Senses are derived from François Boucher (1703–70), but an engraved source by way of confirmation of this theory has not been discovered. Conceivably the models may in some way be linked with the *Livre de six feuilles représentant les cinq Sens par différents amusements chinois sur les dessins de F. Boucher* announced by Gabriel Huquier in the *Mercure* for 1740. Sometimes the children from the above groups appear as separate figures: thus the boy from the group representing 'Feeling' is used to symbolise 'Air' (*Pl. 14*).

The Senses appear also in European form. 'Feeling' is a lady in pannier skirt holding a parrot (*Pl. 5(a)*), 'Taste' likewise a lady in pannier skirt, but with a basket of fruit (*Pl. 6*), 'Sight' a man looking at a mirror, 'Smell' a gallant with snuff-box (*Pl. 7*). What form 'Hearing' took is uncertain.[9]

The Seasons like the Senses are represented in two versions, but the contrast is not between Chinese and European figures. In the one form they appear as putti (*Pl. 9*)—the set seems to have been made in two different sizes—whilst in the more ambitious version they comprise four separate pairs of figures. Spring is represented by a gardener and lady companion (*Pl. 10(a)* for the lady), Summer by a pair of harvesters (*Pl. 11(b)* for the man), Autumn by a pair of peasants with grapes (*Pls 4(a)* and *(c)* and *12*), and Winter by an old man (*Pl. 10(b)*) and an old woman (*Pl. 13*), each warming a hand over a brazier. The fact that Autumn appears in two different sizes suggests that the other Seasons were also produced in two sizes.

The Elements likewise appear to have been made in two versions, ie in Chinese form and as classical gods and goddesses. As regards the first version examples of 'Water' and 'Air' have survived and are represented by Chinese boys (*Pl. 14*). The figure symbolising 'Air' is the boy in the Chinoiserie group representing 'Feeling' (*Pl. 1*). 'Earth' and 'Fire' from this series have not so far been recorded. As for the second version of the Elements, Pluto and Cerberus (*Pl. 15*) stand for 'Earth', Neptune riding on a dolphin—or in an alternative version where the dolphin rests at his feet—for 'Water' and Jupiter sitting astride an eagle and clasping a thunderbolt in his left hand for either 'Air' or 'Fire'. The form of the fourth element is unrecorded. Other gods and goddesses from the dry-edge period are also known such as Mars in Roman armour, Venus and Cupid (*Pl. 17(a)*), and Apollo with the emblems of the arts (*Pl. 18*), but they do not appear to be symbolic of anything, other, of course, than 'war', 'love' and 'the arts' respectively. They were reproduced throughout the life of the factory.

Apart from the models already mentioned there are numerous other human figures recorded belonging to the dry-edge period. A further Chinoiserie group is known comprising a rococo candlestick with two Chinese boys, one each side of it,[10] and there exists in the Indianapolis Museum of Art an important Chinoiserie pair of musicians, of whom the lady plays a double drum and the man a lute. An outstandingly fine Chinoiserie model, of which several examples are known, consists of a watchstand with a Chinaman with flying drapery seated high on open scrollwork and a boy below (*Pl. 16*).

The remaining models are European. They include: a shepherd and shepherdess (seemingly in two different sizes), the former playing bagpipes (*Pl. 19*), identifiable with a pair made at Bow and suggestive of a modeller common to both factories (the models may be based on unidentified Meissen originals); a shepherdess with a sheep clambering up her dress together with a recumbent dog, also produced in the later Duesbury period: a companion shepherd has not so far been recorded; a pair of street vendors, made in two sizes and based on two of the Meissen set of 'Paris Cries' issued in 1753 (*Pl. 20*); a mapseller after the Meissen model by Reinicke (based on a drawing by Bouchardon, engraved by Caylus) either directly or via the red-anchor Chelsea version: as this model appears later with a companion it is reasonable to assume that a dry-edge companion was also made; and Kitty Clive (*née* Rafter, 1711–85) in the character of Mrs Riot, a fine lady in Garrick's *Lethe*, of whom it is said in the play: 'she lies in bed all morning, rattles about all day, and sits up at night; she goes everywhere, and sees everything, knows everybody, and loves nobody; ridicules her friends, coquets with her lovers; sets 'em together by the ears, tells fibs, makes mischief, *buys china* [my italics], cheats at cards, keeps a pug-dog, and hates the parsons'.

This last model (after an engraving by Charles Mosley) was produced in two different versions (both non-phosphatic and made by the slip-casting process), the smaller seemingly direct from the Bow model. One example only of the smaller version is recorded, formerly in the S. J. Katz Collection and now in the Boston Museum of Fine Arts. Several examples of the larger version are known, with drapery differing in detail from that of the Bow model, one in the Victoria and Albert Museum, others in private collections. On the star-shaped base of each—quite different from the square base of the Bow equivalent—is a sprig of prunus blossom, similar to that on the 1750 cream jugs referred to at page 11. They are non-phosphatic with 7.2% lead oxide in the body.[11] Kitty Clive in the Bow version is accompanied by Henry Woodward (1717–77) in the character of the fine gentleman, likewise from Garrick's *Lethe* after a mezzotint by James McArdell. In the play the gentleman is made to say, *inter alia*:

Faith, my existence is merely supported by amusements; I dress, visit, study taste, and write sonnets; by birth, travel, education, and natural abilities, I am entitled to lead the fashion; *I am principal connoisseur at all auctions* [my italics], chief arbiter at assemblies, profess'd critic at the theatres, and a fine gentleman—everywhere.

Some years ago a Derby version of Kitty Clive together with a figure of Henry Woodward passed through the hands of the celebrated dealers Delomosne & Son Ltd. Both figures are illustrated here in *Pl. 21*. Although, of course, the chemical composition of this particular model of Woodward was never analysed, there is no reason to suppose that it was other than the genuine companion of the Derby Kitty Clive, in which event this is the only recorded example of a Henry Woodward made at Derby.

Two interesting references to Derby dancers occur in William Duesbury's *London Account Book*. The relevant entries read as follows:

August 21 [1753] 2 pr of Dansers Darby
figars   0-6-0
August 18 [?1753] 1 pr of Dansars Darbey
figars   0-3-0.

Two distinct Derby models of dancers, one male, the other female, have been identified from the dry-edge period. The former holds his cloak in his right hand, whilst his left hand turns inwards on his hip (*Pl. 11(a)*). The lady clasps her flaring skirt with her left hand and holds a mask in her right (*Pl. 22*). Although there would appear to be no reason why the two models should not constitute a pair, they have not so far been recorded as such. In the Untermyer Collection[12] the lady is accompanied by a dancing youth with right hand extended, left hand upraised and left foot thrust out beyond the base. These two actual figures are illustrated in F. Stonor's *Chelsea, Bow and Derby Porcelain Figures* (Pl. 48) as a pair. However, Yvonne Hackenbroch has attributed to the lady the date *c.* 1750 and to the young man the date *c.* 1755, thereby implying that they are not a pair, and possibly suggesting that the latter was turned out after the dry-edge period. The lady appears to have been once in the collection of Mr Forsythe Wickes, New York. The same two models also appear in *The Cheyne Book* (there wrongly attributed to Chelsea) as Figs 133 and 134, Pl. 10 (Hutton Collection), but it is significant that they are not catalogued as a pair. This dissociation of 'the lady with the mask' from the dancing youth is supported by the fact that the latter model was undoubtedly produced in Duesbury's time and was accompanied by a companion different in form (*Pl. 17(b)*) from 'the lady with the mask'. (Such a pair, from the Derby Museum, are illustrated in Barrett and Thorpe's *Derby Porcelain*, Pl. 51.) However, this companion model was according to Barrett and Thorpe (p. 193) also produced during the dry-edge period, in which event presumably the model of the dancing youth likewise had a pre-Duesbury existence.

It was in the dry-edge period that the famous figure of 'St Thomas' or, as it is often known, 'King Lear' or the 'Roman soldier' (*Pl. 23*) first appeared together with its companion 'St Philip' (*Pl. 67* for a Duesbury example). These models, which were also produced during Duesbury's time, are seen in nineteenth-century Staffordshire pottery bearing the specific names 'St Thomas' and 'St Philip' respectively. Dry-edge models also include a group comprising: a huntsman playing a flute to his lady (*Pl. 24*)—the relationship with the pannier-skirted Senses is to be noted; a seated gallant holding an open cage and representing 'Liberty' (*Pl. 5(b)*), possibly taken from the model of 'Smell' (*Pl. 7*)—presumably a companion 'Matrimony' was also produced: in the post-1755 versions 'Liberty' normally (but not always) holds a bird and the lady representing matrimony holds the open cage—a seated cobbler with a shoe in his left hand and the tools of his trade all around him (*Pl. 25*) and two different versions of a standing fluter, one as a man (*Pl. 8(b)*), the other as a boy. Finally, there are also recorded as belonging to the dry-edge period a pair of seated figures, male and female (seemingly in two sizes), each clasping a shell, a seated lady holding a musical score, possibly representing 'Hearing' from the European Senses, and a pair of theatrical figures in the form of Harlequin and Columbine (*Pl. 26*).

Animals

During the dry-edge period quite a range of animals came to be produced. Included are the famous pair of boars (*Pl. 27*), one running, the other sitting. The sitting boar was based on an antique marble statue known as 'The Florentine Boar' in the Uffizi Gallery in Florence. The title page of Francis Barlow's *Aesop's Fables*, London 1665, contains a similar boar. The original differs in that the head has a less pronounced turn and the hindquarters are somewhat slimmer, whilst the acorns generally appearing on the Derby model do not feature at all. On certain of the later dry-edge examples the raised acorns have disappeared.[13]

A particularly interesting pair of Derby wild boars in white are known where the running boar has incised under the base the initials 'IW', or, if the piece is reversed, 'MI'. (The correct reading is more likely to be 'IW'.) In William Duesbury's *London Account Book* 1751–3 reference is made to a pair of 'Boors', sent to him for decoration; they are not specifically described as being from Derby: '1752 October 27 Mr Michell 1 pr of Boors 5s od', but it would be surprising if they did not come from Derby. The models were continued for a number of years, and a smaller version was produced in the 1760s.

In addition to boars there were turned out at Derby a pair of charging bulls in varying sizes (after similar Meissen animals based on an engraving by Johann Elias Ridinger),[14] a stag and doe at lodge (*Pl. 28*), another version of a recumbent stag and doe (*Pl. 29*), a pair of goats, the nanny suckling a kid (*Pl. 30*), and a further pair comprising a goat and kid and a ewe and lamb. Sheep in various forms (*Col. Pl. C(b)* and *Pl. 31*) and a pair of lions (*Pl. 32*) are recorded. In the Victoria and Albert Museum are to be found a boy milking a goat (*Pl. 33*) and a pug dog scratching (*Pl. 34*). Birds are also known. A single finch in white perched on a tree-stump is recorded. So too is a group consisting of two finches on branches with a spaniel dog below springing upwards with bared teeth. Sometimes the latter group appears with metal branches and porcelain flowers, an example in the Victoria and Albert Museum having in addition a tulip-shape sconce (*Pl. 35*). Finally there is also recorded as belonging to the dry-edge period a bird looking like a parrot perched on a tree-stump.

It will be recalled that Samuel Keys in his various statements cited earlier on the origin of porcelain production at Derby referred to the founder of the factory as having made (to quote one account only) 'small articles in China—such as Birds—Sheep—Lambs—Dogs—Cats and other trifling ornamental toys'.[15] On any footing this statement does not accurately reflect the position, at least from 1750 onwards. Human figures as well as animals were produced, some of them as groups and some quite large. Ironically, so far from being trifling ornamental toys they were some of the finest things ever to be produced at Derby or, for that matter, at any English factory. Even the animals cannot be said to be particularly small. They were certainly no smaller than animals turned out at other times at Derby. In comparison with those of the second quarter of the nineteenth century, with which Samuel Keys would be familiar, they were very much larger. For example, whereas the 'dry-edge' sheep are about 101mm (4in long), the corresponding nineteenth-century examples are about 50mm (2in).

Useful ware

There are very few recorded examples of useful ware from the dry-edge period. There are the three cream jugs referred to earlier (*Pl. 36*). (Incidentally, the prunus blossom on these jugs is similar to that on the known examples of the larger figure of Kitty Clive (*Pl. 2*).) But apart from the cream jugs, a pair of white-glazed shell salts resting on coral and tiny shells are recorded, as is also a white-glazed sweetmeat dish composed of three shells likewise resting on coral and tiny shells (*Pl. 37*). There also exist a white-glazed cabbage tureen and cover (*Pl. 38*) and a coloured partridge tureen and cover, the bird resting on a nest of applied twigs and feathers. Three white cups from the dry-edge period are to be seen in the Victoria and Albert Museum. They are circular with a branch handle and wavy rim, the sides moulded with flowers. An interesting selection of white-glazed individual flowers has also survived. It would seem that only at Derby were porcelain flowers produced during the period 1750–5.

Not service ware, but nevertheless conveniently classified under the present heading, are two different forms of white-glazed wall brackets from the dry-edge period. A pair (*Pl. 39*) with elaborate rococo scrollwork ending in a shaped platform with stepped profile are to be seen at the Victoria and Albert Museum and in the Untermyer Collection[16] at the Metropolitan Museum of New York. The other form of wall bracket, of which an example is in the Untermyer Collection, has scroll and foliage mouldings and volutes at each side ending in a rectangular platform with shaped front. Doubtless, other examples of dry-edge useful and similar ware will surface in the course of time.

As explained earlier, in all probability almost all of the useful ware ever made during the dry-edge period has been used, ultimately damaged and, unlike figures (which when this fate befalls them are frequently repaired and preserved), thrown away. That a considerable amount of useful ware was originally made is demonstrated by the contents of the various sales of Derby porcelain advertised in public journals in 1756.[17] There can be little doubt that the useful ware there referred to was manufactured before William Duesbury took over the factory, and the inference must be that it was made in quantity, at least in the latter part of the dry-edge period.

Appendix 1

In Appendix 1 an attempt has been made to list some of the items which are known to have been produced in the pre-Duesbury period. The list does not in any way purport to be exhaustive. Even if it were possible to include every recorded model or shape, the list would immediately become out of date on the discovery of some further model or shape hitherto unknown. However, the Appendix gathers under one head many of the items produced in the dry-edge period. In a book of this size it would be wholly impractical to illustrate all of the relevant models and shapes. However, an illustration is infinitely more valuable than mere description. Accordingly, against each piece, if not shown here, reference has been made, wherever possible, to one or more publications containing a suitable illustration. Measurements are approximate, and unless otherwise stated relate to height.

Decoration

A great number of dry-edge pieces are found in the white, ie without any decoration at all. It may be that in some instances these items were originally decorated, but with unfired pigments, which have long ago worn off. Indeed, on occasion traces of such pigments can still be seen in protected crevices. But some pieces have survived which have been decorated with fired pigments. The interesting question immediately arises as to whether they were decorated at the factory or sent to London to be painted by such people as William Duesbury, who functioned as a London decorator from 1751 to 1753. It would appear from Duesbury's *London Account Book* that the pieces sent to him for decoration did not normally come directly from the factory of origin, but from various dealers who had purchased the items in question in the white. Accordingly, if the Derby factory was in the habit of selling dry-edge figures in the white to the London dealers, and if it was the practice of such dealers to procure these figures to be enamelled at the various decorating establishments then operating, we would perhaps not expect to see very often the same hand appearing twice running on flower-decorated dry-edge pieces. For it would seem from the different styles of handwriting appearing in Duesbury's *London Account Book* that he employed a variety of different artists, and if a multiplicity of different enamellers was a common feature of other decorating establishments, then the number of different hands that we would expect to find on dry-edge pieces, if they were enamelled solely in London, ought in all probability to be very considerable indeed. However, in the case of the fifteen flower-decorated figures here illustrated it is clear that the same hand has been at work on more than one occasion. Thus, artist A is clearly responsible for the decoration of 'Feeling' and 'Liberty' (*Pl. 5*), the 'Fluter' (*Pl. 8(b)*) and the 'Huntsman and companion' group (*Pl. 24*), artist B for the decoration of 'Spring' and 'Winter' (*Pl. 10*) and the 'Shepherdess' (*Pl. 19*), artist C for the decoration of 'Winter as an old woman' (*Pl. 13*) and the 'Dancer with a mask' (*Pl. 22*), artist D for the decoration of 'Venus and Cupid' (*Pl. 17(a)*) and 'Apollo' (*Pl. 18*), and artist E for the decoration of the pair of 'Standing Goats' (*Pl. 30*) and the pair of 'Standing Sheep' (*Pl. 31*). Moreover, it may well be that there were in fact less than five artists who painted the flowers on the above pieces. The foregoing identification has proceeded on a conservative basis, and it may be

that some of the painting attributed to two or more separate hands should in reality be attributed to one only. There is always the danger of underrating an artist's versatility. Accordingly, the number of artists responsible for the flower-painting (or, for that matter, any other form of enamelling) on dry-edge pieces may possibly at any one time have been only two or three, in which event on the balance of probability the artists concerned were in fact employees of the factory.

It should be remembered that the number of pieces of Derby origin sent to William Duesbury for decoration during the period from November 1751 to August 1753 (even if we include items whose Derby provenance is not certain) was not particularly large, and there is no positive evidence that any other decorating establishment in London undertook any enamelling work on dry-edge pieces. Moreover, it would be improbable in the extreme if the management of the 'China Works near Mary Bridge' did not quickly take into employment competent enamellers rather than continue indefinitely to supply high quality figures in the white. Admittedly, it may well be the case that enamelling at the factory did not start until a year or two after the commencement of manufacture. However, there is no real evidence to support the view that dry-edge pieces were largely or even to a significant extent enamelled in London.

Dating

In dating the dry-edge pieces here illustrated no attempt has been made to be unduly specific. For the reasons given above the enamelled examples may for the most part have been made after (say) 1752, and many of the white figures may have been produced (particularly where unfired pigments have been used) in the first year or two of production. However, the frequency of white examples suggests that the factory found a ready market for figures in the white throughout the whole period 1750-5. Accordingly, it is dangerous to try to attribute a date solely on the basis of decoration or the absence of it. In the case of the 'Absinth Seller' and companion, as these are based on the small 'Paris Cries' series issued by Meissen in 1753, we can be more precise, and attribute to them the date 1754–5.

It is perhaps tempting to approach the whole problem of dating by reference to the sophistication of the modelling. Thus simple sheep and other animals would be expected to antedate such elaborate models as the 'Chinaman with flying drapery' (*Pl. 16*). But there is really no hard evidence to justify this course. In any event, even a time span of 1750–5 is not excessive.

3

THE 'GIRL-ON-A-HORSE' FACTORY

There exists a small group of figures attributable on stylistic and other grounds to a date around 1755. Their distinctive characteristics are that they are light in weight, have a paste that is rather opaque, a glaze that is somewhat dirty and speckled, and a rough unglazed dirty surface under a base which is scrolled and rococo in form. Some of the models have a mark consisting of a circle (seemingly created by the use of a compass, as the circle is perfect) containing a triangle, which in turn contains what some have regarded as a further triangle but the more observant as the letter Y (*Pl. 150(a)*). All the examples so far recorded are modelled with a remarkable artistic flair in a style not seen elsewhere in English porcelain.

These figures (which can for convenience be called after the model illustrated in *Col. Pl. A* the 'Girl-on-a-horse' factory figures) have been attributed to Derby by Arthur Lane in his *English Porcelain Figures of the Eighteenth Century* (p. 100) and have been classified by him as an intermediary group created between the end of the 'Planché period' and the time when Duesbury assumed control of the factory. This attribution may have been encouraged by the absence of bone-ash in the Victoria and Albert Museum's 'Dancer' (*Pl. 41*). Moreover, this view has been generally accepted. However, is this 'traditional' attribution really tenable?

The difficulty that confronts acceptance is that the figures in question do not have the characteristics of either the dry-edge or the Duesbury models. They are a group seemingly *sui generis*. Admittedly, they might, as Lane suggests, be the results of a short-lived experimental change in the paste. But against this, it is to

be noted that none of the models is to be found either as a dry-edge or Duesbury figure. This complete isolation from what went before and what came after is indeed remarkable if a Derby attribution is correct. For continuity is a feature of the factory and some at least of the dry-edge models are repeated after 1755. Of course, the explanation could be that Duesbury simply did not care to produce the models again, but their absence in later years does invite doubt whether they were of Derby origin in the first place.

Now if the 'Girl-on-a-horse' factory figures do not emanate from the enterprise which Duesbury took over, the intriguing question arises as to where exactly their origin is to be found. Manifestly, they do not belong to any of the major contemporary factories such as Bow, Chelsea, Longton Hall or Worcester. However, could they conceivably have come from one of the handful of porcelain factories whose names are known to us, but whose products have so far never been identified? Of these the best authenticated, namely Limehouse and Newcastle-under-Lyme, discontinued production well before 1756. Isleworth, referred to by Jewitt,[1] did not commence porcelain manufacture until 1760, and the others to which fleeting contemporary reference is made, if they had any real existence at all, are, with one exception to be mentioned later, so inadequately documented that there is simply no basis on which even to attempt to make attributions.

Of course, the problem of identification can be complicated still further if the possibility is envisaged of a workman from one of the recognised factories (including any of the soft-paste concerns in France, eg St Cloud) starting up production on a small scale for (say) twelve or eighteen months and then disappearing for all time without trace. If this happened, then our quest is doomed to failure.

However, before abandoning the task of identification as hopeless, it is worthwhile at least to consider such evidence as there is and to see what, if any, inference can be drawn. There are two factories which could be linked with the group of figures under examination.

Cockpit Hill pottery

The first is the Cockpit Hill pottery, whose origin and activities have been discussed in Chapter 1. Could it be that this particular pottery had seen how the factory run by Planché was developing and had decided that it too could produce porcelain figures? Could it be that by about 1755 it had, albeit in a small way, actually commenced the production of a range of porcelain figures? Were the black specks and other impurities found in the 'Girl-on-a-horse' factory figures the consequence of too close an association during manufacture with the pottery's coarse earthenware? Did Duesbury suddenly view with alarm the possibility of the Cockpit Hill works establishing itself in serious competition with the factory that he intended to take over, and did he quickly negotiate a partnership agreement with Andrew Planché and John Heath with the object of stopping in its tracks such unwelcome and unexpected competition? It is not without significance that the draft partnership agreement contains a covenant against competition on the part of the partners. Although the general view is that Duesbury needed Heath for his financial support, it must be remembered that by 1 January 1756 Duesbury had, apart from any accumulation of personal savings, acquired the entire estate of his father in consideration of paying him an annuity, and it may be that the predominant motive for bringing Heath into partnership was to ensure that competition from the Cockpit Hill works was stopped for ever. It is interesting to note that the 'Girl-on-a-horse' factory figures were only produced for a short period of a year or so. But an attribution to the Cockpit Hill pottery is purely speculative. There is no concrete evidence in support.

Crisp's factory

An alternative theory is that the 'Girl-on-a-horse' factory figures originated at Crisp's porcelain factory in Lambeth or Vauxhall. There is good documentary evidence for the existence of such a factory, and in certain of the letters of Cookworthy, the founder of the Plymouth porcelain factory, Crisp's undertaking is bracketed with those at Chelsea and Bow.[2] The natural inference is that the concern was of some standing, and the intriguing thought suggests itself that the figures with which we are concerned may have no Derby connection of any sort, either with Duesbury's factory or with the Cockpit Hill pottery, but instead may have originated in London. It is interesting to note the observations (quoted in Chaffers, *Marks and Monograms*[3]) of Rouquet:[4] 'In the neighbourhood of London *there are three or four manufactories of porcelain* [my italics], among which that of Chelsea is the most considerable.'

The known facts about Nicholas Crisp have been assembled by J. V. G. Mallett in an article appearing in the *Journal of the Royal Society of Arts* (Parts 1–3, 1972; January and February 1973). He was born in 1704 and started his business life as a jeweller (it is interesting to note that Andrew Planché was trained as a goldsmith). However, in about 1751 Crisp ceased trading in London as a jeweller and started to engage in the porcelain business in Lambeth or Vauxhall. Although Crisp is referred to as being of Bow Churchyard, Cheapside, a description which appears to have mistakenly linked him in the eyes of some writers with the Bow factory, his porcelain factory was in fact at Lambeth or Vauxhall, albeit the exact location is unknown. The great sculptor John Bacon was apprenticed to him in 1755. According to a notice in the *British Magazine and Review* for October 1782 Bacon was first encouraged to become a sculptor through seeing on his occasional visits to Lambeth the terracotta models which the various sculptors had sent in for baking to a pottery at the same premises where Crisp's porcelain factory was located. This account is expanded in the *Gentleman's Magazine* of 1799 and Bacon is stated to have actually worked *in* Crisp's china factory. Further elaboration on Bacon's connection with the factory is to be found in Cecil's *Memoir of Bacon* (1801) and Cunningham's *Lives of the Most Eminent British Sculptors and Architects* (1830). The latter writer, in referring to Bacon's apprenticeship to Nicholas Crisp, speaks of the master as being 'an eminent maker of porcelain, who taught [Bacon] the art of modelling various groups and figures such as the Deer and the Holly Tree, the Bird and the Bush, the Shepherd and Shepherdess, and birds of all shapes and beasts of every kind yet made for show or for use in our manufactories'. However, we are not here concerned with the exact extent of Bacon's activities at the factory or of his indebtedness to Crisp. What is germane to the present investigation is that there is evidence that a porcelain factory run by Nicholas Crisp did actually exist.

Crisp was one of the founder members of the Royal Society of Arts and he took a great deal of interest in its multifarious activities. He seems to have been a man of great inventiveness and ingenuity, but as a businessman 'a born loser'. On 17 November 1763 he became bankrupt. He ceased after March 1764 to pay his two guineas annual subscription to the Royal Society of Arts. However, his membership of the Society seems to have remained unchallenged. He last attended on 13 January 1767. His absence thereafter can be explained by his removal to Bovey Tracey in Devonshire, where he eventually died and on 9 July 1774 was buried.

Whilst he was at Bovey Tracey his services were enlisted by William Cookworthy to assist in devising the best method for producing real or hard porcelain. Crisp's experience had, of course, been with artificial or soft porcelain, but, as is shown by his catholic interest in the far-ranging activities of the Royal Society of Arts, he was quite equal to a new challenge, and although Josiah Wedgwood speaks somewhat disparagingly of his efforts—'A Mr Crisp from London endeavoured to make a kind of porcelain here [ie at Bovey Tracey], but did little more than make some experiments, and those unsuccessful ones'—there is no reason to suppose that his work was that ineffective. Certainly he had a small staff at Bovey Tracey, the three principal members of which Cookworthy somewhat unscrupulously enticed away

from him. In his letter to Thomas Pitt dated 20 December 1767 (reproduced by Geoffrey Wills in an article on 'The Plymouth Porcelain Factory' in *Apollo*[5]) Cookworthy refers to a modeller—by implication from other letters, Hammersley—and painter—by like implication, John Brittan (1735–1804)—formerly working for Crisp at Bovey Tracey, whom Cookworthy has taken into his pay, and states that 'these two have been Employ'd for years in the Chelsea, Bow and Vauxhall China Potteries'. Now, the bracketing together of the Chelsea, Bow and Vauxhall factories suggests that the last-named concern was of more than ephemeral duration and that its output was of a quality that could stand comparison with the products of Chelsea and Bow.

Moreover, Jewitt tells us that Duesbury purchased the Vauxhall china works. He says:[6] 'Mr Duesbury, who not only held the Derby China Works, but had purchased those at Chelsea, Giles's and one at Vauxhall, thus became the proprietor of the Bow works as well.' Jewitt repeats the above statement later in his book in the following terms:[7] 'Mr Duesbury himself, after a long and useful life, in the course of which he not only established the Derby China Works, but became the purchaser of those of Chelsea, Bow, Vauxhall, and Kentish Town, died at Derby. . .' Once again there is a clear coupling of the china works at Vauxhall (clearly Crisp's concern is meant) with those at Chelsea and Bow, which must indicate that it was a factory of some significance.

It is possible, then, that the 'Girl-on-a-horse' factory figures came from the original Crisp china works at Lambeth or Vauxhall. Their quality entitles them to comparison with figures from Chelsea or Bow, and it is difficult to point to any other unattributed pieces meriting this distinction. If they do emanate from Crisp's factory, then they have absolutely nothing to do with Derby. However, the case is not proven. Before leaving this subject one further point can usefully be made. The modelling of the 'Girl-on-a-horse' factory figures (allowing for the substitution of porcelain for pottery and the opportunity thereby given to the modeller for a greater delicacy in his work) has a remarkable affinity in feeling with that of the Astbury-

Whieldon pottery figures of *c*. 1740. For example, the 'Girl on a horse' illustrated in *Col. Pl. A* is similar in pose and general concept to the Astbury-Whieldon lady on horseback shown in Pl. 3 of Mankowitz and Haggar, *The Concise Encyclopaedia of English Pottery and Porcelain*. Accordingly, the possibility of the 'Girl-on-a-horse' factory figures emanating from somewhere in Staffordshire cannot be discounted. The whole subject of where these figures originated is perhaps one of the most interesting unsolved mysteries of English ceramics.

The figures

The figures comprising the 'Girl-on-a-horse' factory group are extremely rare. Recorded examples are listed below.

A girl on a horse (152mm (6in) high; 114mm (4½in) long) (*Col. Pl. A*). The rider sits in riding habit on a high-stepping horse, its head turned to the left. On the moulded trappings of the horse are to be found small encrusted flowers in colour. The horse itself is decorated with a distinctive chocolate brown. Some individualistic flower painting appears on the coat of the girl rider. The base has a rococo moulding with a central shell.

A seated man with a dog (152mm (6in) high) (*Col. Pl. B*). This model consists of a seated man without a hat, but wearing a white coat, breeches painted with floral sprays and an orange waistcoat. The base is very similar to that of the 'Girl on a horse', and is outlined in puce. The dog, which is jumping up onto the man's lap, is decorated with the same chocolate brown found on the horse of the preceding model, and the flower-painting comes from the same hand that was responsible for the decoration on the coat of the girl riding on that horse. Furthermore, there is the same rococo base on both models. Another example of the 'Seated man with a dog' model is to be found in the Fitzwilliam Museum.

A seated man with a dog, but wearing a hat and holding a bird, together with a companion in the form of a seated girl with a sheep (152mm (6in) and 139mm (5½in) high respectively) (*Pl. 40*). The man is the same model as the immediately preceding one except that he wears a hat and has a bird on his right arm. The flower decoration would seem to be by the same artist whose work is seen on the preceding models.

The only known pair are in the British Museum. An interesting feature is that the hat and shoes of the man and the markings on his dog are of *matt* black. The lady has incised under the underglazed base the 'circle and triangle' mark.

A dancer (184mm (7¼in) high) (*Pl. 41*). He stands beribboned on the same rococo-style base seen on the preceding models, and has the mark illustrated in *Pl. 150(a)*. The same decorator referred to above would appear to have been at work. The only recorded example belongs to the Victoria and Albert Museum.

An exotic crested pheasant (215mm (8½in) high) (*Pl. 42*). Four examples of this model are known, three of them coloured. One is illustrated here (*Pl. 42*), now privately owned, and formerly in the A. F. Green Collection. It is really in the form of a candlestick, but the nozzle is now missing. The bird has a puce crest, a yellow beak and white neck. Its breast is yellow and the wings are orange tapering to white, whilst the base is predominantly yellow. The reverse model, albeit not mounted as a candlestick, is to be seen in the Untermyer Collection.[8] Here the crest is multi-coloured, the neck yellow and the body green and rose, the base being edged deep puce. Both birds stand against a flower-encrusted and frilled support and are decorated on the slightly rococo mound base with painted flowers, seemingly by the same artist referred to above. A third coloured example, once in the Eckstein and Foden Collections, the reverse of the example illustrated in *Pl. 42* and in the form of a candlestick, is shown in Barrett and Thorpe's *Derby Porcelain* (Pl. 23). A small vignette of figures takes the place of the flowers on the base. A fourth example of the crested pheasant, again in candlestick form, but this time in white, is recorded in the collection of Mr and Mrs S. J. Katz, Covington, Louisiana.

A candlestick with climbing rabbits. Only one example of this model is recorded, and its present whereabouts are unknown. It was formerly in the possession of the celebrated dealer Winifred Williams.

A candlestick group of a dog chasing a cat up a tree

(175mm (6⅞in) high) (*Pl. 43*). This group in damaged condition is to be found in the Victoria and Albert Museum. Unfortunately, the dog has disappeared leaving behind one paw and traces of where the other paw was once affixed. The cat is beautifully modelled, baring its teeth as it snarls at the missing dog which once leapt up at it. The wide base has a typical scrolled rococo moulding, and beneath it is incised the 'circle and triangle' mark.

4

FIGURES 1756–70

General introduction

In Chapter 2 a description was given of the particular characteristics which serve to identify the figures made at Derby during the period from 1756 to about 1770. The terminal date is fixed by the acquisition in 1769 of the Chelsea factory and the change in the Derby paste made shortly thereafter when the bone element found in Chelsea porcelain came to be introduced by Duesbury into his own formula. Also after 1770 the colours became purer, the turquoise in particular losing the muddied appearance which had hitherto been typical of it. Furthermore, from around 1770 the rococo style in English and continental porcelain fell out of favour and was replaced by the neo-classical. New models were created at Derby in the current fashion such as 'Jason and Medea' and the 'Three Virgins awakening Cupid', and the colours (except for the introduction of a new brownish-red) took on a paler and more subdued quality in tone with the restraint associated with neo-classicism. Moreover, for the first time in England biscuit figures came to be manufactured.

The period after 1770 to the final closure of the Chelsea factory in 1784 has become known to collectors as the 'Chelsea-Derby' period. It lies outside the scope of this book. Indeed, in this country by 1770 the great days of figure production had gone for ever. Duesbury's competitors had given up the struggle. Longton Hall had collapsed in about 1760, and in 1769 the Chelsea undertaking had fallen into the hands of Duesbury himself. He kept the factory going in a small way until about 1784 when he closed it down for good. Admittedly, the Bow factory, strictly speaking, continued until about 1776

(when it is reputed to have been acquired by Duesbury, although there is no conclusive documentary evidence to this effect), but its production after 1770 must have been minimal. Admittedly too, the Plymouth and Bristol factories were yet to come into existence and to produce their somewhat gauche and provincial-looking statuettes, and for a short period in the 1770s even the great Worcester factory turned to producing figures (possibly encouraged by the dearth of competition), but they were generally stiff and lifeless and, though rare, constitute no real contribution to the art of figure-making.

Of the figures produced at Derby before 1770 undoubtedly the finest examples were, for the most part, made in the dry-edge period, but these have already been discussed. Accordingly, it is the purpose of this chapter to consider the output for the period 1756 to 1770. The identifying characteristics of figures of this period have already been described, but no consideration has been given so far to the figures themselves. The number of different models runs into several hundred, and it is impractical to compile a list which could in any sense be said to be definitive. Even if it were a realistic proposition to get together a list of all recorded models, such a list would almost immediately be out of date on the discovery of some further model. However, the mere fact that finality is impossible should not be a bar to listing at least a good cross-section of the figures produced during the period under consideration, and such a list is set out in Appendix 2.

For simplicity the models have been grouped under various headings, namely romantics, theatricals, personalities, birds, animals, classical mythology, street vendors and rustics, symbolic representations and miscellaneous. Sometimes the classification has to be arbitrary, in that a particular figure might equally fall within more than one group, eg a figure could sometimes be regarded as either a romantic or a symbolic representation of a season, or again a particular model might be classified as a theatrical or a personality, as in the case of David Garrick. There is no magic in the classification actually adopted; it is designed for convenience alone.

Particular models were often produced in different sizes, and when this is known to have happened, the relevant measurements have been listed. Of course, measurements are approximate only, and indeed there are frequently minor discrepancies in size between models clearly intended to be of identical proportions. It must be emphasised that the measurements listed in Appendix 2 merely indicate those that have been recorded. They are in no way exhaustive.

An interesting feature of the figures referred to in Appendix 2 is that a distinctive group can be identified whose particular characteristics are that they are light in weight and decorated in predominantly pale colours. Deep colours are employed as well, but the palette used gives an emphasis to a lemon yellow, a crimson pink and a light green. The figures are small in stature, measuring from about 75 to 152mm (3 to 6in) in height—although sometimes they are in the form of candlesticks, in which event the overall height will, of course, be much greater. The detailed modelling of flowers and dress accessories, eg bows, is particularly sharp. The group of figures in question, commonly described as belonging to the 'pale-coloured family', often appear as representatives of the seasons or senses or as romantics, but they are also to be found under other classified heads. Generally speaking, they do not recur later in the strong colours typical of the 1760–70 period. These small pale-coloured figures are comparatively few and far between. Manifestly, from the style of their bases, which vary from the simple pad form to the slightly more elaborate, they are early productions and must have been the first to be turned out after Duesbury took over the factory. This is confirmed by the

inscription under the base of one of the two figures of 'Summer' and 'Autumn'—number I 3(v) in Appendix 2; now in the Derby Museum—of the words 'New D' which almost certainly stand for 'New Dresden'. For it was with Dresden that Duesbury was in the habit of comparing his products in the auction sales advertised in 1756 and 1757. Less probably, the inscription could stand for 'New Derby'. It is unlikely that production of the class of figures under consideration lasted for more than (say) two years, and they can therefore be assigned with reasonable accuracy to the years 1756 and 1757. Figures belonging to this class are identified in the list contained in Appendix 2 by a single asterisk.

However, the 'pale-coloured family' is not limited to the class of figures just described. It extends to a further group, including reissues of some of the dry-edge models, eg 'St Thomas' and 'St Philip'. (These reissues could have been produced at any time during the 1756–9 period, and have against them in Appendix 2 a single asterisk.) Examples of this group are much larger in size often 228 or 254mm (9 or 10in) high and, in one cast at least, 394mm (15½in) high, and many of these models are reproduced in the later period 1760–70 in the contemporary darker palette. Here the bases are generally more sophisticated, assuming a more marked rococo style. It is reasonable, therefore, to date these figures, which again are infrequent, to a comparatively short period, and it is unlikely that we will be far out if we assign them to the two years 1758 and 1759. Examples are identified in the list contained in Appendix 2 by a double asterisk. However, it cannot be overstressed that the absence of a double asterisk or, for that matter, a single asterisk against a particular model does not imply that the model was never produced before 1760. All that it indicates is that it has not been positively so established. An early version could easily come to light.

After about 1760 the pale colours referred to above largely disappear and until the end of the decade a stronger palette manifests itself with its emphasis on turquoise, puce and burnt-orange. It is interesting to note that a figure formerly in the Leverhulme Collection, incised underneath 'George Holmes did this figer 1765', had all the attributes normally associated with figures of the 1760–70 period.

The dating of pieces made in the 1760–70 period is not easy. As the decade advanced, it would seem that models tended to become more fussy and the amount of gilt used increased considerably. Courageous attempts have been made by writers in the past to attribute early Derby pieces to a specific year or to a date around that year, and to support this conclusion by reference to such refinements as the colour of the glaze. The difficulty inherent in this approach is that it assumes that at any one moment of time one batch of porcelain is exactly like another, when it is well known that in the early days of porcelain manufacture there were in fact marked differences. Accordingly, in dating the pieces here illustrated a cautious practice has been adopted.

Certain of the models manufactured at Derby from 1756 to 1770 owe their inspiration to continental products, particularly those from the Meissen factory. When this has definitely been established, reference is made to it in the list of Appendix 2 or, where the model is discussed in the text, then in the text itself, but failure to identify any such connection does not necessarily import a total independence of foreign influence. It may simply be that the connection has as yet been unrealised either because the existence of the relevant continental model has simply gone unnoticed—the products of the Meissen factory, for example, are scattered throughout the world and the opportunity for identification of particular models with their English counterparts has to be considered in this context—or because the relevant continental model is no longer represented by any extant example.

Some Derby figures are clearly after more or less contemporary engravings. A few have been identified, but doubtless there are many more whose origin is to be found in this quarter. It would seem that no systematic attempt has been made to identify particular models with contemporary engravings. Such identification as has in fact taken place seems to be the result of mere accident.

A further source of inspiration for Derby figures can be found in sculpture. Where this is

the case, reference has been made in this chapter or in Appendix 2.

Selected figures

A selection of the figures referred to in Appendix 2 is here illustrated and it may be helpful if brief mention is made of them. It will be convenient to refer to them under the same headings as adopted in the Appendix.

Romantics

A particularly fine example of this genre is the pair of seated musicians illustrated in *Col. Pl. J(a)* and *(c)*. These figures sometimes appear with bocage or with candlesticks or even in an arbour, but they are more attractive without any such embellishment. A large version of the man, now in the British Museum, is important for the fact that under the base there are faintly inscribed the letters 'WDCo', clearly standing for 'William Duesbury and Company' and furnishing support for a Derby attribution, not merely for this particular figure, but for all others sharing its characteristics.

Other examples of romantics are a shepherdess with a sheep at her feet, finely painted with floral bouquets (*Pl.* 44), a well-decorated gallant seated on rockwork holding a basket, with two lambs and a dog lying beside him (*Pl.* 45), an interesting pair consisting of a sportsman and companion (*Pl.* 46), and from the 'pale-coloured family' a pair of sweetmeat

(Opposite)
A. A girl on a horse, 152mm (6in) high; c. 1755 ('Girl-on-a-horse' factory figure). See pages 33, 36

(Overleaf, left)
B. A seated young man with a dog, 152mm (6in) high; c. 1755 ('Girl-on-a-horse' factory figure). See page 36

(Overleaf, right, above)
C.(a) A plate moulded with overlapping leaves and wicker work, 209mm (8¼in) in diameter; c. 1756–9. Decorated by 'the cotton-stem painter'. See pages 55, 56, 65, 200
  (b) A sheep, 95mm (3¾in) high; c. 1752–5. See pages 29, 181

(Overleaf, right, below)
D.(a) A 'spectacle' plate with a centre of overlapping leaves, 184mm (7¼in) in diameter; c. 1756–9. Decorated by 'the cotton-stem painter'. See pages 55, 65, 199
  (b) A finch with partially unfurled wings and up-turned tail, 120mm (4¾in) high; c. 1760. See pages 46, 190

figures of a man and girl seated holding shell-shaped baskets (*Pl. 47*). An extremely interesting pair of figures can be seen in *Pl. 48*. The companion to the girl draped with flowers is normally a hatless gallant (accompanied by his dog) proffering in his right hand a fruit taken from a basket of fruit clasped in his left.[1] However, on this occasion the companion figure, although in all material respects identical with the usual model, has been given a hat. Two further pairs of romantics are illustrated. One comprises a Scottish couple, a boy with tartan breeches playing the bagpipes and his dancing companion with tartan jacket lifting her skirt slightly with her right hand and holding flowers in her left (*Col. Pl. L*), in substance a reissue of the dry-edge models of a shepherd and shepherdess (*Pl. 19*). The other pair consists of a youth and his companion, the former holding a lamb and a basket of flowers, the latter with an apron of flowers and a basket of eggs (*Pl. 49*).

Also shown here (*Pl. 50*) is a rare group of lovers, set against an elaborate bocage, the man seated on a stump playing his flute, whilst his companion, lying beside him, holds the score. Other examples of romantics include a dancing lady (*Pl. 17(b)*) (seemingly based on the Meissen), a pair of candlestick figures of a standing boy and girl, the former playing a flute, the latter holding a flower (*Pl. 51*), a boy seated on a rock with one foot thrust forward in a kicking movement (*Pl. 52*), a girl seated on a rock with her hat in her lap (*Pl. 53(a)*), and a sailor and his lass. The sailor carries a stick and displays three gold coins, whilst his companion, around whose neck there is a ribbon with a pendant consisting of a heart pierced by an arrow, coyly beckons to him (*Pl. 54*). It has been suggested that they are Woodward and Nancy

Dawson in character. Mention should also be made of a pair of pastoral figures, the man wearing a cocked hat and holding a struggling cockerel in his arms, whilst his bare-footed companion clasps a hen (*Pl. 55*) (taken from the Meissen), and of a particularly interesting pair of minuet dancers, the man leaning backwards slightly, the lady holding out her skirt with both hands, modelled after the engraving 'Fêtes Vénitiennes' by Laurent Cars of the painting by Antoine Watteau (*Pl. 56*). Unusual romantics are the candlestick figure of a putto supporting a foliate candle nozzle illustrated in *Pl. 57*, and the attractive centrepiece, shown in *Pl. 58*, modelled as a gallant and companion seated back to back, each holding an oval basket, on a circular scroll-moulded base; these last may be figures from the Italian Comedy.

Theatricals

Included in the theatrical group are all those figures in any way connected with entertainment. Thus, the famous so-called 'Ranelagh figures' have been classified as theatricals because of their association with the Ranelagh Gardens, the famous eighteenth-century place of entertainment. An especially fine pair of these figures are illustrated in *Pl. 59*. An interesting feature is that the man holds a letter inscribed 'Dominae Lucretiae' and the lady wears a locket representing an admission ticket to the gardens. This amount of detail does not appear on most examples of these models. Aubrey Toppin identifies the figure of the lady with a mezzotint of Mary, Duchess of Ancaster, by McArdell after Hudson, published in 1757.[2]

The Meissen factory drew upon the Italian Comedy for many of its models and these in turn have sometimes been copied by English factories. Three examples shown here are a candlestick figure of Punch, masquerading as a nightwatchman holding in his right hand a lantern (*Pl. 60*), a group of Harlequin and Columbine dancing (*Pl. 61*) and a group of a lady, gallant and jester, the two lovers seated beneath a flowering tree embracing, whilst the jester stoops obsequiously to offer them a tray set with two cups. The latter group, which is based on a model by J. J. Kändler *c.* 1745 adapted from the *Mockery of Age*, was produced

(Opposite, above)
E.*(a) A plate with feather-moulded border, painted with exotic birds and insects, 203mm (8in) in diameter; c. 1760–5. See pages 55, 66, 200*

(b) A straight-sided mug or tankard, painted with birds, 127mm (5in) high; c. 1760–5. See pages 54, 55, 66, 199

(Opposite, below)
F. *A pair of oval dishes, their wavy rims moulded in relief with vine-branches bearing grapes and leaves, the bird painting by 'the cotton-stem painter', 209mm (8¼in) long; c. 1756–9. See pages 56, 67, 200*

in an early version in pale colours (*Pl. 62*) and again in a later version, larger in size, with more elaborate bocage, and in deeper colours (*Pl. 63*).

Round about the end of the period with which we are concerned, the factory produced an interesting pair of duet singers (*Pl. 64*). It is a matter of speculation whether they represent well-known singers of the day, whose identity is now lost to us. An actor who has been identified is James Quinn playing the part of Falstaff. This figure (unlike the early Bow model, the actor has a beard) is based on an engraving by James McArdell after Francis Hayman's portrait. A large and fine example is shown in *Pl. 65*.

Personalities

Perhaps the two most well known personalities to be produced at Derby were Shakespeare after Scheemaker's statue in Westminster Abbey and Milton. A much rarer personality is the figure of Lord Chatham leaning against a pedestal (inscribed with a reference to his elevation to the peerage and his office as Lord Keeper of His Majesty's Privy Seal), with a kneeling Red Indian woman and an alligator at his feet, symbolic of America (*Pl. 66*). In 1776 Chatham was raised to the peerage and became Lord Keeper. In the same year he identified himself with a conciliatory policy towards the American colonies. Presumably, then, the date of the model is around 1767. The further personality to be illustrated is the figure generally known as 'St Philip' (*Pl. 67*). It was first produced in the dry-edge period and is the companion to the figure variously called 'St Thomas', 'King Lear' or the 'Roman centurion' or the 'Roman soldier'.

Birds

Derby birds were presumably based on engravings (albeit so far unidentified), but as eighteenth-century engravings of birds were often inaccurate either anatomically or by reason of the colours applied or on both counts, it is not surprising to find the same failings carried over into the three-dimensional porcelain models. The result is that, although sometimes it is perfectly clear what species of bird was intended, there are other occasions when this is not the case. Accordingly, whenever a particular model is identified with a particular species of bird, such identification should be accepted with caution. A list of the different birds so far recorded is contained in Appendix 2, and thirteen of them are illustrated here.

A pair of bluetits (*Pl. 68*), a goldfinch (*Pl. 69*), a woodpecker (*Pl. 70*) and a pair of parrots (*Pl. 71*), whose identity in each case cannot be doubted, are shown here. The fine pair of birds in *Pl. 72*, which the factory also turned out, would appear to be some sort of finch, but here unfortunately precision is wanting. An extremely attractive model with its partially unfurled wings is that illustrated in *Col. Pl. D(b)*. Hitherto unrecorded, it would appear to be some sort of finch. An interesting feature of it is that, although the decoration in red-brown and green appears to be of the period 1760–5, it has a screw-hole base. Perhaps it was produced in the dry-edge period, but not decorated till much later—compare the Chinoiserie figure of 'Taste' referred to at page 26. However, the evidence is not sufficient to justify its inclusion among the authenticated dry-edge models.

The Lady Ludlow porcelain collection at Luton Hoo is rich in birds, and it includes certain rare Derby specimens, which are illustrated here. In addition to a fine pair of what would appear to be green woodpeckers and a bird which is manifestly a canary (*Pl. 73(b)*) the collection includes three other Derby models, each perched on a tree-stump, not easily identifiable with any recognised species of bird. One of them has chocolate-brown and black markings (*Pl. 74(a)*), another mauve spots and a dark mauve tail, its body flecked with browny-orange markings (*Pl. 74(b)*), and the third a yellow and green body, a puce head and mauve barred tail feathers (*Pl. 73(a)*).

Animals

A few of the animals appearing in Appendix 2 are illustrated here. They include a candlestick group of two sheep, the one climbing a tree applied with flowers, the other lying recumbent at the bottom (*Pl. 75(b)*), a lowing cow under an overhanging tree in flower (*Pl. 53(b)*), a pair of leopards (*Pl. 76*), a candlestick figure of a spaniel-type dog looking up at two birds perched on branches of a flowering tree

(*Pl. 75(a)*), a pair of early pugs seated erect on rectangular mound bases (*Pl. 77*) and an extremely rare spaniel standing on its own, barking, its head slightly turned to the right (*Col. Pl. L(b)*).

Classical mythology
Figures depicting the gods and goddesses of classical times and other mythological subjects must have found a ready market in the period 1756–70; for they are reasonably frequent today, although, of course, certain models are rare. Some of these classical figures are large and in relation to their Chelsea equivalent are gauche and provincial-looking. However, it must be remembered that they were not intended for display in cabinets, but were meant to stand out in the open in large libraries, where they would have blended excellently, Illustrated here are Europa and the Bull (*Pl. 78*), the Muse Erato (*Pl. 80*) based on an engraving by J. Daullé after Boucher, Cybele or Earth, wearing a coronet and with a lion and cornucopia at her feet (*Pl. 79*) and, perhaps one of the most attractive of models of this genre, 'Time clipping the wings of Cupid'. At the feet of Father Time are a scythe, hour-glass, crown, sceptre, terrestrial globe and skull and Cupid's quiver. Cupid is giving a lively expression to his feelings (*Pl. 81*).

Street vendors and rustics
Two interesting pairs of street vendors are illustrated here. The first consists of the Jewish pedlar and his companion, the former wearing a fur cap, long greenish-blue fur-lined coat and blue and yellow-striped breeches, with a basket of bottles slung in front of him (after the red-anchor Chelsea[3]), the latter with red cape, purple dress and flowered petticoat, holding a rectangular box of trinkets (*Pl. 82*). The other pair comprises a mapseller and companion (*Pl. 83*). The man holds an open map in one hand and a rolled one in the other, the remainder of his wares being stacked in a case on his back, whilst the woman, wearing a broad-brimmed hat, holds a two-drawered tray. The man was also produced during the dry-edge period. He is after the Meissen either directly or via the red-anchor Chelsea model (see the note against this model in Appendix 2, page 193).

The well-known 'Tithe pig group' is also illustrated here (*Pl. 84*). Seemingly based on an engraving of 1751 by J. S. Muller after Boitard, it consists of three figures, the Rector, the Farmer (holding a pig) and his wife (holding a baby). Very rarely these three figures appear as a set of three independent figures and not as a composite group (*Pl. 85*). Many examples of the composite group are post-1770: a group was sold for sixteen shillings to Philip Egerton Esq. on 7 April 1773,[4] and several such groups were included in the auction sale of 9 March 1785.[5] But undoubtedly some were produced before that date. The subject—the farmer's wife is determined not to part with the tenth pig unless the parson takes the tenth child—occurs on a Sadler-printed Liverpool mug, accompanied by the following ballad:

The Parson comes, the Pig he claims,
And the good Wife with Taunts
    inflames,
But she quite Arch bow'd low and
    smil'd—
Kept back the Pig and held the Child,
The Priest look'd gruff, the wife look'd
    big,
Zounds, Sir, quoth she, no Child, no
    Pig.

Representational
Figures were often used to symbolise such things as the continents, the senses, the seasons or liberty and matrimony. A selection of such representational pieces appears here. They include a set of the continents: Africa represented by a black boy with elephant head-dress kneeling on a lion, Europe by a crowned child holding a globe, Asia by a child standing before a camel, and America by a Red Indian standing beside an alligator (*Pl. 86*)—these were copies of the Chelsea[6] and are more frequently found after 1770; 'Hearing' in the form of a lady in a pannier skirt playing a lute (*Pl. 8(a)*), a model which may also have been produced in the dry-edge period;[7] and a set of the seasons (almost an exact reproduction of the Meissen): Spring as a girl with flowers, Summer as a lady with a sheaf of corn, Autumn as Bacchus, and Winter as an old man, in each case accompanied

by a putto (*Pl. 87*). The seasons were produced in a variety of different forms. Two seated figures, which are illustrated in *Pl. 88*, their heads garlanded with flowers, seem in each case to represent Spring. An interesting pair of similarly seated models, but this time with hats, the girl holding flowers and symbolising Spring, the boy holding fruit and representing Autumn, are shown in *Pl. 89(a)* and *(c)*. Another version of Spring and Autumn is illustrated in *Pl. 90*. This time the figures are standing and hatless. The girl (Spring) with flowered skirt holds in her left hand a posy of flowers, whilst the boy (Autumn) with floral decorated breeches holds grapes in his right hand. Another version of Spring and Autumn, but on this occasion with hats, appears in *Pl. 91*. These two models are particularly attractive. Sometimes seasons take the form of groups of twin figures. Thus the candlestick group of two lovers illustrated in *Pl. 92*, the youth seated, the girl standing, either side of a palm tree, each holding a sheaf of corn, represents Summer, and the group of two lovers, arm in arm surrounded by grapes, shown in *Pl. 89(b)*, symbolises Autumn.

Liberty and matrimony were a favourite subject for representation during the period from 1756 to 1770. Liberty is normally symbolised by a man holding a bird or bird's nest, and matrimony by a woman holding an open cage (*Col. Pl. K*) although, somewhat suprisingly, in some models the man holds the cage and the lady the bird or bird's nest.

Miscellaneous

Included under this classification are figures which do not conveniently fit elsewhere. Illustrated here are the Virgin and St John and Mary Magdalene gathered around the Cross (missing) (*Pl. 93*), the Abyssinian archer and companion (the former holding a bunch of arrows in his right hand and clasping with his left a low-slung belt, from which a dagger protrudes, the latter holding an apple in her raised left hand) (*Pl. 94*), a pair of blackamoors, each kneeling on one knee and supporting a shell on the other, and a group of four black figures (including the two previously mentioned blackamoors) around a central pillar (*Pl. 95*).

The Derby boxes of 1763

It is interesting to note that some of the figures included in the list contained in Appendix 2 are referred to among the contents of forty-two large boxes of china which Jewitt tells us were sent from Derby to London in 1763. He observes as follows:[8]

. . . in 1763, in an account of 'goods sent to London' no less than forty-two large boxes appear at one time to have been despatched to the metropolis, and the proceeds, I presume, of the sale of part of them, on the 2nd of May in that year, amounted to no less a sum than £666 17s 6d. It is very interesting, at this early period of the art, to be enabled to say of what varieties of goods the consignment to London consisted, and I therefore give the list of some of the boxes entire, and also a few from others. . . .

Box No. 41 contained

8	Large Flower Jarrs, at 21s.
3	Large Ink Stands, at 42s.
1	Small ditto, at 24s.
4	Large Britanias, at 36s.
6	Second-sized Huzzars, at 12s.
4	Large Pidgeons, at 7s.
12	Small Rabbets, at 2s.
12	Chickens, at 2s.
16	Small Baskets, at 2s 6d.

Box No. 31

4	Large Quarters, at 40s.
4	Shakespeares, at 42s.
6	Miltons, at 42s.
24	Bucks, on Pedestals, at 2s 6d.

Box No. 29.

4	Large Quarters, at 40s.
2	Jupiters, at 68s.
2	Junos
5	Ledas, at 36s.
1	Europa, at 36s.
2	Bird-catchers, at 10s 6d.
12	Sixth-sized solid Baskets
18	Second-sized Boys, at 1st 6d.

Box No. 11

24	Enammelled, round, fourth-size open-worked Baskets
12	Blue ditto
12	Open-worked Spectacle Baskets

9 Second-size Sage-leaf boats

There were also, of various sizes, blue fluted boats, Mosaic boats, sage-leaf boats, potting pots, caudle cups, blue strawberry pots, fig-leaf sauce boats, octagon fruit plates, vine-leaf plates, coffee cups, flower vases, standing sheep, feeding sheep, cats, sunflower blows, pedestals, honeycomb jars, coffee pots, blue guglets and basins to ditto; butter tubs, Chelsea jars, tea pots, honeycomb pots, figures of Mars and Minerva, sets of the Elements, Spanish shepherds, Neptune, the Muses, bucks, tumblers, roses, Jupiter, Diana, boys, garland shepherd, Spaniards, Chelsea-pattern candlesticks, Dresden ditto, jars and beakers, polyanthus pots, etc, etc.

We have no difficulty in identifying from extant examples referred to in the list contained in Appendix 2 many of the figures mentioned above, eg the Quarters (of the globe, ie the Continents (I2)), the Britannias (I4), Shakespeares (C1), Miltons (C1), bucks (E3, 4, 5), Jupiters (F4, 6), Junos (F5), Ledas (F1), the Europa (F2), cats (E20), Mars (F11, 16), Minerva (F12, 15, 16), Muses (F18, 19), and Diana (F13). Moreover, the pigeon may be a dove (D13) or a pigeon tureen (*Pl. 123*). Standing sheep and feeding sheep (again presumably standing) appear frequently in the post-1770 period. It is clear from their inclusion in the 1763 boxes that these models must have been produced long before 1770. However, so far no example has been recorded of a 'huzzar', rabbit, chicken or bird-catcher—are 'bird-catchers' a reference to 'Liberty' and 'Matrimony'?

There are a large number of models which could properly be described as 'boys', and there are many different figures of shepherds, but which of them, if any, is the 'garland shepherd' is unknown. Likewise the identification of the 'Spaniards' poses difficulty. Another problem is the identity of the tumblers. Incidentally, the identification of the items mentioned of useful and ornamental ware will be attempted in the chapters dealing respectively with those types of porcelain.

Size of the factory

A but cursory glance at the list of figures contained in Appendix 2, and likewise at the lists of useful and ornamental ware contained in Appendices 3 and 4, reveals a wide-ranging variety of output, and suggests a factory operating on a very substantial scale. We would perhaps expect to find that the premises were extensive in size and the number of workmen employed considerable. However, during the period from 1756 to 1770 the factory seemingly covered a remarkably small area. 'The Old China Manufactory' (to distinguish it from 'The New Works' erected on property known as 'Calver Close' at the end of the century and lying to the east of the original site) was enlarged in 1781 and 1783,[9] but even in its completed form it stood on an area no more than 45m by 25m; half the original site on which the factory was erected was taken up by Duesbury's own house and garden, and Haslem very aptly observes that 'in a space so limited the manufactory must have been small, and incapable of accommodating a large number of workmen'.[10] Hutton in his *History of Derby* published in 1790 asserts that seventy people were then employed at the factory, and Haslem does not seek to challenge this figure. In view of the extensions of 1781 and 1783 there were presumably less than seventy employees at all times prior to 1781.

It is not known what size the factory was when Duesbury took over its management in 1756. It is known, however, from a recital in a conveyance dated 1 August 1780[11] that a number of properties immediately adjacent to the original works were on 19 April 1756 transferred to John Heath and 'were ... converted into and then continued to be Workshops used and employed by the Sd W. Duesbury and Company as such in the making of China'. Moreover, there appears in the *Public Advertiser* of 28 January and again of 11 February 1758 the following interesting announcement:

The Proprietors of the Derby *China Company* beg leave to acquaint the Nobility and Gentry that they have fix'd their Porcelain to be sold by their Factor, *Mr Williams*, at his large Foreign China Warehouse up one Pair of Stairs, formerly known by the Name of Oliver Cromwel's Drawing-Room, facing Craigg's Court, near the Admiralty, consisting of a great variety of Figures, the nearest the Dresden, and several curious Pieces for Deserts and all mark'd at the Factory's lowest Prices. As with great Care and Expence this Factory is allowed by all Judges to exceed any Thing of the kind made in England, and the great Demand there is for them, has encouraged the Proprietors to enlarge their Manufactory, and *have engaged double the Number of Hands they used to employ* [my italics], which will enable them to send to the said Warehouse every week great variety of new Goods, and much cheaper than any Thing of equal Quality made in England. . . .

Now, the reference to doubling the number of hands is consonant with the enlargement of the factory, and even allowing for a certain degree of exaggeration in any advertisement there is no need to discount, at least to any significant extent, the assertion that the number of employees had been doubled. Presumably this was effected in 1757, and may have been encouraged by the announcement in an advertisement of 1757[12] that 'the Chelsea Porcelain Manufactory has been very much retarded by the sickness of Mr Sprimont'. Duesbury was a consummate opportunist, and having taken over the china works at Derby and got himself on his feet, he may have seen a golden opportunity to fill a gap brought about by Sprimont's indisposition. It is clear from Mason's statement[13] that the Chelsea factory was closed for two years or so.

Although it is impossible to give any accurate figures, it is perhaps difficult to envisage there ever having been at Derby prior to 1770 any more than (say) sixty workmen. Moreover, at the time Duesbury took over, the hands could have been less than thirty. It is truly remarkable how such a small concern made the impact that it did.

Marketing

Of course, it was not enough for the factory merely to produce fine pieces. It had to market them as well. Presumably during the period with which we are concerned this was done largely through dealers, or, as they were called, chinamen. That there were chinamen resident in Derby is clear from the marriage registers of St Alkmund's and the other Derby churches which conveniently recorded the occupation of the bridegrooms. However, in addition to this quiet channel of disposal through dealers a more dramatic means of marketing was adopted at the beginning of our period. For the factory had resort to auctions, and also sales from a London warehouse.

The earliest auction sale, which took place in June 1756 at 54 Richmond Wells, Surrey, has already been referred to.[14] Notice of the next one appeared in the *Public Advertiser* on 14 December of that same year. It reads as follows:

To be sold by Auction
By MR BELLAMY
By Order of the Proprietors of the
DERBY PORCELAIN Manufactory at a
Commodious House in Prince's Street
Cavendish Square. This and three
following days.
A Curious Collection of fine *Figures*,
Jars, Sauceboats, Services for Deserts, and a
great *Variety* of other useful and
Ornamental Porcelain, after the finest
Dresden models, all exquisitely painted in
Enamel, with Flowers, Insects, India
Plants etc. . .

J. E. Nightingale in his *Contributions towards the History of Early English Porcelain from Contemporary Sources* painstakingly traced in the London journals any reference to Derby sales. He refers, *inter alia*, to a spring sale which took place on 17 May 1757 and quotes from the *Public Advertiser*. The sale notice there appearing refers to 'the largest Variety of the Derby or Second Dresden with Chelsea, Worcester, Bow, Longton hall, Birmingham etc'. The subsequent report on the sale reads as follows:

At the large Auction Room facing
Craig's-court near the Admiralty,
Whitehall, there were Numbers of
Quality and Gentry, who expressed great

satisfaction at seeing the extensive Number of foreign, and the great Variety of the English China Manufactories; and admired at the great Perfection the Derby Figures in particular, are arrived to, that many good Judges could not distinguish them from the real Dresden.

Another sale of 1757 is referred to by Mr Geoffrey Wills in *The Country Life Book of English China* at page 58. It reads as follows:

AT WILLIAMS'S Cool Retreat, formerly Oliver Cromwell's Palace, facing Craig's Court, Charing-cross, being remarkably cooler than most Houses in London, There will be sold by Hand, a few Days longer, all the Remainder of his large Collection of Foreign China, with several new Chinese Curiosities never before exposed to Sale: with great Variety of India Japan Dressing-Boxes in compleat and other sets; Japan Dressing Glasses, and a large Quantity of new-fashion'd Fans; there is also the greatest Variety of the Derby Porcelain or second Dresden Figures, Baskets, Leaves, etc and several curious Pieces for Deserts, all mark'd by the Proprietor's Orders at the lowest Prices, with good Allowance to Dealers; several of the said Goods will be sold under prime cost, rather than risque the moving; for conveniency of Gentlemen and Ladies Carriages, the Door will be open'd in Spring Gardens.

Mr Williams is referred to again in a further notice appearing in the *Public Advertiser* on 28 January 1758 and again on 11 February 1758, cited by Nightingale. The first part of that notice has already been reproduced.[15] It concludes in the following terms:

The said Proprietors [ie of the Derby factory] hope all Gentlemen and Ladies according to the Merit the said Ware deserves will please to encourage their Undertakings, by sending for their Orders to the said Warehouse, where all their Commands will be duly observed and carefully executed, by Gentlemen and Ladies, your most obedient humble Servant to command,

Thomas Williams
Factor for the Derby Porcelain Company

There will be allow'd as great Encouragement to Dealers in this Manufactory as any in England.

To be sold at the said Warehouse, the greatest Variety of Foreign China, India Dressing-Boxes, and Fans; and by Desire of Several Gentlemen and Ladies there is a Door open'd in Spring-Gardens.

On 6 March 1758 Mr Williams announced 'that he has this day unpacked the greatest Variety of new Figures from Derby, allowed by several good Judges to be the nearest to Dresden, and several curious Wares in Leaves, Baskets etc for Deserts, finely painted in Dresden Flowers, and all warranted the true Enamel'.

However, the business at this particular warehouse was shortlived. For the *Public Advertiser* of 6 April 1758 contains the following valedictory notice:

'Tis assured that the large China Warehouse facing Craig's-court, Charing-Cross must now soon be pull'd down to widen the way, by Order of the Hon. the Commissioner, Mr Williams having received Warning to quit the Premises in a short Time. There is to be sold at the above Warehouse the greatest Variety in England of the Derby Porcelain or Second Dresden, foreign China etc. All Gentlemen and Ladies that have not seen that antient Building and Drawing-Room, formerly called Oliver Cromwell's, may now have that Opportunity as well as of purchasing any small Quantity of the said Ware exceeding cheap, rather than risque the moving of them etc.

Thereafter Nightingale can trace no further allusion to the Derby factory in any of the London journals for the next ten or twelve years, ie until after the close of our period. Possibly the factory conducted some direct trade with the public, but presumably the bulk of its output was disposed of through 'chinamen'.

5

USEFUL WARE
1756–70

During the period from 1756 to 1770 useful ware was produced in a considerable variety of shapes. Moreover, as the amount of such ware which has survived can only be a fraction of what was turned out—it was the fate of pieces of this kind, when they became through use cracked or chipped, to be thrown away, and not, as in the case of figures, repaired and preserved—there were doubtless shapes of which we now have no knowledge, all examples having long ago disappeared. A selection of Derby useful ware, classified by shape, is given in Appendix 3. As in the case of the figures described in Appendix 2, the shapes listed are not, nor do they purport to be, exhaustive. However, they constitute a significant representation of the kind of useful ware turned out in the period from 1756 to 1770. The opportunity has been taken to record against each shape, if it is not here illustrated, one or more publications where a suitable illustration can be seen. Recorded measurements are also given, but it should not be inferred from this that the shape in question is not to be found in a variety of other sizes. In this connection it is perhaps pertinent to point out that included in the items stated by Jewitt[1] as having been sent in 1763 from Derby to London are '12 Sixth-sized solid Baskets', indicating that such baskets were produced in at least six different sizes.

Tea and coffee services

It is interesting to note that the various auction and other sales advertised in the press during the period from 1756 to 1758[2] do not refer to tea or coffee services at all. However, it is clear from what has survived that such services were produced from as early as 1756.[3] Moreover, teapots, coffee pots and coffee cups are referred to by Jewitt as being among the items sent from Derby to London in 1763.[4] It would appear from the contemporary auction sales of Chelsea porcelain that a tea and coffee service normally consisted of a teapot, cover and stand, a sugar basin and cover, a slop basin, a cream jug, 8 tea bowls, 8 coffee cups and 8 saucers, and a plate. It would seem from this that a coffee pot and lid were normally an extra. See, for example, the Sale of Chelsea Porcelain conducted by Mr Ford at St James's Haymarket on 29 March 1756, lots 14, 32 and 67 (reproduced in Appendix VIII to George Savage's *18th-Century English Porcelain*). Although at Chelsea a complete service apparently consisted of 8 tea bowls, 8 coffee cups and 8 saucers, we cannot be sure that at Derby a different number was not adopted as the norm.

Teapots and covers
That teapots were manufactured as early as 1756 is apparent from the survival in the Cecil Higgins Art Gallery of a teapot with that date incised under the base. It has a lobed body and scroll handle. It is decorated with Chinoiserie figures, but unlike a similarly shaped and decorated example in the Castle Museum, Norwich, it has lost its cover, which would have been slightly domed and surmounted by a finial probably in the form of an acorn. Another example of a teapot and cover shaped as above is to be seen in the Derby Museum, this time painted with birds. Various other forms of teapot were turned out at Derby. Two are illustrated here in colour (*Col. Pls I* and *J(b)*).

One of them, decorated with flowers painted by 'the cotton-stem painter', has a ribbed melon-shape body, flat scroll handle, and slightly domed cover, also ribbed, surmounted by a conical finial. Two other examples of this shape are in public museums, one (with an acorn finial) in the Castle Museum, Norwich, the other (with flower finial) in the National Museum of Wales. The second teapot here illustrated, with its chained cover, is of great rarity. It has a small globular body, fluted spout, scroll handle and domed cover surmounted by a 'mushroom' finial, and is decorated with exotic birds. A further form of teapot is recorded, in at least two different sizes, with a smooth globular body, smooth spout, loop handle and a slightly domed cover surmounted by a conical or onion-shape finial.

It was an unfortunate characteristic of early Derby teapots that they were likely to crack when filled suddenly with hot liquids. Unlike Worcester teapots, where the paste had a soapstone content, they were not really equal to the purpose for which they were intended. Even the later teapots (by which time calcined bones had been added to the soft-paste formula) were still functionally inadequate. For late in the century it was stated in the correspondence between Joseph Lygo, the factory's agent in London, and William Duesbury the second that teapots 'flew'. It is interesting to note that on 17 December 1790 Duesbury the second had occasion to write to Lygo about a complaint received from Sir John Shaw. He subsequently caused a warning notice to be sent to customers in the following terms:

To prevent Accidents with Tea Pots—Let about a Tea Cupful of Cold Water be sent up in the Tea Pot, and just before you wish to make Tea pour about 2 Tea Cupfulls of boiling water to the cold in the pot and give it a shake round. This will gradually expand the Pot and prepare it for Reception of boiling water to make Tea. It being the expansion of Tea Pots etc by means of boiling water suddenly thrown in rends them.

Presumably coffee pots suffered from a like fault.

Coffee pots and covers

Slightly less rare than teapots are coffee pots. Three different forms were made at Derby. One was of pyramidic shape with scrolled loop handle and domed cover surmounted by a conical finial. A blue and white example, transfer-printed with the ox-herd pattern, is illustrated here (Pl. 96(a)). The other two forms of coffee pot are essentially pear-shape, one with a ribbed body, the other smooth. Two examples of the former are shown here with their domed covers, decorated respectively with exotic birds (Pl. 97) and Chinoiserie figures (Pl. 98). The slight difference in the modelling of the handle is to be noted. A coffee pot of the smooth variety is also illustrated, decorated with birds (Pl. 99(a)).

Tea bowls, coffee cups and saucers and other items

Tea bowls and coffee cups are rare today, and rarer still with their saucers. A factor which partially accounts for the paucity of the last item is that normally in a tea and coffee service each tea bowl and coffee cup had to share a single saucer, the reason being that tea and coffee were not served at one and the same time and whichever beverage was being dispensed the same saucers could always be used. This doubling up of saucers meant that they were exposed to greater risk of damage and eventual destruction. The effect of this on the present-day survival ratio of saucers to cups can be startling. Suppose a set of eight tea bowls, eight coffee cups and eight saucers came to suffer over the years a loss of fourteen pieces, and suppose these losses occurred to cups and saucers equally, then the surviving pieces would amount to nine cups and only one saucer. Particularly distinctive of the factory's output are coffee cups of varying shapes (eg octagonal, circular, and square with shaped canted corners) having as a common feature a handle reminiscent of a wish-bone. Occasionally fluted cups and saucers can be found (Pl. 100(b)). A selection of the different types of bowls/cups and saucers produced by the factory is given in Appendix 3. Illustrated here (Pl. 101) is an interesting two-handled 'trembleuse' cup, together with its stand, painted with flowers; made in two sizes, this is perhaps to be identified with the 'caudle cups' already referred to at page 49. The 'trembleuse', intended for use by invalids, is held in position by the stand's central openwork gallery.

In addition to the items already mentioned a tea and coffee service normally had a sugar basin and cover, a slop basin and cream ewer. Cream ewers are occasionally to be found, but so far no surviving slop basin from our period seems to be recorded, and only one sugar bowl and cover, illustrated in Bradley's *Ceramics of Derbyshire*, Pl. 168. Not exactly part of a tea-service, but intimately connected therewith, are the teapoys and spoon trays that have occasionally survived.

Doubtless some tea and coffee services were enlarged to become breakfast services as well. Certainly butter dishes—which are included in the items mentioned by Jewitt as having been sent in 1763 from Derby to London[5]—survive and presumably these were part of a breakfast service. Three different shapes of dish are recorded, square with fluted corners rectangular with canted corners, and cylindrical They were made with covers and stands. Usually the stands have failed to survive and sometimes this is true of the covers as well. One would have expected honey-pots to have been produced in addition to butter dishes, but no example has been recorded for certain. However, 'honeycomb pots' and 'honeycomb jars' are included in the items despatched from Derby to London in 1763.

Punch pots, kettles and bowls

Very rarely what looks like a particularly large form of teapot is encountered. This must have been used for making not tea but punch, and is therefore properly called a punch pot. Two examples with covers are in the Victoria and Albert Museum and the National Museum of Wales respectively, the former being finely painted with exotic birds (*Pl. 102*). However, what is of exceptional interest and rarity is the punch kettle and cover, illustrated here in colour (*Col. Pl. H*), decorated with exotic birds in landscape, and, on the cover, with moths. The kettle has an ormolu handle. No other example is known. It is particularly interesting to note that Lady Schreiber in Vol. 1 of her *Journals*[6] refers to a visit on 15 September 1869 to Mr Hodges' collection at Lyme where there was a

'Chelsea tea Kettle (I should think unique), painted in birds'. At that time all early Derby pieces were attributed to Chelsea, and it is difficult to avoid the conclusion that the particular kettle to which Lady Schreiber refers and which she professed to covet was in fact the kettle illustrated here. Admittedly, she speaks of it as being a tea kettle rather than a punch kettle, but this is a distinction which perhaps does not automatically, or even readily, spring to mind.

Very occasionally punch bowls are encountered. An important example is illustrated here (*Pl. 103*). It is painted with a group of birds (in flight and on the ground) including a magnificent peacock. The sides are decorated with moths and insects and the interior with a pipe-smoker reclining in a rococo arbour holding a lidded tankard. In the tobacco smoke is to be seen the inscription 'Success to the Mine Innocent' and William Duesbury may well have had an interest in that mine. The bowl now belongs to the Victoria and Albert Museum and can be seen alongside a companion punch bowl also decorated on the outside with birds.

Jugs, tankards and goblets

Jugs are recorded in two basic shapes—ovoid and pear-shaped, sometimes with a pointed lip, sometimes with a mask spout, the handle, it seems, invariably scrolled. Three examples of pear-shaped jugs are here illustrated (*Col. Pl. G* and *Pls 104* and *105*), two decorated with birds, the other with flowers, and each with a different kind of spout. The spout of the jug of *Col. Pl. G* is not in the usual pointed form, but is moulded in a way so far not elsewhere recorded.

Tankards or mugs were also produced at Derby in the period 1756–70. They were barrel-shape with raised moulded straps, ovoid shape, inverted bell-shape (sometimes in truncated form) or very rarely straight-sided. A barrel-shape tankard is illustrated in *Pl. 96(b)*. It is decorated with a Chinoiserie scene in blue and white. Two examples of tankards with bird decoration are also shown here, the one ovoid in form (*Pl. 106*), the other of inverted bell-shape (*Pl. 99(b)*). An example of the truncated version (decorated with birds) is also illustrated (*Pl. 107*). The straight-sided form of tankard, of which a fine specimen decorated with birds is shown in *Col. Pl. E(b)*, is extremely rare. Only one other example has so far been recorded, this time decorated in blue and white.[7]

Akin to tankards or mugs are goblets, of which a pair, ovoid in shape, each standing on a small foot, are to be seen in the Victoria and Albert Museum. They are decorated with a spray of narcissus and other flowers.

Dinner/dessert services

The Derby factory produced the necessary pieces that go to make up a dinner/dessert service.

Plates

Plates were turned out in the period 1756–70 in a variety of different forms, although on occasion, notwithstanding detailed modification, the same basic shape can be seen. For example, one particular type of dessert plate ('spectacle'), whose border is edged with linked circles (compare the 'spectacle baskets' referred to below at page 56), has a centre sometimes moulded with three overlapping leaves, and sometimes left smooth, whilst its rim, sometimes pierced, sometimes not, is applied with one or three rows of florettes. It is not certain whether every permutation and combination of the above alternatives was employed in connection with this plate, but some of the variations positively recorded are set out in Appendix 3. One of the above variations is illustrated here in *Col. Pl. D(a)*. It is decorated by the hand of 'the cotton-stem painter'.

The 'overlapping leaves' motif referred to above occurs again on another type of plate, where the shaped borders are moulded with wicker work. An example is shown in *Col. Pl. C(a)*, again decorated by 'the cotton-stem painter'. A variant of this shape is recorded where the border is pierced and one or two rows of florettes are applied. Indeed, applied florettes are a characteristic feature of early Derby plates (and of baskets as well). They occur again on the trellis diaper moulding of another type of plate where the centre is smooth, but the rim is moulded with the above-mentioned trellis diaper pattern and with raised scrolling to take painted vignettes. The same style of plate is also found with a pierced rim. It may be that one or

other of the above designs incorporating the 'overlapping leaves' motif is to be identified with the 'vine-leaf plates' referred to earlier at page 49.

Two other shapes are worthy of comment. The characteristic feature of the one is its shaped twelve-sided rim, and of the other its feather-moulded border. Three examples of the latter are illustrated here. One is painted with cherries and foliage and insects (*Pl. 113(a)*), another with birds and insects on the rim and more insects in the centre (*Pl. 109*). These two plates do not appear to have been decorated by the same artist, and indeed it is not easy to identify the hand on the second example with painting on other Derby pieces, except, of course, on plates of the same service.[8] This is unfortunate because we know part of the artist's name. For on the wing of one of the insects of the plate illustrated he has painted 'Thos F' or 'Thos Fl'. It is not clear whether the 'F' is followed by an 'l' because of the inconvenient presence of a scale of the insect's wing. It has not proved possible to identify this particular artist with any name connected with the factory. The third feather-moulded plate illustrated here (*Col. Pl. E(a)*) is painted in the centre with two fine exotic birds.

A quite different form of plate, again painted in the centre with two exotic birds, one of them this time dishevelled, is shown in *Pl. 108(a)*. The wavy-edge ten-sided border is decorated with stylished flowers in blue and puce.

Dishes

During the period under consideration the Derby factory was responsible for producing a variety of different shapes of dish. They include a 'silver-patterned' design with fluted rim moulded with shells (after the Chelsea version from the raised anchor period), a diamond-shaped dish (the border moulded with four shells and with panels of four-petalled flowers divided by hoops), a dish of lobed oval form, and two interesting designs based on a leaf motif, the one with a border moulded with a basket-weave pattern—a pair of such dishes are illustrated here in *Pl. 110*—the other modelled in the form of five overlapping leaves with the stalk as the handle. Particularly attractive are the rare sunflower and peony dishes (*Pls 111* and

112). The sunflower dishes are presumably to be identified with the 'sunflower blows' referred to by Jewitt as being among the items sent in 1763 from Derby to London.[9]

Three other designs are recorded. One is oval, with serrated edge, moulded with floral and other motifs. The second, also oval in shape, has as its distinctive feature an elaborate twirled moulding at each end at the edge of the rim. The third design, again basically oval in form, has a wavy-edge rim moulded in relief with vine branches bearing grapes and leaves. A pair of such dishes are illustrated here (*Col. Pl. F*). They are painted in distinctive style, in the one case with a magpie and two chicks and in the other with two peacocks and a bird in the distance. It would seem that the artist was 'the cotton-stem painter'.[10] A variant dish is sometimes seen where the crinkled rim is less pronounced.

Baskets

Baskets were produced in different shapes and sizes, and many, if not all of them, undoubtedly formed part of a dessert service. They were normally made with stands, although most surviving baskets are now without them. Particularly elegant are the 'shallow oval' baskets with wavy rim, moulded on the exterior with a diagonal wicker-work pattern (sometimes pierced, sometimes solid) applied with florettes at the intersections, or with a close basket-weave pattern applied with one row of florettes at the top of the rim. The twin handles have sometimes single, sometimes double, ropes. A pair of solid baskets with close basket-weave moulding are shown in *Pl. 114*, together with two stands, of which only one would seem to match the baskets. They are finely decorated with fruit and insects, and may be the type of baskets to which the description '12 Sixth-sized solid Baskets' (mentioned earlier at page 48) refers. Equally attractive are the 'deep circular' shaped baskets, which the factory also turned out, seemingly after the Viennese.[11] An example, together with its stand, decorated with flowers, is illustrated in *Pl. 115*. The pierced sides and the adoption of the same motifs used on the 'shallow oval' baskets should be noted. The 'deep circular' type of basket is presumably to be identified with

24 Enammelled, round fourth-size, open-worked Baskets
12 Blue ditto

stated by Jewitt to have been included in Box No. 11 of the forty-two boxes sent to London in 1763.[12] Incidentally the stand is similar to the pierced version of the plate illustrated in *Col. Pl. C(a)*.

Sometimes the pierced version of the 'shallow oval' type of basket has a rim consisting of a chain of pierced circles or discs linked one with another by a bridge, giving the appearance of a row of spectacles. All the examples recorded to date have *double-rope* handles. However, it could easily be the case that the factory also produced the design with single-rope handles, but a specimen has simply not survived or been recorded. One of a pair of these 'spectacle' baskets, decorated with cherries, foliage and insects, is illustrated in *Pl. 113(b)*. But this was not the only type of 'spectacle' basket to be produced at Derby. The 'deep circular' basket was sometimes modified so that it too had an outer rim consisting of a chain of pierced circles or discs giving the appearance of spectacles (*Pl. 116*). In this case each of the twin handles has a single rope only. But once again this assertion is dependent for its accuracy on the recorded examples correctly reflecting the factory's practice.

Of the forty-two boxes sent to London in 1763, Box No. 11 contained in addition to the items mentioned above '12 Open-worked Spectacle Baskets'. Unfortunately it is not possible to say to which of the two varieties of spectacle basket the above reference relates.

A further type of basket produced at Derby during the period 1756–70 is oval in shape with wavy everted rim, twin double-rope handles and an exterior moulded with a diagonal wicker-work pattern. An example, together with its matching stand, is illustrated in *Pl. 117*. It is finely painted with fruit and insects.

Chestnut baskets were turned out in two versions and examples of both are illustrated in *Pls 118* and *119*. The circular basket in blue and white is decorated in the centre with a Chinoiserie scene. It is particularly interesting because the cover is inscribed on the inside 'August 1762'; the stand, which is missing, would have been similar in form to the pierced version of the plate with rim moulded with raised scrolling interspersed between diagonal wicker work. The pair of oval baskets, complete with covers and stands, are finely painted with insects on the covers and exotic birds on the stands.

The Derby factory also turned out eel-baskets. A group of three are illustrated in *Pl. 121*. They are oviform in shape, and moulded with wicker work. Their flared necks and sleeves are pierced, and the twin handles are modelled in the shape of bulrushes. The rock-work bases are applied with two ducks. The baskets carry the Chelsea red anchor mark, which Duesbury did not scruple to appropriate to himself whenever he wished to pass off his own goods as those of the more fashionable Chelsea factory.

Three further types of basket should be mentioned, all of them rare. Two are oval in form, their distinctive features being in the one case the fluted sides (applied at the rim with one row of florettes) and in the other the single, centrally positioned handle. The sides of the latter basket are moulded with a basket-weave pattern and encrusted at the top with flowers. A particularly fine pair decorated with birds and small 'Gainsborough-type' figures are shown in *Pl. 120*. The third type of basket, of which a pair are illustrated in *Pl. 122*, is circular in form, the sides moulded on the outside with a diagonal wicker-work design applied with florettes at the intersections. It stands on a rococo foot, but the really distinctive feature is the cover surmounted by a bird among leaves and flowers. The only recorded examples are in the Victoria and Albert Museum where they are described as 'sugar baskets'. It is highly improbable that *pairs* of sugar basins were produced. Each tea and coffee service had only *one* sugar basin. Furthermore, as each of the above baskets is pierced, it would be an unsuitable receptacle for sugar. However, what was the true function of the pair of baskets is problematical. Possibly they were potpourri baskets, useful in days of indifferent sanitation.

Tureens

Tureens together with their covers normally take the form of pigeons (*Pl. 123*) or partridges (*Pl. 124*) sitting on a nest. The stands have only rarely survived. Tureens of quatrefoil shape with domed covers surmounted by a cherry resting on leaves were also produced at Derby. A pair without their stands but with their ladles—the ladles are normally missing; collectors of ladles as such have contributed to their scarcity—are illustrated in *Pl. 125*, decorated in puce and gilding with a 'banded hedge pattern' together with sprigs and flowers, after the continental.[13] A rare small tureen and cover in the form of a bunch of grapes resting on and partially covered by vine leaves, all in natural colours, are also shown here in *Pl. 126*.

Sauce-boats

The Derby factory produced a variety of differently shaped sauce-boats, often decorated in blue and white. Only very rarely has the stand survived. Some shapes are recorded only in blue and white and sometimes in these cases a Derby attribution cannot be accepted with complete confidence. A further complication is that such pieces cannot always be dated with certainty. Accordingly in Appendix 3 there have only been included those shapes which can with reasonable assurance be regarded as having been produced at Derby during the period with which we are concerned. Several examples of different types of sauce-boats are illustrated here. Most interesting are the pair of boats (together with their covers) in the form of plaice (*Pl. 127*). More common are the pair of leaf-shaped boats (decorated by 'the cotton-stem painter'), each with a curled leaf handle (*Pl. 128*). Also illustrated is a lobed sauce-boat with scalloped rim and looped handle, standing on a pedestal foot, painted with oriental-type flowers (*Pl. 100(a)*). It is interesting to note that among the items sent in 1763 from Derby to London are 'blue fluted boats', 'Mosaic boats', 'sage-leaf boats' and 'fig-leaf sauce boats'.

Centrepieces

Centrepieces of two distinct kinds are recorded. The more attractive is modelled with two or three tiers of scallop shells, and stands on an erection of rock-work and weeds encrusted with smaller shells. Sometimes the whole edifice is surmounted by a kingfisher or a figure, and in the latter instance the figure sometimes holds a shell above the head. Some specimens were made in two parts. An example of the 'king-fisher' version of this type of centrepiece is illustrated in *Pl. 129*. The shells are decorated with insects. The other kind of centrepiece is in the form of a shaped round pillar or column with square holes from which extend metallic supports holding porcelain flowers.

Ice pails

These are extremely rare. A fine example of four-lobed shape with two scroll handles immediately below the circular rim is illustrated in Bradley's *Ceramics of Derbyshire* (Col. Pl. at p. 46 and Pl. 108). It is decorated with birds and insects.

Cruet sets

A full cruet set consists of a vinegar bottle, oil bottle, sugar sifter, pepper pot and mustard pot. An example is illustrated here (*Pl. 130*) decorated with flowers. The carrier is made of wood, and the silver handle is marked 'Birmingham 1782/3'. Presumably the carrier was acquired subsequently to the set. Originally mustard was brought to the table in its dry state, so that it required a container similar to a sugar caster. However, later it was the practice for mustard to be served already mixed with water and a different sort of receptacle was called for. To meet this need the Derby factory produced a mustard pot cylindrical in shape with reeded exterior and smooth sleeve, the cover (likewise reeded) surmounted by a floral knop and with a cut-out to take a spoon.

Salts

Salts were produced in a variety of shapes.

Illustrated in *Pl. 131* is one of an interesting pair from the Victoria and Albert Museum. It is of depressed globular form with twin satyr's mask handles, standing on a high-domed foot, its moulded cover surmounted by a floral knop. Further types include a design in the form of three deep scallop shells resting on a coral and shell-encrusted base, another in the form of a shallow cup with applied flowers standing on three lion-paw feet, and a further model consisting of a globular bowl with wish-bone-shape handle on a circular pedestal foot.

Broth bowls

A pair of broth bowls are recorded, circular in shape with double scroll handles, the slightly domed cover surmounted by a flower finial.

Miscellaneous items

In addition to the shapes already mentioned, the factory turned out a miscellany of other items, often in blue and white and generally at the end of or after the period with which we are concerned. For example, a type of pickle dish was produced in the form of geranium leaves with a rustic loop handle, and the factory also turned out a design of asparagus butter boat moulded as a leaf, with rustic handle and standing on trefoil feet. Sometimes it is difficult to define the exact purpose for which a particular piece was made. Thus, examples are recorded of a small curved dish of lobed form with cut-out or shaped handle, but it has been variously described as a pickle dish, oyster dish, sweetmeat dish and wine-taster. Asparagus dishes are also recorded, but no example so far can be assigned with any confidence to a date earlier than 1770.

6

ORNAMENTAL PORCELAIN
1756–70

If ornamental porcelain, which in this chapter does not include figures, was produced during the dry-edge period, it does not seem to have survived. It was not until Duesbury took over the factory that this type of porcelain came to be made at Derby. Most ornamental porcelain during the period from 1756 to 1770 took the form of vases, some of which, particularly the heavier ones, carry under the base the patch marks associated with figures. Some twenty-seven different types of vases are described in Appendix 4 and of these the fifteen types here illustrated are particularly worthy of comment.

The three vases shown in *Pl. 132* are of a kind which seem invariably to be decorated with painting of an exceptionally high order (usually incorporating figures or birds) on a mazarine blue ground. With their flower-knopped covers they were once thought to emanate from Longton Hall, but they were in fact produced at Derby. It has been suggested that the decoration was carried out in London. However, there is no concrete evidence to support this view.[1] Another kind of vase, more readily associated with Longton Hall, but in fact of Derby origin, is of eight-lobed form, filled with a variety of large and small flowers (*Pl. 133(b)*). It is accompanied in the illustration by a pair of potpourri vases of bulbous shape, the sides pierced with scrollwork and the covers high-domed. They are decorated with birds, flowers and insects (*Pl. 133(a)* and *(c)*). This same type of vase was also produced with scrolling *unpierced* and with encrusted flowers. In this form it was manifestly not a potpourri vase. Similar in style is the vase illustrated in *Pl. 108(b)* with its cover. Whether or not it is a

potpourri vase is uncertain. The body is unpierced, but the cover does have one or two holes through which the perfume might escape. The decoration on the example illustrated takes the form of painted birds, insects and flowers, all from the hand of 'the cotton-stem painter'.[2] This type of vase was also produced with a high waist and short neck.

Frill vases, named after the frill of shell-shaped leaves projecting from the lower part of the body of each vase, are found in Derby porcelain. The fact of their being pierced suggests that they were a form of potpourri vase. A garniture of such vases, painted with insects, is illustrated in *Pl. 135*. An important documentary vase, now in the Victoria and Albert Museum, has inscribed under it 'Jonathan Boot 1764'. A flanking vase, from another type of garniture, is illustrated in *Pl. 136*. It, too, has a frill but of different form from that of the vases of *Pl. 135*.

Asymmetrical vases with elaborate rococo moulding were also produced at Derby. They appear in a variety of different shapes. A pair topped with flowers are shown here, each decorated on one side with a painted bouquet of flowers and on the other with a figure of a woman (*Pl. 137*). Are items of this kind the 'Large Flower Jarrs' or 'flower vases' referred to earlier at pages 48 and 49? A further specimen of this shape is also shown, this time without the flowers in relief, but finely painted with figures (*Pl. 138*). It belongs to the British Museum. Likewise decorated with figures is the asymmetrical vase with elaborate rococo fluting and moulding appearing in *Pl. 143*.

An important vase of elaborate form with a

figure of Venus on one side and Cupid on the other is illustrated in *Pl. 139*. It is painted with insects by a hand not frequently seen at Derby. A similar style of vase has as its distinguishing feature twin Dolphin handles (*Pl. 140*).

Totally different in feeling is the urn-shaped vase shown in *Pl. 141*. It has a fluted neck and foot, and the pierced cover has a fruit knop. In the Victoria and Albert Museum is a small flower-filled vase, the basic shape of which is rather like a sugar sifter. It is particularly interesting for the painted leopard that appears on it (*Pl. 142*).

However, ornamental porcelain was not confined at Derby to vases. It covers a wide range of objects (more particularly described in Appendix 4) including: inkstandishes—'3 Large Ink Stands, at 42s. 1 small ditto, at 24s' (Box No. 41)[3]—(a larger and a smaller version) (*Pl. 144*); guglets (*Pl. 145*) and basins;[4] toilet boxes— of which those in the form of a rose should perhaps be identified with the 'roses' referred to earlier at page 13—and covers (*Pls 146* and *147*); flower pots (*Pl. 148*)—compare the 'polyanthus pots' and 'potting pots' referred to earlier at page 49; dovecots; wall pockets; chamber candlesticks (*Pl. 149*) and pastille-burners. However, they are far from common.

(Opposite)
G. *A pear-shaped jug with unusually shaped spout, painted with exotic birds, 228mm (9in) high; c. 1760–5. See pages 54, 66, 199*

(Overleaf, left)
H. *A punch kettle and cover, with ormolu handle, painted with birds and insects, 260mm (10¼in) high; c. 1760–5. See pages 54, 66, 199*

(Overleaf, right, above)
I. *A smooth teapot and cover with fluted spout, painted with birds and insects, 127mm (5in) high; c. 1760–5. See pages 52, 66, 197*

(Overleaf, right, below)
J.(a) and (c) *A pair of seated musicians, 203 and 190mm (8 and 7½in) high respectively; c. 1760–5. See pages 24, 25, 40, 183*
   (b) *A ribbed teapot and cover painted with flowers by 'the cotton-stem painter', 139mm (5½in) high; c. 1756–9. See pages 52, 65, 197*

7

DECORATION 1756–70

Derby painting during the period 1756–70 is seen at its best on useful and ornamental porcelain. The broad surfaces brought into play provide the decorative artist with a splendid opportunity to display his skill. (In contrast, where figures are concerned, the scope for his talent is necessarily restricted.) The subject-matter of early Derby painting can be classified under (1) flowers, (2) birds, (3) fruit, (4) insects, (5) figures, and (6) oriental subjects. In addition some pieces are found decorated in underglaze blue or with printed patterns. We will consider each decorative form under a separate head.

Flower-painting
Examples of flower-painting are prolific, appearing on figures as well as on useful and ornamental ware. During the period from 1756 to 1770 several different flower-painters were at work. Of these perhaps the most distinctive hand is that of the artist who has come to be dubbed 'the cotton-stem painter' from his practice of giving to his flower-groups thread-like stalks. Examples of his work as a flower-painter can be seen in *Col. Pls C(a)*, *D(a)* and *J(b)* and *Pls 101, 128, 133(a)* and *(c)* and *145*. It is to be noted that his work appears on the

earliest of post-dry-edge porcelain, including figures, clearly indicating that he must have been at the factory from or shortly after the time when William Duesbury first took control.

Except where, as in the case of 'the cotton-stem painter', an artist has a particularly distinctive style, the task of distinguishing between different hands painting similar subjects on porcelain poses extremely difficult, if not insoluble, problems. The difficulty is graphically illustrated by the observations of John Haslem, himself an artist working at the factory towards the end of its existence. For whilst he was able to identify the work of 'those who painted [flowers] from about 1820 until the close of the factory in 1848', he went on to say with reference to the earlier flower-painters (Billingsley and the elder Pegg excepted) as follows:[1]

Probably, however, there is no one now living who could distinguish with certainty the flowers of Clavey, Stanesby, Bancroft, Cresswell, Pegg the younger, and one or two others from each other, as there is a sort of family likeness in their several productions.

Coming from such a source as Haslem with all his intimate knowledge of the technique of painting on porcelain, these are strong words indeed.

Flowers on early Derby porcelain are painted sometimes naturalistically, sometimes in a stylised manner after the Meissen. It is to the latter form of decoration that the sales notices of 1756–8 are referring when they speak of ware being 'finely painted in Dresden flowers'.

(Opposite, above)
K. 'Matrimony' and 'Liberty', 228mm (9in) high; c. 1760–5. See pages 48, 195

(Opposite, below)
L.(a) and (c) A Scottish girl dancing to the piping of her Scottish companion, 165 and 158mm (6¼ and 6¼in) high respectively; c. 1756–7. See pages 45, 184
(b) A spaniel dog barking, 76mm (3in) long; c. 1760–5. See pages 47, 191

Bird-painting

Some of the most attractive decoration takes the form of exotic birds. These are creatures of pure imagination, brightly coloured, the like of which have never appeared on earth. They derive their origin from the *Fantasievögel* of Meissen, which in turn appears to have developed from a cross between the golden pheasant and the phoenix. The concept was later perfected at Sèvres.

A selection of pieces decorated with exotic birds can be seen in *Col. Pls E, G, H* and *I* and *Pls 99, 102, 106, 107, 108(a), 109, 116, 119, 132* and *141*. Sometimes the exotic birds are replaced with naturalistic birds such as finches, or at least birds resembling finches (*Pls 97* and *104*), peacocks (*Pl. 103*) or kingfishers. A careful examination of bird-painted pieces reveals that only one or possibly two hands were responsible for most of the decoration assuming this particular form. Some of the bird scenes are done with a darker palette than others (albeit the same essential style is maintained), suggesting that there may have been two painters rather than one.

Generally speaking, Derby birds have smooth feathers, but occasionally they appear to a greater or lesser extent agitated or dishevelled. The fact that an artist should choose to change the plumage in this way would not normally call for any comment. It is a natural variation, to which any artist might be expected to resort. However, the practice has sprung up in recent years among the *cognoscenti* of regarding *all* dishevelled birds, of whatever factory, as having been executed in London, probably at the Giles studio. See, for example, the comments on Pls 51 and 61 of Winifred Williams, *Early Derby Porcelain*.

The reason for this attribution finds its origin in the alleged identification of a distinctive hand on pieces from a variety of different factories—the decorator responsible is generally known as 'the artist of the dishevelled birds'—and the attribution to this same hand of the dishevelled birds found on Derby porcelain. The case for the existence of 'the artist of the dishevelled birds' seems to date as far back as 1910 when R. L. Hobson in his *Worcester Porcelain* illustrated in Pl. LXXXVII six alleged examples of the work

of that particular artist on Worcester, Bow, Chelsea, Longton Hall and Bristol porcelain. The theory was later taken up by W. B. Honey in the first edition (published in 1928) of his *Old English Porcelain* and in an article in *ECC Transactions* 1937.[2] However, whereas R. L. Hobson took the view that 'the artist of the dishevelled birds' was itinerant, working for short periods at each of the relevant factories, W. B. Honey preferred to think—and his opinion has prevailed generally—that the artist in question carried on his work in London and probably at the Giles studio. Moreover, in support of his view he claimed to have identified the relevant hand on Chinese porcelain. We are not in this book concerned with the controversy as to where 'the artist of the dishevelled birds' actually worked or, for that matter, whether all the pieces attributed to this hand by the various protagonists are truly his. Suffice it to say that the dishevelled birds, illustrated here (see, for example, *Col. Pls E(a)* and *H*, and *Pls 108(a), 109* and *119*) and, for that matter, those appearing on other Derby pieces are of a totally different style from any of the birds on the items in the Victoria and Albert Museum, whose decoration is claimed by W. B. Honey to be the work of 'the dishevelled bird painter'.[3] The dishevelled birds at Derby were executed by the same factory artist or artists who was or were responsible for the smooth-feathered birds.

Furthermore, there is no evidence to suggest that *any* bird-painting on Derby porcelain was carried out in London, still less that the Giles studio was responsible. Admittedly, as Aubrey J. Toppin has shown,[4] the ledgers of Giles reveal that he received from 'Wm. Duesbury & Co., parcel Derby China, on Sale or Return', a 15% discount being allowed. But the words 'on Sale or Return', which imply that the goods in question will, if not sold, be returned in the condition in which they were received, suggest that what was being supplied was something that needed no further speculative decoration on the part of the Giles atelier.

It is to be conceded that the auction sales of 1756–8,[5] although referring to other forms of decoration, make no mention of birds. However, this omission only shows that at that stage bird-painting had not, at least to any noticeable extent, got under way, and it is consistent with this that pieces decorated with birds seem to date from after 1758.

As has been stated above, most of the bird-painting on Derby porcelain was undertaken by one or possibly two artists ('the principal bird-painter(s)'). However, a further hand, whose bird-painting appears far less frequently, can also be identified. His work can be seen on the vase illustrated in *Pl. 108(b)*, on the two vine-shaped dishes shown in *Col. Pl. F*, where the centres are naturalistically, but somewhat sketchily, painted, in the one case with chickens and a magpie and in the other with peacocks, both in rustic settings, and on a further vase, a detail of which is reproduced in *Pl. 134*. The similarity of subject appearing in this detail and on the centre of one of the two dishes is to be noted. This same hand with its lighter and somewhat more sketchy treatment of birds can also be seen on the pieces illustrated in *Pls 133(c)* and *145*. The artist responsible can conveniently be styled 'the secondary bird painter'.

Exotic and natural birds are not infrequently accompanied by butterflies and moths and sometimes flowers. It is hard to avoid the conclusion that the artist who was responsible for the birds was also responsible for the insects and flowers. Reference has been made earlier to 'the cotton-stem painter' whose hand can easily be distinguished on useful and ornamental ware and on figures. Now, the flower-painting of this artist sometimes accompanies bird-painting of 'the secondary bird-painter'. Thus on the vase illustrated in *Pl. 108(b)*, on the further vase from which the detail shown in *Pl. 134* has been taken, and on the pieces illustrated in *Pls 133(c)* and *145*, there are to be seen, in addition to the bird-painting already referred to, the distinctive flowers of 'the cotton-stem painter'. The obvious inference is that the latter artist and 'the secondary bird-painter' are one and the same person. Moreover, the same artist was presumably also responsible for the butterflies, moths and other insects that occasionally are to be found in company with his flowers or birds.

Fruit-painting

More than one hand is to be seen employing fruit as a decorative motif. However, one particular artist seems to be responsible for the major part of this type of work—'the principal fruit-painter'. Examples of his work can be seen in *Pls 113, 114* nd *117*. Fruit-decoration includes cherries, apples, pears, peaches, nuts, strawberries and, very rarely, blackberries.

Insect-painting

During the period 1756–70 several hands can be identified in connection with the painting of moths, butterflies, bees and other insects (including caterpillars). Writers and cataloguers are in the habit of referring to 'the moth-painter' as though there were only one artist answering to this description. There are at least four. Insects regularly accompany the bird-painting of 'the principal bird-painter(s)' and of 'the secondary bird-painter'/'the cotton-stem painter', and they must presumably be attributed to the same hand as was responsible for the birds. Likewise insects often appear with the fruit of 'the principal fruit-painter' and they are presumably the work of that particular artist. Another insect painter altogether was responsible for the moths, butterflies, caterpillars and a particularly fine bee on the rare vase illustrated in *Pl. 139*. It is to be assumed that he also executed the distinctive flowers on the seated Venus that accompanies the vase.

Figure-painting

Occasionally, Derby pieces are decorated with painted figures. Often they are small and 'Gainsborough-like' in style. Examples of this charming form of decoration are shown in *Pls 138* and *143*. A pair of early baskets are recorded (*Pl. 120*) where figures of the above kind are painted in conjunction with birds—particularly a magpie, not shown in the illustration, similar to the bird appearing in *Col. Pl. F* (right-hand dish)—that seem to come from the hand of 'the secondary bird-painter' (ie 'the cotton-stem painter'). The inference must be that this particular artist was also responsible for the 'Gainsborough-type' figures.

Sometimes figures of a more elaborate kind are encountered, particularly on vases of the mazarine blue variety—see *Pl. 132*; see also the Cupids of the vase illustrated in *Pl. 140*, the reverse of which is decorated with birds. Figure scenes appearing on such vases are generally accompanied on other panels by birds, and the implication must be that the artist who painted the birds also painted the figures. Although it has been suggested[6] that the elaborate decoration generally found on mazarine blue vases was executed in London, there is no evidence in support of this view. The birds were done at the factory; so too presumably were the figure scenes. Not exactly a figure scene, but conveniently classified under this head, is a scene of hare-coursing on a jug illustrated in Pl. 46 of Barrett and Thorpe, *Derby Porcelain*; see also the leopard of the vase of *Pl. 142*.

Oriental subjects

A variety of Chinese subjects appear on Derby useful and ornamental ware of 1756–70, particularly on the early pieces. For example, on a coffee pot illustrated in Gilhespie's *Derby Porcelain*, Pl. 51, and on two teapots respectively in the Cecil Higgins Art Gallery, Bedford, and the Castle Museum, Norwich, and shown in Bradley's *Ceramics of Derbyshire* in Pls 48 and 47 (all three items being dated around 1756), the principal decoration consists of a Chinaman standing, and a Chinese woman seated, by a table laden with fruit and flowers, a large jar set in front of them. Other examples of decoration with Chinese figures can be seen on two coffee pots, one illustrated here (*Pl. 98*), the other (belonging to the Derby Museum) shown in Barrett and Thorpe's *Derby Porcelain*, Pl. 38, and *Ceramics of Derbyshire*, Pl. 61. The Chinoiserie motif, however, occurs with reasonable frequency in enamel decoration on ware produced throughout the entire period from 1756 to 1770. A bell-shaped cup with undulating rim and flat pierced handle, illustrated in Winifred Williams' catalogue of *Early Derby Porcelain*, Pl. 74, with its saucer, and in *Ceramics of Derbyshire*, Pl. 70, without it, is decorated with an overglaze design taken from the Chinese *famille verte*.

Some overglaze decoration owes its inspiration to Japanese Kakiemon designs taken over via Meissen. An example is the 'banded hedge' pattern, which can be seen on a pyramidic coffee pot and cover and on a punch pot and cover illustrated in *Ceramics of Derbyshire* in Pls 60 and 63 respectively. The punch pot and cover are also shown in Gilhespie's *Derby Porcelain* in Pl. 41, immediately below a Derby fluted cup which stands adjacent to a Meissen tea-bowl and saucer, and on each piece the same decorative pattern has been used.

Underglaze blue

So far we have considered decoration in the form of enamel colours applied over the glaze. However, the Derby factory along with its principal competitors also produced ware decorated in underglaze blue. These pieces, some of which are transfer-printed, are referred to as 'blue and white'. A fine selection of blue and white examples can be seen in *Ceramics of Derbyshire*, Pls 135 to 230, although many of the illustrations relate to items that are post-1770. They are comparatively scarce, but so too are Derby polychrome wares. Blue and white pieces are mentioned in the lists of items stated by Jewitt[7] to have been sent in 1763 from Derby to London. It will be remembered that Box 11 contained, *inter alia*, '12 Blue round fourth-size open-worked Baskets'. Included in the items sent to London were blue fluted boats, blue strawberry pots and 'blue guglets and basins to ditto'. The designs on blue and white ware are multifarious, too numerous to list here. Frequently they have a Chinoiserie motif. They are often to be seen on sauceboats, and are particularly effective on scallop-shell centrepieces. The quality of the underglaze blue varies considerably, possibly because of the difference in purity between different batches of cobalt or because of unstable kiln conditions or because of a combination of both factors. Sometimes the blue has a dry appearance, sometimes a soft tone of considerable attractiveness, whilst at other times it assumes a very dark violet-blue. These variations would appear to be contemporaneous.

It would seem that blue transfer-printing did not properly commence until the mid 1760s, ie until after Richard Holdship's arrival. However, an on-glaze coronation mug of George III and Queen Charlotte is dated 1761, and Chaffers, *Marks and Monograms*, 8th edn (1897), refers to an interesting cup with a lilac underglaze bust of the King of Prussia (together with the words 'Derby 1757') on one side, and the figure of

Fame with two trumpets on the other. The last-mentioned piece was apparently experimental as Fame changed in the kiln from lilac to brown.

A variety of distinct patterns of blue transfer-printing have been identified, eg 'boy on a buffalo', 'spinning maiden', 'buffalo beside the river with a Chinese sailing junk', 'three oriental figures minding oxen in a landscape', 'open zig-zag fence' and 'buck at lodge' (in fact the arms of the town of Derby). Apart from the 'stag at lodge' none of the patterns appears peculiar to Derby. An example of the 'boy on a buffalo' pattern is shown on the coffee pot illustrated in *Pl. 96(a)*. There are a few pieces where on-glaze transfer-printing has been applied. It occurs in black or pink, eg a mug with portrait busts in black of King George III and Queen Charlotte celebrating the coronation which took place on 22 September 1761[8]—the piece is in the Royal Crown Derby Museum—and a further mug with a portrait of the King of Prussia in pink. However, the attribution of these pieces to the Nottingham Road factory is not certain.

In any event printing (whether underglaze or on-glaze) on Derby porcelain fell far short of its competitors in quality, and it is not surprising that it was not produced in any quantity. Duesbury exploited success; he did not back projects rooted in failure.

Dating

In dating useful or ornamental ware the same essential criteria can be adopted as are applicable in the case of figures. The use of colours associated with figures of 'the pale-coloured family' indicates that the piece in question was made around 1756-9. Attempts at greater precision based on such subtleties as the colour of the glaze proceed on the highly questionable premise that at one period of time each batch of porcelain produced was the same as another.

The deeper colours point to the subsequent period 1760-70. A feeling of primitiveness and the presence of blemishes suggest an early date of origin, whilst sophistication in design and a high degree of technical accomplishment indicate a date later in our period. However, precision is impossible. Dating is still very largely a subjective issue, with perhaps a temptation to assign pieces to an earlier date than is really justified. How many items are by convention dated *c*. 1760-5, and how few *c*. 1765-70!

8

ARTISTS

Painters

It is an unfortunate fact that little is known of the artists who decorated Derby porcelain during the first twenty years of the factory's life. They were never allowed to sign their work, and for the most part they have passed into oblivion. Nevertheless it has at least proved possible to unearth the names of some artists and to ascertain a little about them.

Two artists are particularly important, as they commenced employment with the factory early in its life and continued until the close or nearly the close of the period with which we are concerned. They are Constantine Smith and William Billingsley (the elder).

Constantine Smith

The researches of W. H. Tapp show[1] that, along with George Holmes, Constantine Smith was a ratepayer in Clerkenwell in 1746 and 1747 and was described in the rate books as an enameller. Tapp argues that he received his training in enamelling from Thomas Hughes of Clerkenwell. We do not know what happened to Constantine Smith immediately after 1747, but we can be certain that by July 1757 he was working at Derby as a china painter. For it appears in the records of All Saints Church, Derby, that on 11 July 1757 he married Hannah Storer. He is there described as a 'china painter'.

As has already been pointed out,[2] there is evidence that George Holmes was at Derby from late 1747 or early 1748, and it is possible that Constantine Smith was with him. If this was so, it is interesting to reflect on where exactly he worked. One intriguing possibility is that he was employed at the dry-edge factory, in which

70

event we would expect to see his hand on pieces from the pre-Duesbury period. However, it may be that he went to work at the Cockpit Hill pottery, painting in fired enamels the earthenware products of that factory.

In any event there can be no doubt that by July 1757 Constantine Smith had arrived at Derby and was working for William Duesbury. Moreover he was still there in 1770, because, as is shown by a document formerly in the possession of Jewitt, he witnessed[3] an agreement made 17 September 1770 between Pierre Stephan and William Duesbury. Incidentally, he is described by Jewitt[4] as a 'preparer of colours and porcelain painter and enameller', 'one of the best "hands" at the Derby works'.

On 28 October 1773 his son William was bound apprentice to him. The implication of this must be that Constantine had by this date become an independent decorator. Otherwise William would have been apprenticed to Duesbury. According to Jewitt[5] he did in fact finish his time with Duesbury, so that presumably his father died before the expiry of his apprenticeship. This is confirmed by the existence in the Duesbury Collection of Manuscripts in the Derby Public Library of an agreement between William Smith and Duesbury dated 23 November 1778 under which, in addition to contracting to make colours for painting upon china, William undertook to support his mother:

I do hereby promise to pay to my mother, Hannah Smith, weekly and every week, out of the wages I may get under Messrs Duesbury & Co., the sum of eighteen shillings, to commence from this date and expire the 28th Oct. 1780.

This particular undertaking on his part strengthens the view that his father had died.

If Constantine Smith did not commence working for Duesbury at the time the latter took over the factory, he must have started shortly thereafter. We do not know exactly how long he stayed before he took up employment as an independent contractor, but the fact that he did become an independent contractor may possibly be confirmed by a teapot (referred to by J. Twitchett in his *Derby Porcelain*) which belongs to the Royal Crown Derby Porcelain Museum and is signed on the cover 'Smith enammeller Derby'. The difficulty is that the reference may be to his son William. However, he was still at the factory in 1770, so that he was decorating for Duesbury throughout most, if not all, of the period with which we are concerned. In the light of this it is interesting to reflect on whether or not he could conceivably be 'the cotton-stem/secondary bird-painter' (hereinafter called for convenience merely 'the cotton-stem painter') referred to earlier. Undoubtedly some of the work of 'the cotton-stem painter' is to be seen early on in the factory's life under Duesbury, and his hand appears frequently on useful and ornamental ware and on figures of the period under consideration. 'The cotton-stem painter' shows great versatility, being capable of painting flowers, birds, insects and figures, and this degree of accomplishment fully entitles him to be called, as was Constantine Smith by Jewitt, 'one of the best "hands" at the Derby works'. However, although it is interesting to contemplate the possibility of 'the cotton-stem painter' being Constantine Smith, the evidence is only circumstantial and far from conclusive.

A controversy has arisen as to whether it was Constantine or his son, William, who was responsible for 'Smith's blue'. Haslem unequivocally credits William with the invention:[6]

On leaving the old works, [William] Smith commenced enamelling china on his own account, in a court in St. Alkmund's Church yard, Derby, where he erected an enamelling kiln. He afterwards removed to Spring Gardens, London Road and, lastly, to Robin Hood Yard, Iron Gate. Smith was also a maker of enamel colours, and a dark blue, which went by his name, was a good rich colour. It is the well-known blue so much used on Derby china before the general adoption of cobalt under the glaze.

Exactly when William Smith left the factory is uncertain. He subscribed the notices dated respectively 23 November 1787 and 24 September 1788, in 1790 he entered into a further agreement with Duesbury, a term of which was that his wages were raised from twenty-one to twenty-five shillings a week, and around 1794 his name was included in a factory order requiring the artists then employed to mark the articles finished by them with their respective numbers.

Commentators other than Haslem have contended that as the form of decoration in question, 'Smith's blue', appears on Chelsea-Derby pieces 'which must have been made in the earliest years of William's apprenticeship',[7] the true inventor must have been Constantine. The problem about accepting this view is that it is singularly difficult to assign any particular Chelsea-Derby piece to a period of a few specific years, and William was expressly employed by Duesbury to make colours for painting on china. There seems no overriding reason for rejecting Haslem's version.

William Billingsley
The second artist who seems to have been at Derby from the very early days of the factory under Duesbury is William Billingsley. The name 'William Billingsley' is, of course, for ever linked in the ceramic world with his far more distinguished son. However, the son and his famous roses lie outside the period with which we are concerned. It is the father alone who features in the early days of the factory.

The researches of W. H. Tapp show[8] that William Billingsley's name appears in the Chelsea rate books in March 1756: 'William Billingsley Area 2 Rent 14-14-0 Rates 14/- Mch 1756'. More important, the records of St Werburgh's Church, Derby, reveal that William Billingsley, described as a china painter, married there on 9 October 1757 Mary Dallison (Tapp confuses the church with St Alkmund's). Their son, William junior, was baptised on 12 October 1758 and eventually apprenticed to Duesbury on

26 September 1774. William senior died in 1770 and was buried in St Alkmund's Church, Derby, on 4 March 1770.

W. H. Tapp refers to a notice appearing in one of the Derby journals some three years before William Billingsley's death, which reads as follows:

BILLINGSLEY
Painter and Japanner
Sells in his Button Warehouse in Bridge
Gate Derby all sorts of metal buttons &c
Wholesale or Retail at the lowest prices.
N.B. All sorts of Japanning done after
the neatest manner.

Exactly when Billingsley arrived at Derby is not known. Clearly it was after March 1756, but before October 1757. In any event he was clearly an early painter who continued working at the factory until about 1767. Seemingly, he is just as likely a candidate for identification as 'the cotton-stem painter' as is Constantine Smith. Major Tapp refers to his being 'a flower-painter'. This is probably true, but there is no direct evidence in support. The fact that his son was an outstanding flower-painter perhaps suggests, but it certainly does not prove, that the father was a flower-painter as well. Of course, if he is to be considered 'the cotton-stem painter', it will have to be shown that he was capable of painting birds, moths and figures as well as flowers. However, it is reasonable to assume that in the early days of a porcelain factory's life the artists had to be extremely versatile, and we ought to be slow to impose any limitation on the range of their decorative powers. The age of specialisation came much later when techniques had become more sophisticated.

Apart from Constantine Smith and William Billingsley there are two other artists of whom we must now take notice. They worked at Derby in the early 1760s. Their names are William Pardoe and a certain Mason. What is known of them is set out below.

William Pardoe

He was the father of the more widely celebrated Thomas, who for a time worked at the Cambrian Pottery, Swansea, decorating that factory's earthenware, and who subsequently became an independent decorator of porcelain at Bristol, being responsible for flower-painting on the products of the Swansea, Nantgarw, Caughley, Coalport and other factories. There is a reference to William Pardoe in the parish documents of All Saints Church, Derby. For he is recorded as having married on 29 August 1769 Alice Burford. (Their son was born on 3 July 1770.) He is described on the register as a 'china painter'. He is also described as a widower, so that somewhere there must be a record of his earlier marriage. It is of particular interest, then, to note from the church records that on 30 November 1761 a certain William Pardoe, parishioner of St Alkmund's, married at St Peter's Church, Derby, Sarah Buxton. Unfortunately, the occupation of this William Pardoe is not given, which would have put the matter beyond dispute, but it is highly probable that the two William Pardoes were one and the same person, in which event he was working at Derby at least as early as November 1761. Unfortunately we do not know his style of painting.

Mason

We are indebted to Chaffers, *Marks and Monograms on Pottery and Porcelain*, for our information on Mason:[9]

I think the Chelsea China Manufactory began about the year 1748 or 1749. I went to work about the year 1751. It was first carried on by the Duke of Cumberland and Sir Everard Fawkener, and the sole management was entrusted to a foreigner of the name of Sprimont, report says, at a salary of a guinea per day, with certain allowance for apprentices and other emoluments. I think Sir Everard died about 1755, much reduced in circumstances, when Mr Sprimont became sole proprietor; and having amassed a fortune, he travelled about England, and the manufactory was shut up about two years, for he would neither let it or carry it on himself. I then went to work at Bow for a short time, which was carried on by a firm, but I don't recollect their names. I went to

*1. 'Feeling', from the Chinese Senses, 235mm (9¼in) high;
c. 1750–5. See pages 26, 27, 178
(Victoria and Albert Museum Crown Copyright)*

2. 'Taste', from the Chinese Senses, 222mm (8¾in) high;
c. 1752–5. See pages 26, 178
(Victoria and Albert Museum Crown Copyright)

3. 'Hearing', from the Chinese Senses, c. 1752–5, 203mm
(8in) high. See pages 25, 27, 178 (Note: this model in the
past has been erroneously called 'Sight'.)
(By courtesy of Christie Manson & Woods Ltd)

4.(a) and (c)   A pair of grape sellers representing Autumn, 181mm (7⅛in) high; c. 1752–5. See pages 27, 179

(b) 'Smell' from the Chinese Senses, 222mm (8¾in) high; c. 1752–5. See pages 27, 178

(By courtesy of the Trustees of the Werner Collection, Luton Hoo)

5.(a) 'Feeling', from the European Senses, 165mm (6½in) high; c. 1752–5. See pages 27, 31, 178

(b) 'Liberty' as a seated gallant balancing an open cage on his right knee, 165mm (6½in) high; c. 1752–5. See pages 29, 31, 180

(By courtesy of Sotheby Parke Bernet & Co)

6. 'Taste', from the European Senses, 165mm (6½in) high;
c. 1752–5. See pages 26, 27, 178
(Victoria and Albert Museum Crown Copyright)

7. 'Smell', from the European Senses, 158mm (6¼in) high; c. 1752–5. See pages 27, 29, 179 (By courtesy of Christie Manson & Woods Ltd)

8.(a) Lady with a lute, presumably representing 'Hearing', 139mm (5½in) high; c. 1756. See pages 47, 179, 193 (Note that the decoration is by the same hand as was responsible for the decoration on the dancer of Pl. 17(b).)
   (b) A fluter, 158mm (6¼in) high; c. 1752–5. See pages 26, 29, 31, 181 (By courtesy of Sotheby Parke Bernet & Co)

9. A set of Seasons, represented by seated putti, 108–133mm
(4¼–5¼in) high; c. 1750–5. See pages 27, 179
(By courtesy of Sotheby Parke Bernet & Co)

10.(a) Spring as a young girl, 184mm (7¼in) high;
c. 1752–5. See pages 27, 31, 179
   (b) Winter as an old man, 158mm (6¼in) high;
c. 1752–5. See pages 27, 31, 179
(By courtesy of Christie Manson & Woods Ltd)

11.(a) A dancer, 171mm (6¾in) high; c. 1750–5. See pages
28, 180
   (b) Summer represented by a harvester, 171mm (6¾in)
high; c. 1750–5. See pages 27, 179
(By courtesy of Sotheby Parke Bernet & Co)

12. *A grape seller representing Autumn, 133mm (5¼in)
high, standing on a tole peinte base with branches holding up
porcelain flowers; c. 1752–5. See pages 27, 179
(By courtesy of Christie Manson & Woods Ltd)*

13. *Winter represented by an old woman, 158mm (6¼in)
high; c. 1752–5. See pages 27, 31, 179
(Victoria and Albert Museum Crown Copyright)*

14. 'Air' and 'Water' as Chinese boys, with metal branches
holding porcelain flowers and metal sconces, 203mm (8in) high
overall; c. 1752–5. See pages 27, 179
(By courtesy of Christie Manson & Woods Ltd)

15. Pluto and Cerberus, 168mm (6⅝) high; c. 1750–5. See
pages 26, 27, 179, 192
(By courtesy of Sotheby Parke Bernet & Co)

16. A Chinaman with flying drapery, together with a Chinese boy, 241mm (9½in) high; c. 1752–5. See pages 26, 27, 32, 179
(By courtesy of Christie Manson & Woods Ltd)

17. (a) *Venus and Cupid, 190mm (7½in) high; c. 1752–5.
See pages 26, 27, 31, 179*
    (b) *A dancer holding a corner of her apron in her right
hand, 171mm (6¾in) high; c. 1756–7. See pages 29, 45, 180,
184 (Note that the decoration is by the same hand as was
responsible for the decoration on the figure of Pl. 8(a).)
(By courtesy of Sotheby Parke Bernet & Co)*

(Opposite page)
18. *Apollo with the emblems of the arts, 165mm (6½in)
high; c. 1752–5. See pages 26, 27, 31, 180, 195
(By courtesy of Albert Amor Ltd)*

19. *A shepherdess and shepherd, 178 and 190mm (7 and 7½in) high respectively; c. 1752–5. See pages 27, 31, 45, 180 (By courtesy of Sotheby Parke Bernet & Co)*

20. *An absinthe seller and companion vegetable seller, 171 and 181mm (6¾ and 7⅛in) high respectively; c. 1754–5. See pages 28, 180 (Victoria and Albert Museum Crown Copyright)*

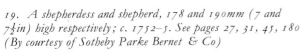

21. *Henry Woodward and Kitty Clive as the characters of the*
Fine Gentleman and the Fine Lady from David Garrick's
Lethe, *273 and 247mm (10¾ and 9¾in) high respectively;*
c. 1750–5. See pages 28, 30, 180
(By courtesy of Delomosne & Son Ltd)

22. *A dancer holding a mask, 165mm (6½in) high;*
c. 1752–5. See pages 28, 31, 180
(By courtesy of the Trustees of the British Museum)

23. 'St Thomas', 241mm (9½in) high; c. 1750–5. See pages
26, 29, 180
(Victoria and Albert Museum Crown Copyright)

24. A seated huntsman playing a flute to his companion,
158mm (6¼in) high; c. 1752–5. See pages 29, 31, 180
(By courtesy of Christie Manson & Woods Ltd)

25. *A seated cobbler, 175mm (6⅞in) high; c. 1750–5. See pages 29, 180*
(Victoria and Albert Museum Crown Copyright)

26. *A pair of theatrical figures comprising Columbine and Harlequin, 120mm (4¾in) high; c. 1750–5. See pages 29, 181*
(By courtesy of Klaber & Klaber)

27. *A pair of wild boars, 123 and 118mm (4⅞ and 4⅔in)*
high respectively; c. 1752–5. See pages 26, 29, 181
(By courtesy of the Trustees of the British Museum)

28. *A stag and doe at lodge, each with metal stand, branches*
and sconces, and coloured porcelain flowers, 308mm (12⅜in)
high overall; c. 1752–5. See pages 29, 181
(By courtesy of Sotheby Parke Bernet & Co)

29. *Alternative version of a stag and doe at lodge, 73 and 92mm (2⅞ and 3⅝in) high respectively; c. 1750–5. See pages 29, 181*
(By courtesy of the Trustees of the British Museum)

30. *A pair of standing goats, 108 and 165mm (4¼ and 6½in) high; c. 1752–5. See pages 29, 31, 181*
(Victoria and Albert Museum Crown Copyright)

31. *A pair of standing sheep, 114mm (4½in) long;*
c. 1752–5. See pages 29, 31, 181
(By courtesy of Christie Manson & Woods Ltd)

32. *A pair of recumbent lions, 89mm (3½in) high;*
c. 1750–5. See pages 29, 181
(By courtesy of Sotheby Parke Bernet & Co)

33. *A boy milking a goat, 206mm (8⅛in) high; c. 1750–5.*
See pages 29, 181
(Victoria and Albert Museum Crown Copyright)

34. *A pug dog scratching, 92mm (3⅝in) high, c. 1750–5. See*
pages 29, 181
(Victoria and Albert Museum Crown Copyright)

35. *A group of two finches on branches with a dog below
springing up baring his teeth, 158mm (6¼in) high, with metal
branches and leaves and with porcelain flowers and tulip sconce,
254mm (10in) high overall; c. 1750–5. See pages 29, 181
(Note the similarity of the tulip sconce with that supported by
the putto of Pl. 57.)
(Victoria and Albert Museum Crown Copyright)*

36. *A cream jug with moulded strawberries and leaves around
the base, 89mm (3½in) high. Incised under the base 'D.1750'.
See pages 11, 30, 181
(Victoria and Albert Museum Crown Copyright)*

94

37. *A sweetmeat dish, 98mm (3⅞in) high; c. 1750–5. See pages 30, 181*
(By courtesy of Christie Manson & Woods Ltd)

38. *A cabbage tureen and cover, 127mm (5in) high; c. 1750–5. See pages 30, 182*
(By courtesy of Winifred Williams, London)

39. *A pair of wall brackets, 149mm (5⅞in) high;
c. 1750–5. See pages 30, 182
(Victoria and Albert Museum Crown Copyright)*

40. *A seated man with a dog and bird, and a girl with a sheep,
152 and 139mm (6 and 5½in) high respectively; c. 1755
('Girl-on-a-horse' factory figures). See page 36
(By courtesy of the Trustees of the British Museum)*

41. *A dancer, 184mm (7¼in) high; c. 1755 ('Girl-on-a-horse' factory figure) (face-on view and side view). See pages 33, 36*
(Victoria and Albert Museum Crown Copyright)

42. *An exotic crested pheasant (in candlestick form, the nozzle and the top of the stick now missing), 178mm (7in) high; c. 1755 ('Girl-on-a-horse' factory figure). See page 36 (By courtesy of Winifred Williams, London)*

43. *A candlestick group of a dog (missing) chasing a cat up a tree, 175mm (6⅞in) high; c. 1755 ('Girl-on-a-horse' factory figure). See page 37 (Victoria and Albert Museum Crown Copyright)*

(Opposite page)
44. *A shepherdess and sheep, 260mm (10¼in) high; c. 1760. See pages 40, 183*

98

45. *A gallant seated on a rock with a dog and two lambs,*
247mm (9¾in) high; c. 1760–5. See pages 40, 184 (Note
that the basket is of the same design as that shown at
Pl. 114).)
(By courtesy of Christie Manson & Woods Ltd)

46. *A sportsman and companion, 222mm (8¾in) high;*
c. 1765–70. See pages 40, 184
(By courtesy of Christie Manson & Woods Ltd)

47. *A pair of sweetmeat figures, each holding a shell-shaped*
basket, 178mm (7in) high; c. 1756–7. See pages 45, 184
(By courtesy of Christie Manson & Woods Ltd)

48. *A girl draped with flowers, and gallant holding out a fruit*
from a basket, with a dog at his feet, 203 and 222mm (8 and
8¾in) high respectively; c. 1758–9. See pages 45, 183
(By courtesy of Delomosne & Son Ltd)

49. *A youth with a lamb and a basket of flowers, and a companion with an apron of flowers and basket of eggs, 222mm (8¾in) high; c. 1760–5. See pages 45, 184*

50. *A group of lovers, 190mm (7½in) high; c. 1765. See
pages 45, 184. (A reissue of the group of Pl. 24)
(By courtesy of Christie Manson & Woods Ltd)*

51. *A pair of candlestick figures of a standing girl and boy,*
the former holding a flower, the latter playing a flute, 247mm
(9¾in) high; c. 1756–7. See pages 45, 184
(By courtesy of Delomosne & Son Ltd)

52. *A boy seated on a rock kicking, 139mm (5½in) high; c. 1756–7. See pages 45, 185 (Victoria and Albert Museum Crown Copyright)*

53.(a) *A girl seated on a rock, her hat in her lap, with her right leg bent and her foot stretched out in front of her, 133mm (5¼in) high; c. 1756–7. See pages 45, 185*
  (b) A lowing cow recumbent under an overhanging tree, 76mm (3in) long; c. 1765–70. See pages 46, 190

54. *A sailor and his lass, 247 and 241mm ($9\frac{3}{4}$ and $9\frac{1}{2}$in)*
high respectively; c. 1765–70. See pages 45, 185
(By courtesy of Sotheby Parke Bernet & Co)

55. *A pair comprising a bare-footed woman grasping a hen and a man holding a struggling cockerel, 152mm (6in) high; c. 1760. See pages 45, 185 (Victoria and Albert Museum Crown Copyright)*

56. *Minuet dancers, 273 and 282mm (10¾ and 11⅛in) high respectively; c. 1760–5. See pages 45, 186 (Victoria and Albert Museum Crown Copyright)*

57. *A candlestick figure of a putto supporting on his head a tulip candle nozzle, 254mm (10in) high; c. 1760. See pages 45, 187 (Compare the candle nozzle with that of Pl. 35)*

(Opposite page)

58. *A centrepiece as a gallant and companion sitting back to back, each with an oval basket, 235mm (9¼in) high; c. 1760–5. See pages 45, 187*
(By courtesy of Christie Manson & Woods Ltd)

*59. A pair of 'Ranelagh figures', 289 and 314mm (11$\frac{3}{8}$ and
12$\frac{3}{8}$in) high respectively; c. 1760. See pages 45, 187
(Victoria and Albert Museum Crown Copyright)*

60. *A candlestick figure of Punch as a nightwatchman,*
247mm (9¾in) high; c. 1760. See pages 45, 188
(Victoria and Albert Museum Crown Copyright)

(Opposite page)
61. *A group of Harlequin and Columbine dancing, 158mm*
(6¼in) high; c. 1756–7. See pages 45, 188
(By courtesy of Sotheby Parke Bernet & Co)

62. *A group of lady, gallant and jester, early version, 184mm (7¼in) high; c. 1756–7. See pages 45, 188 (Note: the jester should be holding a tray with two cups) (Victoria and Albert Museum Crown Copyright)*

63. *A group of lady, gallant and jester, later version, 279mm (11in) high; c. 1765. See pages 45, 188 (By courtesy of Sotheby Parke Bernet & Co)*

64. *Duet singers, 203 and 196mm (8 and 7¾in) high*
respectively; c. 1765–70. See pages 45, 188
(By courtesy of Sotheby Parke Bernet & Co)

65. *James Quinn as Falstaff, 330mm (13in) high; c. 1765.*
See pages 46, 188
(Victoria and Albert Museum Crown Copyright)

(Opposite page)
66. *Lord Chatham, 368mm (14½in) high; c. 1767. See pages*
46, 189
(Victoria and Albert Museum Crown Copyright)

On the plinth:

VISCOUNT
PITT OF BURTON
PYNSENT,
EARL OF CHATᴹ,
LORD KEEPER
OF HIS MAJESTYˢ
PRIVY SEAL

67. *St Philip, 241mm (9½in) high; c. 1760–5. See pages 29, 46, 180, 189*

68. *A pair of bluetits, 127mm (5in) high; c. 1760–5. See
pages 46, 189
(By courtesy of Sotheby Parke Bernet & Co)*

69. *A goldfinch, 127mm (5in) high; c. 1760–5. See pages
46, 189
(By courtesy of Sotheby Parke Bernet & Co)*

70. A woodpecker, 158mm (6¼in) high; c. 1760–5. See
pages 46, 190
(By courtesy of Sotheby Parke Bernet & Co)

71. *A pair of parrots, 225mm (8⅞in) high; c. 1760–5. See pages 46, 190*
(Victoria and Albert Museum Crown Copyright)

72. *A pair of finches, 152mm (6in) high; c. 1760–5. See
pages 46, 189*
(By courtesy of Sotheby Parke Bernet & Co)

73.(a) *A yellow and green bird with puce head and mauve
barred tail feathers, 135mm (5 5/16 in) high; c. 1760–5. See
pages 46, 190*
   (b) *A canary, 122mm (4 13/16 in) high; c. 1760–5. See
pages 46, 189*
*(By courtesy of the Trustees of the Werner Collection, Luton
Hoo)*

74.(a) A finch (?) with black and brown markings, 114mm
(4½in) high; c. 1760–5. See pages 46, 190
    (b) A bird with mauve spots and dark mauve bars on the
tail, 100mm (3¹⁵⁄₁₆ in) high; c. 1760–5. See pages 46, 190
(By courtesy of the Trustees of the Werner Collection, Luton
Hoo)

75.(a) A candlestick group of a spaniel-type dog looking up
at two birds on branches, 209mm (8¼in) high; c. 1765. See
pages 47, 191
    (b) A candlestick group of two sheep, one climbing a tree
applied with flowers, 228mm (9in) high; c. 1765. See pages
46, 190

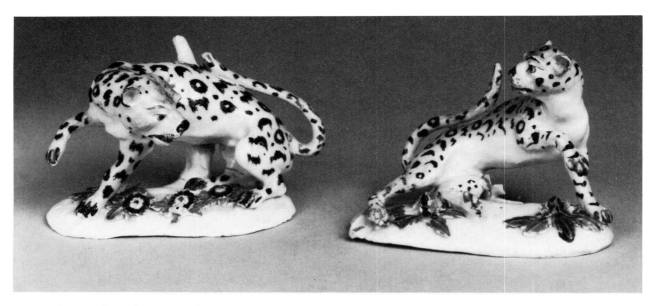

76. *A pair of leopards, 89mm (3½in) high; c. 1760. See*
pages 46, 191
(Victoria and Albert Museum Crown Copyright)

77. *A pair of early pug dogs, 89mm (3½in) high; c. 1756–7.*
See pages 47, 190
(By courtesy of Christie Manson & Woods Ltd)

78. *Europa and the Bull, 289mm (11⅜in) high; c. 1760–5.*
See pages 47, 191
(Victoria and Albert Museum Crown Copyright)

79. Cybele or Earth, 215mm (8½in) high; c. 1756–7. See pages 47, 180, 192
(Victoria and Albert Museum Crown Copyright)

(Opposite page)
81. Time clipping the wings of Cupid, 311mm (12¼in) high; c. 1760–5. See pages 47, 193

80. The Muse Erato, 228mm (9in) high; c. 1760–5. See pages 47, 193
(By courtesy of the Trustees of the British Museum)

82. *A Jewish pedlar and companion, 254 and 260mm (10 and 10¼in) high respectively; c. 1760–5. See pages 47, 193 (Victoria and Albert Museum Crown Copyright)*

83. *A mapseller (right) and companion, 158mm (6¼in) high; c. 1760–5. See pages 47, 180, 193 (By courtesy of Sotheby Parke Bernet & Co)*

84. The 'Tithe pig group', as a composite entity, 165mm
(6½in) high; c. 1765. See pages 47, 193
(Victoria and Albert Museum Crown Copyright)

85. The 'Tithe pig group', as separate individuals, 152mm
(6in) high; c. 1765–70. See pages 47, 193
(By courtesy of Delomosne & Son Ltd)

86. *A set of Continents, 178mm (7in) high; c. 1765–70. See pages 47, 194*
(By courtesy of Christie Manson & Woods Ltd)

87. *A set of the Seasons, 215mm (8½in) high; c. 1760–5. See pages 47, 48, 194*
(By courtesy of Christie Manson & Woods Ltd)

88. A pair of seated children representing Spring, 95mm (3¾in) high; c. 1756–7. See pages 48, 194 (By courtesy of Christie Manson & Woods Ltd)

89.(a) and (c) A pair of seated figures of Autumn and Spring, with hats, 133 and 127mm (5¼ and 5in) high respectively; c. 1756–7. See pages 48, 194
    (b) A group of two lovers representing Autumn, 158mm (6¼in) high; c. 1758–9. See pages 48, 195
(By courtesy of Sotheby Parke Bernet & Co)

90. *A pair of standing figures of Autumn and Spring, without hats, 165 and 152mm (6½ and 6in) high respectively; c. 1756–7. See pages 48, 194 (By courtesy of Sotheby Parke Bernet & Co)*

91. *A pair of standing figures of Spring and Autumn, with hats, 152mm (6in) high; c. 1756–7. See pages 48, 194 (By courtesy of Delomosne & Son Ltd)*

92. *Two candlestick groups of two lovers representing Summer,*
292mm (11½in) high; c. 1758–9. See pages 48, 194
(By courtesy of Christie Manson & Woods Ltd)

93. *The Virgin with St John and Mary Magdalene, 266mm*
(10½ in) high; c. 1760–5. See pages 48, 195
(Victoria and Albert Museum Crown Copyright)

94. *An Abyssinian archer (right) and companion, 318mm*
(12½in) high; c. 1765. See pages 48, 196
(Victoria and Albert Museum Crown Copyright)

95. *A centrepiece with four blackamoors with shells for holding sweetmeats, 235mm (9¼in) high; c. 1765. See pages 48, 196*
(By courtesy of Christie Manson & Woods Ltd)

96.(a) *A conical shaped coffee pot and cover, blue and white, printed with the ox-herd pattern, 209mm (8¼in) high; c. 1765. See pages 53, 69, 197*

(b) A barrel-shaped mug, blue and white, decorated with pagodas in a rocky landscape, 171mm (6¾in) high; c. 1765. See pages 54, 199

(By courtesy of Christie Manson & Woods Ltd)

97. *A pear-shaped coffee pot and cover, ribbed, and with scrolled handle, 222mm (8¾in) high; c. 1760–5. See pages 53, 66, 197*

(By courtesy of Christie Manson & Woods Ltd)

98. *A pear-shaped coffee pot and cover, ribbed, and with
scrolled handle, but with a turned-up thumb terminal, 254mm
(10in) high; c. 1760. See pages 53, 68, 197
(By courtesy of Winifred Williams, London)*

99.(a) A pear-shaped coffee pot and cover, smooth, with
scrolled handle and standing on a pedestal foot, 228mm (9in)
high; c. 1760–5. See pages 53, 66, 197
    (b) An inverted bell-shaped mug with scrolled handle,
152mm (6in) high; c. 1760–5. See pages 54, 199
(By courtesy of Christie Manson & Woods Ltd)

100.(a) A lobed sauce-boat, 127mm (5in) long; c. 1765. See
pages 57, 202
    (b) A fluted coffee cup and saucer, cup 76mm (3in)
high; c. 1760–5. See pages 53, 197
(By courtesy of Sotheby Parke Bernet & Co)

101. A 'trembleuse' cup and stand decorated by 'the cotton-stem painter', cup 50mm (2in) high, saucer 139mm (5½in) in diameter; c. 1760–5. See pages 53, 65, 198
(By courtesy of Christie Manson & Woods Ltd)

102. *A punch pot and cover, 215mm (8½in) high; c. 1760–5.*
See pages 54, 66, 199
(Victoria and Albert Museum Crown Copyright)

103. *A punch bowl, 254mm (10in) in diameter; c. 1760–5.*
See pages 54, 66, 199
(Victoria and Albert Museum Crown Copyright)

104. *A pear-shaped jug with pointed spout, 215mm (8¼in)*
high; c. 1760–5. See pages 54, 66, 199
(Victoria and Albert Museum Crown Copyright)

105. *A pear-shaped jug with mask spout, 165mm (6½in)
high; c. 1760–5. See pages 54, 199
(By courtesy of Christie Manson & Woods Ltd)*

106. *An ovoid-shaped mug with simple loop handle, 114mm*
(4½in) high; c. 1760–5. See pages 54, 66, 199
(By courtesy of Delomosne & Son Ltd)

107. *A truncated version of the inverted bell-shaped mug,*
117mm (4⅝in) high; c. 1760–5. See pages 54, 66, 199
(By courtesy of Sotheby Parke Bernet & Co)

108.(a) A shaped ten-sided plate, 206mm (8⅛in) in
diameter; c. 1765–70. See pages 55, 66, 200
    (b) A long-necked pear-shaped vase and cover, standing
on a circular base, decorated by 'the cotton-stem painter',
190mm (7½in) high; c. 1760–5. See pages 59, 67, 204

109. A plate with a feather-moulded border, painted by an
artist signing himself 'Thos F' or 'Thos Fl', 209mm (8¼in)
in diameter; c. 1760–5. See pages 55, 66, 200
(Victoria and Albert Museum Crown Copyright)

110. *A pair of leaf-shaped dishes with wicker-work border, 254mm (10in) long; c. 1760–5. See pages 55, 200 (By courtesy of Christie Manson & Woods Ltd)*

111. *A sunflower dish, 165mm (6½in) long; c. 1756–9. See pages 55, 200 (By courtesy of Christie Manson & Woods Ltd)*

112. *A peony dish, 209mm (8¼in) long; c. 1756–9. See pages 55, 200*
(By courtesy of Sotheby Parke Bernet & Co)

113.(a) *A plate with a feather-moulded border, painted with fruit and insects, 203mm (8in) in diameter; c. 1760–5. See pages 55, 67, 200*
   (b) *A 'spectacle' basket of shallow oval form with twin double-rope handles, 152mm (6in) long; c. 1760–5. See pages 56, 201*

114. *A pair of solid baskets with close basket-weave moulding on the exterior and with twin double-rope handles, and two stands, the baskets 152mm (6in) long; c. 1760–5. See pages 56, 67, 201*
(By courtesy of Delomosne & Son Ltd)

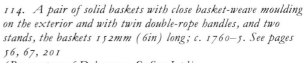

115. *A deep circular basket, pierced, with twin single-rope handles, and matching stand, the basket 155mm (6⅛in) in diameter; c. 1760–5. See pages 56, 201*
(Victoria and Albert Museum Crown Copyright)

116. *A 'spectacle' basket of deep circular form, pierced, having twin single-rope handles, 120mm (4¾in) in diameter; c. 1760–5. See pages 56, 66, 201*
(By courtesy of Albert Amor Ltd)

117. *A solid oval basket with everted rim and twin double-rope handles, the exterior moulded with a diagonal wicker-work pattern, and matching stand, 247mm (9¾in) long; c. 1760–5. See pages 56, 67, 201 (By courtesy of Sotheby Parke Bernet & Co)*

118. *A circular chestnut basket, in blue and white, the domed cover inscribed on the inside 'August 1762', 193mm (7⅝in) in diameter. See pages 56, 201 (By courtesy of Sotheby Parke Bernet & Co)*

119. *A pair of oval chestnut baskets, covers and stands, the stands 260mm (10¼in) long; c. 1760–5. See pages 56, 57, 66, 201*
(By courtesy of Christie Manson & Woods Ltd)

120. *A pair of deep oval baskets with central handle, 152mm (6in) long; c. 1756–9. See pages 57, 67, 201*
(By courtesy of Albert Amor Ltd)

121. *Three eel baskets, oviform and moulded with wicker-work, the two larger ones 241mm (9½in) high, the smaller 215mm (8½in) high; c. 1765–70. See pages 57, 201 (By courtesy of Christie Manson & Woods Ltd)*

122. *A pair of deep circular baskets, each with a cover surmounted by a bird, 127mm (5in) high; c. 1760–5. See pages 57, 201 (Victoria and Albert Museum Crown Copyright)*

123. *A pair of pigeon tureens and covers, 215mm (8½in)*
long; c. 1760. See pages 49, 57, 202
(By courtesy of Christie Manson & Woods Ltd)

124. *A pair of partridge tureens and covers, 152mm (6in)*
long; c. 1760. See pages 57, 202
(By courtesy of Sotheby Parke Bernet & Co)

125. *A pair of quatrefoil-shaped tureens and covers, together with a ladle, 127mm (5in) high; c. 1760–5. See pages 57, 202*
(By courtesy of Christie Manson & Woods Ltd)

126. *A tureen and cover in the form of grapes, 120mm (4¾in) long; c. 1756–9. See pages 57, 202*
(By courtesy of Sotheby Parke Bernet & Co)

127. *A pair of plaice sauce-boats with covers, 241mm (9½in)*
long; c. 1760–5. See pages 57, 202
(By courtesy of Sotheby Parke Bernet & Co)

128. *A pair of leaf-shaped sauce-boats decorated by 'the*
cotton-stem painter', 184mm (7¼in) long; c. 1760–5. See
pages 57, 65, 202
(By courtesy of Christie Manson & Woods Ltd)

129. *A shell centrepiece surmounted by a kingfisher, 158mm*
(6¼in) high; c. 1760–5. See pages 58, 202
(By courtesy of Christie Manson & Woods Ltd)

*130. A cruet set, the pieces 108 to 158mm (4¼ to 6¼in)
high; c. 1760–5. See pages 58, 203
(By courtesy of Christie Manson & Woods Ltd)*

131. *A salt with satyr's mask handles, 92mm (3⅝in) high;*
c. 1760–5. See pages 58, 203
(Victoria and Albert Museum Crown Copyright)

132. *Three mazarine blue vases and covers, two flanking, one*
centre, 266mm (10½in) high; c. 1760–5. See pages 59, 66,
67, 204
(By courtesy of Christie Manson & Woods Ltd)

133.(a) and (c) A pair of 'parfum' burners and covers,
decorated by 'the cotton-stem painter', 241mm (9½in) high;
c. 1760. See pages 59, 65, 67, 204
    (b) An eight-lobed vase, the top applied with flowers,
222mm (8¾in) high; c. 1756–9. See pages 59, 204
(By courtesy of Sotheby Parke Bernet & Co)

134. A scene painted on a long-necked pear-shaped vase,
depicting a pair of chickens and a pheasant by 'the cotton-stem
painter'; c. 1756–9. See page 67

135. *A garniture of baluster-shaped frill vases with covers,*
241, 292 and 241mm (9½, 11½ and 9½in) high respectively;
c. 1765. See pages 59, 204
(By courtesy of Sotheby Parke Bernet & Co)

136. *A flanking vase from a garniture of asymmetrical frill*
vases, 190mm (7½in) high; c. 1765–70. See pages 59, 205
(Victoria and Albert Museum Crown Copyright)

137. *A pair of asymmetrical vases with rococo moulding, filled
with a cluster of flowers, 117mm (4⅝in) high; c. 1765. See
pages 59, 205
(Victoria and Albert Museum Crown Copyright)*

138. *An asymmetrical vase with rococo moulding, but without
applied flowers, 171mm (6¾in) high; c. 1760. See pages 59,
67, 205
(By courtesy of the Trustees of the British Museum)*

139. A large vase of elaborate rococo form with the figure of Venus on one side, and that of Cupid on the other, 305mm (12in) high; c. 1760. See pages 60, 67, 205

140. *A large vase of elaborate rococo form with twin handles
in the form of dolphins, 260mm (10¼in) high; c. 1760. See
pages 60, 67, 205
(Victoria and Albert Museum Crown Copyright)*

141. *An urn-shaped vase and cover, 318mm (12½in) high;*
c. 1765. See pages 60, 66, 205
(By courtesy of Sotheby Parke Bernet & Co)

142. *A flower-filled vase in the shape of a sugar-caster,*
171mm (6¾) high; c. 1760. See pages 60, 205
(Victoria and Albert Museum Crown Copyright)

143. *An asymmetrical vase with elaborate rococo fluting and*
moulding, 196mm (7¾in) high; c. 1765. See pages 59, 67,
205
(Victoria and Albert Museum Crown Copyright)

164

144. *An elaborate inkstand dish on scroll feet, 260mm (10¼in) long; c. 1760–5. See pages 60, 206 (By courtesy of Sotheby Parke Bernet & Co)*

145. *A pair of guglets decorated by 'the cotton-stem painter', 235mm (9¼in) high; c. 1760. See pages 60, 65, 67, 206 (Victoria and Albert Museum Crown Copyright)*

146. *A toilet box and cover in the form of a rose, 76mm*
(3in) high; c. 1756–9. See pages 60, 206
(By courtesy of Christie Manson & Woods Ltd)

147. *A toilet box and cover in the form of a peach, 76mm*
(3in) high; c. 1756–9. See pages 60, 206
(Victoria and Albert Museum Crown Copyright)

148. *A pair of flower pots containing bouquets of flowers in full relief, 178mm (7in) high; c. 1765. See pages 60, 206 (Victoria and Albert Museum Crown Copyright)*

149. *A chamber candlestick, 158mm (6¼in) long; c. 1765. See pages 60, 207 (By courtesy of Christie Manson & Woods Ltd)*

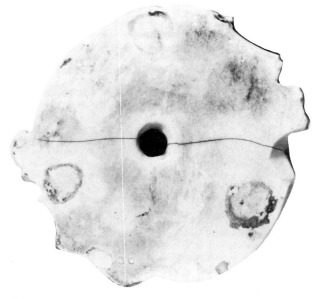

150. (Top) (a) 'Girl-on-a-horse' factory mark. See pages 33, 36 (Victoria and Albert Museum Crown Copyright)

(Centre) (b) Counter-sunk 'screw-hole' found on some dry-edge pieces. See page 25

(By courtesy of the Trustees of the British Museum)

(Bottom) (c) Patch marks. See page 24

work again at Chelsea for Mr Sprimont after being absent between two and three years, where I stopped till I engaged with Mr Duesbury to go to Derby, which was about the year 1763. I think there was very little business done there after that time. What time Mr Duesbury made a purchase of it I don't recollect, but some of the materials were taken to Derby.

Mason is not entirely accurate as regards certain of the details given by him. For example, Sir Everard Fawkener died on 16 November 1758 (the Duke of Cumberland survived him till 31 October 1765). The reason why Sprimont suspended trading round about 1758 and 1759 was not because he had amassed a large fortune, but because he was seriously ill. William Duesbury acquired the Chelsea factory in 1769. However, none of these mistakes undermines Mason's account of *his own* activities, with which he would be only too familiar. The fact emerges that he went to Derby in about 1763.

Unfortunately, he does not go on to say how long he stayed there. The name 'Mason' appears twice over in the list of workmen subscribing the notice of 23 November 1787,[10] in one case preceded by the initial 'M'. In the list of workmen subscribing the notice of 24 September 1788,[11] the only 'Mason' appearing is 'M. Mason'. Jewitt gives[12] a short biography of M. Mason: 'was an apprentice to Mr Duesbury as a painter. He left Derby and engaged himself to Mr Barr of Worcester, in October, 1792.' Clearly then, M. Mason is not the Mason who made the statement recorded in Chaffers, but presumably he was his son. Jewitt also gives[13] a short biography of a Thomas Mason who was a 'China or Porcelain repairer' who bound himself to Duesbury for four years by an agreement dated 2 September 1772. Apparently there was also a Thomas Mason who was a 'time-keeper'. Manifestly, then, the 'Mr Mason' is not Thomas Mason, and there is really nothing to show that he was the 'Mason' referred to in the list of 1787. Doubtless, he had left Derby before 1787, but exactly when is unknown.

In theory at least, assuming that sufficient pieces decorated by Mason have survived, it ought to be possible to see his work on Chelsea, Bow and Derby porcelain, and the identification of a distinctive hand appearing at all three factories on pieces of the relevant dates could suggest that the hand in question was that of Mason. However, quite apart from the inherent difficulties of the task, the whole exercise would be undermined if, as is probably the case, more than one artist operating at Derby during part of the period from 1756 to 1770 also worked at other periods at Bow and Chelsea.

The itinerant character of artists and others engaged in the production and decoration of porcelain and pottery is vividly illustrated in a letter dated 23 May 1770 from Josiah Wedgwood to his London partner Thomas Bentley:

The man I mention'd to you from Derby will do us no good. He told the Man he work'd along with that he wod. stay abot. a month here, wod. then go to Liverpool which wod. complete his Tour over all the works in England, & he wod. then embark for America. He has been drinking three days & I have ordd. him off, that he may proceed upon his intended Tour.

Apart from the artists already mentioned, there are certain others who worked at Derby during part at least of the period with which we are concerned. Unfortunately, we know little of them except for their names. They are Fidèle Duvivier, Thomas Edlin, Thomas Strong and William Taylor.

Fidèle Duvivier (1740–1817)

Fidèle Duvivier, who lived to a quite advanced age, was a painter at Chelsea in 1764. He did not leave that factory for Derby until 1769, so that he only just falls within our period. An agreement was made between him and William Duesbury bearing the date 31 October 1769. According to Jewitt[14] he became the principal flower-painter. The register of marriages at All Saints Church, Derby, records his marriage on 4 December 1769 to Elizabeth Thomas. He is there described as a 'china painter'.

Thomas Edlin

We know nothing of Thomas Edlin except that

he was at Derby sometime before July 1767. For the register of marriages of All Saints Church refers to his marriage on 5 July 1767 to Elizabeth Rowse and he is styled a 'china painter'.

It has proved impossible so far to identify his hand.

Thomas Strong

Nothing is known of Thomas Strong apart from the fact that in the records of All Saints Church he is described as a 'china painter' on his marriage on 22 December 1765 to Mary Tomlinson. Again, his work has not been identified.

William Taylor

That William Taylor was working during at least the last part of our period is established from the record of his marriage at St Werbergh's Church, Derby, on 2 February 1768 to Elizabeth Wright, where he is described as a 'china painter'. He was still operating at Derby in 1787 and the following year because his name appears among the various workmen who acknowledged receipt of the two notices dated respectively 23 November 1787 and 24 September 1788.[15] (He is also stated by Jewitt to have 'painted the centre of a service of plates for Dr Digby in 1784'.[16]) More important, he was still working at Derby in about 1794, since Jewitt quotes[17] a document in his possession requiring William Taylor to mark underneath each article finished by him (except for blue and white) the number 11. Later still, probably about 1796, William Taylor signed along with other workmen draft heads of agreement concerning the employment of painters.

It is interesting to note that a William Taylor is recorded as having been apprenticed in 1756 to 'Edw Wingfield of Deritend Birmingham, engrav. £21'. Jewitt says[18] of our William Taylor as follows: 'At first a blue painter, afterwards became a clever arabesque and Indian pattern painter.' In the fourth edition of Chaffers, *Marks and Monograms*,[19] he is described as a painter of 'Oriental subjects and patterns'. Now, could our William Taylor be the William Taylor who was apprenticed in 1756 to an engraver?

In any event he would seem to have been one of the earlier blue and white decorators, and

doubtless his hand is to be seen on some at least of the blue and white ware produced before the end of 1770 and, for that matter, on much of the ware produced thereafter.

There are two further Derby decorators who may have worked at the factory during part of the period with which we are concerned. They are Richard Askew and George Complin.

Richard Askew

In an article in *The Connoisseur* of June 1934[20] W. H. Tapp points out that the name of Richard Askew, the figure-painter (he occasionally did landscapes as well) appears in the Chelsea poll books. He is recorded as having lived in Church Lane West—'Rent £11 – Taxes 19/-'—in 1761 and Kings Road Chelsea—'Rent £12 – Taxes 21/-'—in 1764. Tapp infers from this that Richard Askew was probably at Derby in 1762 and 1763 and again in 1765, though he goes on to say that after 1765 he worked steadily at the Chelsea factory right up to 1780.

While admittedly the omission of his name from the Chelsea poll books for the years 1762 and 1763 suggests the possibility that he may have gone to Derby, it certainly does not prove it. In the absence of any corroborative evidence the assumption that Richard Askew spent 1762 and 1763 at Derby is nothing more than mere speculation.

Likewise there is nothing to corroborate the suggestion that Richard Askew was at Derby in 1765. Jewitt is able to show[21] that he was at Chelsea at the time Duesbury took over the factory, and he goes on to assert that he was transferred from Chelsea to Derby in 1772. He bases this assertion on the 'weekly bills' for Chelsea in his possession. There is no particular reason for doubting the accuracy of Jewitt's statement, but in any event we are not concerned with what happened after 1770.

The possibility of Richard Askew's being at Derby in the 1760s is speculative in the extreme.

George Complin

It is just conceivable that George Complin was employed at Derby in 1758 when the activities of the Chelsea factory were temporarily suspended owing to the illness of Sprimont. For it is possible that Complin was recruited by Sprimont to work at Chelsea in about 1755 and that during the temporary closure of the factory he was constrained to seek employment at Derby.

Undoubtedly, Complin's name appears several times in the Derby pattern books and he seems to have worked in that town from about 1785 to 1798, painting birds, animals, fruit and landscapes. However, there is no real evidence that he was at Derby during the period with which we are concerned.

A decorative form not greatly practised at Derby was that of printing. However, it was carried on at least to a small extent and the person responsible for its initiation (but note the early, possibly experimental, pieces referred to above at page 68) was Richard Holdship, one of the original proprietors of the Worcester factory.

Richard Holdship

Jewitt refers[22] at length to articles of agreement made in 1764 between Richard Holdship on the one hand and Duesbury and Heath on the other, after he had become bankrupt in 1761 and had sold his interest in the Worcester concern for five shillings. He undertook, *inter alia*, 'to supply . . . soapy rock' (steatite) and to 'print or cause to be printed all the china or porcelain ware which the said John Heath and William Duesbury, their heirs etc, shall from time to time have occasion to be printed'. According to Jewitt 'the printed ware did not appear to meet Mr Duesbury's views, or to be so advantageous as the higher class of goods painted by hand, for which he was famed, and thus there were constant complaints and recriminations passing between Holdship and his employers'. Holdship remained at the factory until at least 1769.

It is reasonable to assume that all the printing on Derby porcelain at the period with which we are concerned was carried out by or at the direction of Richard Holdship. Sometimes he added his rebus, an anchor.

Figure-makers

There must have been a considerable number of modellers and repairers working at the factory during the period with which we are concerned.

A repairer was responsible for assembling the various separate casts that made up a particular figure. Within limits the pose of the figure could be varied at the discretion of the repairer, and it was often his practice to mould hand-modelled ornament in the form of flowers, leaves, etc. The quality of the figure would depend to a large extent on the skill of the repairer. A repairer would also be needed to put together ornamental or useful ware. Although we know little of these modellers and repairers, what is known appears under their respective names.

Isaac Farnsworth

This name appears in a manuscript affidavit referred to by William Bemrose in his *Bow, Chelsea and Derby Porcelain*.[23] The relevant passage reads as follows:

Isaac Farnsworth, Ornamental China Repairer, saith he was brought up in the business of a repairer of ornamental china and china figures, and has continued in such business to the present time. That for nearly 40 years prior and down to the partnership of Duesbury and Kean in 1795, and afterwards up to the sale of the works to Bloor in 1811.

The implication of this is that Isaac Farnsworth was one of the hands employed by William Duesbury when he took over the factory in 1756. He often marked his work with an incised asterisk. He is said to have died in 1821.

Joseph Hill, Stephen Lawrence and Richard Whitaker

Haslem links the above three with Farnsworth. He says:[24]

When Farnsworth first began to work at the factory, Joseph Hill [he sometimes marked his work with an incised triangle[25]], Stephen Lawrence and Richard Whitaker were the three principal figure-makers, and had been employed at the works from their commencement, at which time, and for several years afterwards, small figures only were made.

The reference to 'small figures' seems to tie in with the man 'in very poor circumstances, living in Lodge Lane', who 'made small articles in china, such as birds, cats, dogs, sheep and other small ornamental toys'[26] and the implication must be that Haslem regarded Hill, Lawrence and Whitaker as having worked at the factory during the dry-edge period. However, as Haslem's knowledge of the early years is sketchy, no great reliance can be placed on his assertion that the workmen in question were at the factory at its commencement. It is possible that they were employed by William Duesbury from a time shortly after he took over, when doubtless with the rapid expansion of the concern there was a sudden demand for repairers (and to a lesser extent modellers: perhaps some of the models were imported from London), but we simply have no details. Apparently, Isaac Farnsworth arrived somewhat later than the others referred to.

I.W.

On one of a pair of white boars of the dry-edge period there are incised the letters 'I W' (or conceivably, but less likely, the letters 'M I', if the piece is reversed). Unfortunately, so far it has not been possible to identify the repairer with these initials. It may be that he inscribed his initials on the boar in question on his completing his apprenticeship. In all probability he was responsible for other work at the factory.

George Holmes

In his article on 'Thomas Hughes, First Enameller of English China, of Clerkenwell'[27] W. H. Tapp pointed out that in the Clerkenwell rate books for the years 1746 and 1747 George Holmes and Constantine Smith were recorded as enamellers. Further, in a letter written on 1 January 1775 by Josiah Wedgwood to Bentley a reference is made to an interruption whilst writing 'by a Man from the Derby China works who wants to be hired—He is a Derby Man, has a Wife and Family there and has work'd at the Factory 28 Years. His name is Holmes.'

Now the inference to be drawn from the rate books and Wedgwood's statement that Holmes claimed to have been at Derby for twenty-eight years must be that he was working there around

late 1747 or early 1748. He could well have worked at the factory during the dry-edge period. (He could, of course, instead have been employed at Cockpit Hill.) In any event, he was certainly working for Duesbury in 1765 because a figure formerly in the Leverhulme Collection is incised under the base 'George Holmes made this figer 1765'. Furthermore, his name appears in 1787 among the workmen who subscribed the notice of 23 November 1787.[28]

What is particularly interesting about George Holmes is that, according to the Clerkenwell rate books, he was in 1746 and 1747 an enameller, whereas his subsequent career was as a repairer. Assuming, of course, that George Holmes the enameller and George Holmes the repairer were one and the same, he seems to have been one of those versatile people who could turn their hand to more than one skill. It is interesting to reflect on whether, if he did work at the factory during the dry-edge period, he was responsible for any of the decoration on the figures then produced.

John Laurence or Lawrence

Jewitt speaks[29] of John Laurence (Lawrence) in the following terms: 'John Lawrence, "repairer", was one of the earlier hands, and in 1772 he, along with Robert Askew the younger, absconded while under article of agreement, and was advertised [three different times[30]] in the Birmingham papers.' His name appears among the subscribers of the notice of 23 November 1787,[31] but by 1790 he had left Derby for employment by 'Mr Turner, the Salop china manufactory'.[32]

The fact that John Laurence was under articles of agreement in 1772 in itself suggests that he may well have been working at the factory before 1770. A pair of candlestick figures of a shepherd playing bagpipes with a dog at his feet and of a shepherdess with a sheep beside her, which were sold at Sotheby's on 20 May 1969, Lot 243—their present whereabouts are unknown—had inscribed under the scroll base 'John Laurence'. Unfortunately, the catalogue does not give the date of the figures, but as they are not described as being Chelsea-Derby and there was no incised number under the base, which, where it occurs, invariably indicates a post-1770 origin, on the balance of probability they were produced in the 1760–70 period, in which event John Laurence can be said to have been working during the period with which we are concerned.

Perhaps he was the son or other relative of Stephen Lawrence referred to by Haslem.

Jonathan Boot

A frill vase, illustrated in Winifred Williams' catalogue of *Early Derby Porcelain*, Pl. 48, and now in the Victoria and Albert Museum, is incised under the base 'Jonathan Boot 1764'. Clearly the signatory was a repairer.' A gravestone in St John's Churchyard, Hanley, shows that he was born in 1745 and died in 1806. In 1800 and 1802 he was a toymaker and modeller at Cobridge.[33]

Charles Bullock

This name appears incised under the figure of a piper with his dog (*c.* 1765–70), which has been in the British Museum since 1931. Presumably he was a 'repairer' and conceivably this was his 'passing-out' piece on completion of his apprenticeship. The records of St Michael's Church, Derby, show that on 2 November 1777 a certain Charles Bullock, parishioner of St Alkmund's, chinaman, married Martha Toplis. Presumably this was the same person who signed the figure now in the British Museum, in which case it would appear that he left the factory sometime before 1777 to become a dealer in china. Whether or not he was any relation of Joseph Bullock who according to Jewitt[34] was 'bound apprentice on the 23rd September 1765 to learn the Art of Painting upon China or Porcelain ware' is unknown.

NOTES

1 The Origin and Early History of the Factory

1 *Ceramic Art in Great Britain*, Vol. 2, p. 67.
2 See William Bemrose, *Bow, Chelsea and Derby Porcelain*, p. 7.
3 For a discussion of Thomas Hughes of Clerkenwell see Major W. H. Tapp's article in *ECC Trans*, 1939, Vol. 2, No. 6, p. 60.
4 Herbert Jenkins, *William Duesbury's London Account Book* (1751–3), English Porcelain Circle, 1951.
5 *Ceramic Art in Great Britain*, Vol. 2, p. 68.
6 ibid., p. 67.
7 Revealed by Mrs Donald MacAlister in her introduction (p. xi) to *William Duesbury's London Account Book*.
8 *Ceramic Art in Great Britain*, Vol. 2, p. 68.
9 *Bow, Chelsea and Derby Porcelain*, pp. 17, 18.
10 See Bernard Watney, *Longton Hall*, p. 61.
11 *Ceramic Art in Great Britain*, Vol. 2, p. 67.
12 Chaffers, *Marks and Monograms on Pottery and Porcelain*, 4th edn, p. 790.
13 At p. 97.
14 See *post* at p. 28.
15 See *post* at p. 21.
16 See *Apollo*, August 1933, p. 101, Fig. XII.
17 See *post* at p. 172.
18 At p. 14 *et seq*.
19 Vol. 2, p. 66.
20 See *post* at p. 21.
21 At p. 97.
22 See *post* at pp. 50, 51.
23 Vol. 2, p. 110.
24 *Ceramic Art in Great Britain*, Vol. 2, p. 63.
25 See, for example, the 4th edn at p. 790.
26 At pp. 104, 105.
27 1927, pp. 228–9.
28 At p. 105.
29 Op. cit., 4th edn, pp. 790, 791.
30 At pp. 26–30.
31 *Royal Society's Journal Book*, 10 February 1742–3.
32 'The Earliest Days of the Derby China Factory', *Apollo*, August 1933, p. 97.
33 At p. 87.
34 'Thomas Briand—A Stranger', *ECC Trans*, Vol. 7, Part 2, pp. 87–99.
35 Vol. 2, at p. 65.
36 'The Earliest Days of the Derby China Factory', *Apollo*, August 1933, pp. 96–105.
37 'The Early Works of Planché and Duesbury', *EPC Trans*, 1929, No. II, pp. 50–9.
38 *Ceramic Art in Great Britain*, Vol. 2, p. 65.
39 See *post* at pp. 34, 35.
40 At p. 104.
41 *Ceramic Art in Great Britain*, Vol. 2, p. 111.
42 ibid., p. 102.
43 At p. 6.
44 At pp. 34, 35.
45 At p. 19.
46 At p. 105.
47 At p. 105.
48 Reproduced in full in *Ceramic Art in Great Britain*, Vol. 2, p. 59.
49 ibid., at p. 59.

2 'Dry-edge' Porcelain 1750–55

1 At p. 95.
2 'Early Derby Porcelain', Vol. XLIX, 1926, pp. 292–302.
3 At pp. 13–15.
4 The list was first published in John Haslem's *The Old Derby China Factory* (1876). Another version with variations is given by Bemrose

in his *Bow, Chelsea and Derby Porcelain*, pp. 67–85.

5 At pp. 3–11.

6 At. p. 25.

7 In the Untermyer Collection. See *post* at p. 26.

8 Yvonne Hackenbroch's *Chelsea and Other English Porcelain, Pottery and Enamel in the Irwin Untermyer Collection* (1957).

9 See note in Appendix 1 at p. 179.

10 A later example dated 1755–8 is illustrated in Stonor's *Chelsea, Bow and Derby Porcelain Figures*, Pl. 49.

11 See Hugh Tait, 'Some Consequences of the Bow Exhibition', *Apollo*, Vol. LXXI, 1960, pp. 42–3; Bernard Watney, 'Pre-1756 Derby Domestic Wares', *Burlington Magazine*, Vol. CIX, No. 766, 1967, p. 19.

12 Fig. 271, Pl. 96.

13 See Sotheby's sale, 16 June 1981, Lot 160; Untermyer Collection, Yvonne Hackenbroch, op. cit., Pl. 104, Fig. 279.

14 In *Entwurff Einiger Thiere . . .*, Part III, Augsburg 1738, Pl. 37.

15 See also the statement attributed to Locker quoted at p. 15.

16 Yvonne Hackenbroch, op. cit., Pl. 93, Fig. 291.

17 See at pp. 13, 50.

3 The 'Girl-on-a-horse' Factory

1 *Ceramic Art in Great Britain*, Vol. 1, p. 161.

2 See *post* at p. 35.

3 4th edn, p. 913.

4 *Present State of the Arts*, 1755 edn.

5 December 1980, p. 384.

6 *Ceramic Art in Great Britain*, Vol. 1, p. 202.

7 ibid., Vol. 2, p. 68.

8 Yvonne Hackenbroch, op. cit., Pl. 106, Fig. 280.

4 Figures 1756–70

1 See Stonor, Pl. 52.

2 *ECC Trans*, 1951, Vol. 3, Part I, p. 70.

3 See Yvonne Hackenbroch, op. cit., Fig. 43, Pl. 27.

4 Chaffers, *Marks and Monograms*, 4th edn, p. 801.

5 Jewitt, *Ceramic Art in Great Britain*, Vol. 2, pp. 78–83.

6 See Arthur Lane, *Eighteenth Century English Porcelain Figures*, Pls 22B, 23B.

7 See *ante* at p. 27.

8 *Ceramic Art in Great Britain*, Vol. 2, pp. 68, 69.

9 Derby Co-operative Society Deeds, conveyance, 20 November 1840.

10 *The Old Derby China Factory*, pp. 33, 34.

11 Duesbury MSS at the British Museum (Bemrose Collection).

12 Reproduced in Chaffers, *Marks and Monograms*, 4th edn, p. 914.

13 Cited *post* at pp. 72, 169.

14 *Ante* at p. 13.

15 *Ante* at pp. 49, 50.

5 Useful Ware 1756–70

1 *Ceramic Art in Great Britain*, Vol. 2, p. 69.

2 See *ante* at pp. 50, 51.

3 See below.

4 See *ante* at p. 49.

5 See *ante* at p. 49.

6 At p. 37.

7 Illustrated in Bradley, *Ceramics of Derbyshire*, Pl. 217.

8 See Winifred Williams, catalogue of *Early Derby Porcelain*, Pl. 53.

9 See *ante* at p. 49.

10 See *post* at p. 65.

11 See Cushion's *Continental Porcelain*, Pl. 13.

12 See *ante* at p. 48.

13 For the Chantilly version (*c.* 1740) see Ducret's *The Colour Treasury of Eighteenth Century Porcelain*, Fig. 73.

6 Ornamental Porcelain 1756–70

1 See *post* at pp. 67, 68.

2 See *post* at pp. 65, 67.

3 See *ante* at p. 48.

4 See *ante* at p. 49.

7 Decoration 1756–70

1 *The Old Derby China Factory*, p. 100.

2 *ECC Trans*, V, 1937, p. 7; see also H. R. Marshall, *ECC Trans*, III, 1951, Part I, p. 2, etc.

3 See Schreiber Collection, Nos 107, 546–9 and 755; and Herbert Allen Collection, No. 262.

4 *ECC Trans*, 1933, pp. 31–8.

5 See *ante* at pp. 50, 51.
6 See, for example, Barrett and Thorpe, *Derby Porcelain*, p. 28, n. 2.
7 See *ante* at pp. 48, 49.
8 *Ceramics of Derbyshire*, Pl. 133.

8 Artists

1 See 'Thomas Hughes, First Enameller of English China, of Clerkenwell', *ECC Trans*, 1939, Vol. 2, No. 6, p. 60.
2 See *ante* at p. 12.
3 *Ceramic Art in Great Britain*, Vol. 2, p. 97.
4 ibid., at p. 112.
5 ibid., at p. 113.
6 *The Old Derby China Factory*, p. 135.
7 Barrett and Thorpe, *Derby Porcelain*, p. 103.
8 *The Connoisseur*, January 1933, p. 28.
9 4th edn, pp. 913, 914.
10 *Ceramic Art in Great Britain*, Vol. 2, p. 102.
11 ibid., at p. 103.
12 ibid., at p. 111.
13 ibid., at p. 111.
14 ibid., at p. 97.
15 ibid., at p. 102.
16 ibid., at p. 113.
17 ibid., at p. 103.
18 ibid., at p. 113.
19 At p. 794.
20 At p. 359.
21 *Ceramic Art in Great Britain*, Vol. 2, p. 98.
22 ibid., Vol. 1, pp. 232, 233.
23 At p. 129.
24 *The Old Derby China Factory*, at p. 163.
25 ibid.
26 See *ante* at p. 15.
27 *ECC Trans*, 1939, Vol. 2, No. 6, p. 60.
28 *Ceramic Art in Great Britain*, Vol. 2, p. 102.
29 ibid., at pp. 110, 111.
30 ibid., at p. 99.
31 ibid., at p. 102.
32 ibid., at p. 111.
33 Reginald G. Haggar, *Staffordshire Chimney Ornaments*, 1955, at p. 119.
34 *Ceramic Art in Great Britain*, Vol. 2, p. 108.

ABBREVIATIONS
USED IN APPENDICES

Christie Manson & Woods Ltd's sale (date), Lot (No.)	C (date) L (No.)
Sotheby Parke Bernet & Co.'s sale (date), Lot (No.)	S (date) L (No.)
Franklin A. Barrett and Arthur L. Thorpe, *Derby Porcelain*	B. & Th.
Peter Bradshaw, *18th-Century English Porcelain Figures 1745–95*	Bradshaw
J. L. Dixon, *English Porcelain of the Eighteenth Century*	Dixon
English Ceramic Circle, Commemorative Catalogue of an Exhibition held at the Victoria and Albert Museum May 5–June 20 1948	ECC Exh.
English Ceramic Circle Transactions	ECC Trans
English Porcelain Circle Transactions	EPC Trans
F. Brayshaw Gilhespie, *Crown Derby Porcelain*	Gil., CDP
——, *Derby Porcelain*	Gil.
Yvonne Hackenbroch, *Chelsea and other English Porcelain, Pottery and Enamel in the Untermyer Collection*	Untermyer Col.
R. L. Hobson, *Catalogue of the Collection of English Porcelain in the British Museum*	Hobson
W. B. Honey, *Old English Porcelain* 3rd edn	Honey

F. Hurlbutt, *Old Derby Porcelain*	Hurlbutt
Arthur Lane, *English Porcelain Figures of the Eighteenth Century*	Lane
William King, *English Porcelain Figures of the Eighteenth Century*	King
Bernard Rackham, *Catalogue of the Schreiber Collection of English Porcelain*	Schr. Col.
Frank Stonor, *Chelsea, Bow and Derby Porcelain Figures*	Stonor
John Twitchett, *Derby Porcelain*	Twitchett
Winifred Williams, Catalogue of *Early Derby Porcelain 1750–70*	W.W.
Colour Plate	Col. Pl.
Plate	Pl.
Figure	Fig.
Museums	Mus.
Derby Museum and Art Gallery	Derby
Fitzwilliam Museum, Cambridge	Fitzwilliam
Cecil Higgins Art Gallery, Bedford	Cecil Higgins
Metropolitan Museum of New York	Metropolitan
Royal Crown Derby Porcelain Museum	Royal Crown Derby
Untermyer Collection	Untermyer Col.
Victoria and Albert Museum	V. & A.
Werner Collection Luton Hoo	Luton Hoo

APPENDIX 1 — 'DRY-EDGE' MODELS
1750–55

This appendix contains a list of models belonging to the 'dry-edge' period (1750–5) which have been recorded to date. It does not purport to be exhaustive. References to colour and black and white plates in this book appear in italics. Where a particular model is not illustrated in this book a reference has been made to one or more illustrations published elsewhere. Where an example of a particular model is known to be in the possession of a particular public museum, this is indicated. However, in some instances the examples in question are only on loan and can therefore be withdrawn at any time. Abbreviations are explained on page 177. Measurements are approximate only and unless otherwise stated relate to the height of the object. Other examples may have been produced whose measurements differ from those recorded.

Human figures
1. Senses
A. Chinoiserie
(i) *Feeling* A Chinaman about to chastise a boy, 235mm (9¼in). *Pl. 1. Mus.* Cecil Higgins; V. & A.

(ii) *Taste* A Chinaman holding up a phial of medicine, whilst a boy leans over a basket of medicines, a bottle in his right hand, 203 or 222mm (8 or 8¾in) (sometimes called 'the Quack Doctor and his Assistant'). *Pl. 2. Mus.* Metropolitan (Untermyer Col.); V. & A.

(iii) *Hearing* A Chinese woman holding out her left hand and clasping a trumpet in her right* whilst an elderly Chinaman sits listening beside her, 178 or 203mm (7 or 8in).

*Two examples, one in the British Museum (illustrated in B. & Th., Pl. 16), the other in the Untermyer Collection (Fig. 269, Pl. 100), have such a trumpet. See also Twitchett, Pl. 15. An example illustrated in Dixon, Pl. 34, has a bird resting on the woman's right hand.

(Note: this model has hitherto universally been called 'Sight'. Manifestly, it represents 'Hearing'.)

Pl. 3. Mus. British; The Gubbay Collection, Clandon Park, Surrey; Metropolitan (Untermyer Col.); V. & A.

(iv) *Smell* A Chinese lady with flowing robe and pointed hat holding flowers to her nose, whilst a Chinese boy leaning backwards on a seat seeks to grasp the flowers, 215 or 222mm (8½ or 8¾in). *Pl. 4(b). Mus.* British; Fitzwilliam; Luton Hoo; Metropolitan.

(v) *Sight* A standing Chinese lady looking into a mirror held in her right hand, accompanied by a seated child, 219mm (8⅝in). S 26 May 1938, L 317 (Wallace Elliot Collection).

B. European
(i) *Feeling* A lady in pannier skirt, holding a parrot, 165mm (6½in). *Pl. 5(a). Mus.* Fitzwilliam.

(ii) *Taste* A lady in pannier skirt selecting fruit from a basket of fruit on her lap, 152 to 165mm (6 to 6½in). *Pl. 6. Mus.* Fitzwilliam; V. & A.

(iii) *Sight* A gallant looking at a mirror, 158mm (6¼in). *Apollo*, Dec. 1928, p. 322, No. IX; Gil., Pl. 14 (in white, together with 'Feeling', 'Taste' and 'Smell'); Bradshaw, Col. Pl. M.

(iv) *Smell* A gallant with a snuff-box, 158mm (6¼in). *Pl. 7.*

(v) *Hearing* The exact form of 'Hearing' is unknown. An early patch-marked figure of a seated lady in a pannier skirt with a lute (*Pl. 8(a)*) may be a re-issue of a dry-edge model.

Alternatively, the model of a seated lady holding a musical score (see *post*, No. 16) may represent 'Hearing'.

2. Seasons
(i) Represented by four seated putti, respectively:
   (a) taking flowers from a basket of flowers (Spring), 123mm (4⅞in);
   (b) clasping a sheaf of corn (Summer), 120mm (4¾in);
   (c) holding grapes (Autumn), 133mm (5¼in); and
   (d) warming hands over a brazier (Winter), 95 or 108mm (3¾ or 4¼in).
   Pl. 9. Mus. Derby (Autumn); V. & A.

(ii) Represented by four standing pairs:
   Spring A gardener holding a basket of flowers with his left hand and a single flower in his right, and a companion holding flowers in her apron and a single flower in her left hand, a bee-hive at her feet, 178 and 171mm (7 and 6¾in) or 190 and 184mm (7½ and 7¼in) respectively. *Pl. 10(a)* (lady). Gil., *CDP*, Fig. 183 (man); Stonor, Pl. 47; B. & Th., Pl. 14 (man). *Mus.* Fitzwilliam.
   Summer A pair of harvesters, 171mm (6¾in) (male) and 152mm (6in) (female). *Pl. 11(b)* (man). B. & Th., Pl. 6 (woman); Bradshaw Col., Pl. J. *Mus.* Derby.
   Autumn A pair of grape-sellers, 133 or 181mm (5¼ or 7⅛in). *Pls 4(a)* and *(c)* and *12* (woman, 133mm (5¼in), standing on a tole peinte base with branches holding up porcelain flowers). *Mus.* Luton Hoo.
   Winter A pair comprising an old man and old woman, each warming a hand over a brazier, 158mm (6¼in). *Pls 10(b)* and *13. Mus.* Royal Crown Derby (woman); V. & A. (woman).

3. Elements
A. Chinoiserie
Air and water, each in the form of a Chinese boy, 101mm (4in), *Pl. 14* (their pierced backs holding metal branches, carrying porcelain flowers and metal sconces, 203mm (8in) overall).

B. Classical gods and goddesses
(i) Pluto and Cerberus, symbolic of Earth, 168mm (6⅝in). *Pl. 15. Mus.* V. & A.

(ii) (a) Neptune with a dolphin at his feet, 171mm (6¾in). Gil., Pl. 2.
   (b) Neptune riding on a dolphin. *The Connoisseur*, Sept. 1927, p. 13, Pl. VI. Each model symbolic of Water.

(iii) Jupiter riding on an eagle and brandishing a thunderbolt, symbolic of Air or Fire. *The Connoisseur*, Sept. 1927, p. 13, Pl. VI.

4. Miscellaneous Chinoiserie figures
(i) A rococo candlestick with two Chinese boys, one on either side, 260 or 266mm (10¼ or 10½in). F. Hurlbutt, *Chelsea China*, Pl. 13 (ascribed to Chelsea); Untermyer Col., Pl. 107, Fig. 289; Stonor, Pl. 49 (later version). *Mus.* Metropolitan (Untermyer Col.).

(ii) A Chinaman with flying drapery perched high on open scrollwork and a boy below, designed as a watch stand, 235 or 241mm (9¼ or 9½in). *Pl. 16. Mus.* British (patch-marked).

(iii) Pair of Chinese musicians, the lady playing a double drum, the man a lute, 152 and 127mm (6 and 5in) respectively. Twitchett, Pl. 24. *Mus.* Indianapolis Museum of Art.

5. Classical gods and goddesses (not representing the elements)
(i) Mars in Roman armour, 168mm (6⅝in). *ECC Exh.*, No. 306, Pl. 67; Gil., Pls 3 and 27 (a candlestick figure, 228mm (9in)); Bradshaw, Pl. 93.

(ii) Venus and Cupid, 190mm (7½in). *Pl. 17(a).*

(iii) Apollo with emblems of the arts, including

a palette, and several large books of music, 165mm (6½in). *Pl. 18. Mus.* Fitzwilliam; Royal Crown Derby.

(iv) Cybele or Earth, wearing a coronet and with a lion and cornucopia at her feet, 165mm (6½in). *Pl. 79* (for later, somewhat larger, patch-marked example). *ECC Trans.* 1968, Vol. 7, Pt. I, Pl. 57(d).

6. Shepherds and shepherdesses

(i) The youth playing bagpipes, whilst a dog sits at his feet, his companion holding aside her skirt with her left hand, whilst a sheep lies recumbent at her feet, 171 and 165mm (6¾ and 6½in) or 190 and 178mm (7½ and 7in) respectively. *Pl. 19. Mus.* Fitzwilliam; V. & A. (shepherdess).

(ii) A shepherdess with her left hand outstretched and her right hand holding up her apron, whilst a sheep tries to clamber up her and a small dog lies curled at her feet, 241mm (9½in). W.W., Pl. 11.

7. Street sellers

(i) A male absinthe seller holding a lantern in his left hand, and a female vegetable seller, 133 and 139mm (5¼ and 5½in) or 171 and 181mm (6¾ and 7⅛in) respectively. *Pl. 20. Mus.* City Museum and Art Gallery, Plymouth (absinthe seller); V. & A.

(ii) A mapseller holding an open map in one hand and a rolled one in the other, with his wares in a case on his back, 152 or 158mm (6 or 6¼in). *Pl. 83* (for later patch-marked example); Gil., Pl. 13; Bradshaw, Pl. 90.

8. Henry Woodward and Kitty Clive

In the characters of the Fine Gentleman and the Fine Lady from David Garrick's *Lethe*, 273 and 247mm (10¾ and 9¾in) respectively. *Pl. 21. Mus.* V. & A. (Kitty Clive).

(Note: Kitty Clive is known to have been produced also in a smaller version—Boston Museum of Fine Arts.)

9. Dancers

(i) A female dancer clasping her flared skirt with her left hand and holding a mask in her right,

165mm (6½in). *Pl. 22. Mus.* British; Metropolitan (Untermyer Col.).

(ii) A moustached male dancer holding his cloak in his right hand, his left hand turned inwards on his hip, 171mm (6¾in). *Pl. 11(a). Mus.* V. & A.

(iii) A female dancer holding in her right hand a corner of her apron, her left hand bent and raised, 171mm (6¾in). *Pl. 17(b)* (the patch-mark version).

According to Barrett and Thorpe, *Derby Porcelain*, p. 193, an example of this model in dry-edge porcelain was once in the possession 'of the late Mr W. Pease, of Nottingham'.

10. Saints

(i) 'St Thomas' or 'King Lear' or the 'Roman soldier'. Standing figure of a long-haired bearded man with a long cloak thrown loosely over a tunic and with Roman-type sandals, an orb and broken sword at his feet, 241mm (9½in). *Pl. 23. Mus.* V. & A.

(ii) 'St Philip'. Standing figure of a long-haired bearded man with bare feet looking at a crucifix in his right hand, 241mm (9½in). *Pl. 67* (for a later patch-marked example). Lane, Pl. 59. *Mus.* V. & A.

11. Huntsman group

Group comprising a seated huntsman playing a flute to his companion who holds in her left hand a sheet of music, 158mm (6¼in). *Pl. 24. Mus.* Fitzwilliam.

12. 'Liberty'

A seated gallant balancing an open cage on his right knee, 165mm (6½in). *Pl. 5(b).*

13. Cobbler

A seated cobbler with a shoe in his left hand and the tools of his trade all about him, 175mm (6⅞in). *Pl. 25. Mus.* V. & A.

14. Fluters

(i) A boy with tricorn hat standing without shoes playing a flute, 139mm (5½in). Gil., Pl. 9.

(ii) A man without a hat standing playing a flute, 158mm (6¼in). *Pl. 8(b)*.

15 Sweetmeat figures
A pair of seated figures, male and female, each clasping a shell, 158 or 184mm (6¼ or 7¼in). Twitchett, Col. Pl. 2 (male), Pl. 7 (female).

16. Seated lady holding a musical score
133mm (5¼in). Twitchett, Col. Pl. 1. *Mus.* Royal Crown Derby.

17. Theatrical figures
A pair comprising Harlequin and Columbine, 120mm (4¾in). *Pl. 26*.

Animals and birds

1. Pair of wild boars, one running, the other sitting, on oval bases applied with acorns and/or leaves. (These models vary in size between about 101 and 133mm (4 and 5¼in) high.) *Pl. 27. Mus.* British; Cecil Higgins; Metropolitan (Untermyer Col.); V. & A.

2. Pair of charging bulls, 60, 114 or 139mm (2⅜, 4½ or 5½in). Gil., Pl. 7; Stonor, Pl. 43; Untermyer Col., Pl. 104, Fig. 278; B. & Th., Pl. 20; Twitchett, Pl. 12. *Mus.* Derby; Metropolitan (Untermyer Col.); Royal Crown Derby (single bull).

3. Stag and doe at lodge, 127, 139 or 171mm (5, 5½ or 6¾in). *Pl. 28* (with metal stand, branches and sconces and coloured porcelain flowers, 308mm (12⅛in)). *Mus.* Derby.

4. Alternative version of stag and doe at lodge, 73 and 92mm (2⅞ and 3⅝in) respectively. *Pl. 29. Mus.* British.

5. Pair of standing goats, the billy with his head turned to the left, the nanny suckling a kid, 165 and 108mm (6½ and 4¼in) respectively. *Pl. 30. Mus.* Fitzwilliam (billy goat); V. & A.

6. Pair comprising a recumbent goat suckling a kid, and recumbent ewe and lamb, 120 and 89mm (4¾ and 3½in) respectively. S 13 Oct. 1970, L 213. *Mus.* Fitzwilliam (ewe and lamb, 123mm (4⅞in)).

7. Pair comprising a standing ram and ewe, 114mm (4½in) long. *Pl. 31*.

8. Standing ram, very solid in appearance, 95mm (3¾in). *Col. Pl. C(b)*.

9. Standing sheep, 89mm (3½in). W.W., Pl. 5.

10. Pair of recumbent lions, 89mm (3½in). *Pl. 32. Mus.* V. & A. (single).

11. A boy milking a goat, 206mm (8⅛in). *Pl. 33. Mus.* V. & A.

12. Pug dog scratching on an oblong base, 92mm (3⅝in). *Pl. 34. Mus.* V. & A.

13. Finch perched on a tree-stump. George Savage, *18th-Century English Porcelain*, Pl. 58(b).

14. Group of two finches on branches with a spaniel dog below springing upwards baring his teeth, 158mm (6¼in). *Pl. 35* (with metal branches and leaves and with porcelain flowers and a tulip sconce, 254mm (10in) overall). *Mus.* V. & A.

15. Parrot standing on a tree-stump, 165mm (6½in). William Duesbury, *London Account Book* (1751–3), English Porcelain Circle monograph, 1931, Pl. IV (b).

Useful and allied ware

1. Cream jugs
With moulded strawberries and leaves around the base, 89mm (3½in). *Pl. 36. Mus.* British; Colonial, Williamsburgh; V. & A.

2. Salts
A pair of single shells, resting on coral and tiny shells, 44mm (1¾in). W.W., Pl. 7.

3. Sweetmeat dishes
In the form of three shells, resting on rock-work and coral base, 98mm (3⅞in). *Pl. 37*.

4. Coffee cups
Circular, with shaped rim and branch handle, the sides moulded with flowers. No published illustration. *Mus.* V. & A.

5. Tureens

(i) Cabbage tureen and cover, 127mm (5in). *Pl. 38.*

(ii) Partridge tureen and cover, the bird resting on a nest of applied twigs and feathers, 127mm (5in) long. No published illustration (item 8 in W.W.).

6. Flowers

For a selection of individually moulded flowers see W.W., Pl. 6.

7. Wall brackets

(i) With elaborate rococo scrollwork ending in a shaped platform with stepped profile, 149mm (5$\frac{7}{8}$in). *Pl. 39. Mus.* Metropolitan (Untermyer Col); V. & A.

(ii) With scale and foliage mouldings and volutes at each side, ending in a rectangular platform with shaped front, 139mm (5$\frac{1}{2}$in). Untermyer Col., Pl. 93, Fig. 290; *EPC Trans*, No. 3, 1931, Pl 17, opp. p. 81, Fig. c. *Mus.* Metropolitan (Untermyer Col.).

APPENDIX 2—FIGURES 1756–70

This appendix contains a cross-section of the factory's output of figures during the period from 1756 to 1770. For convenience the list is sub-divided under various headings. Where a particular model is known to have been produced as early as 1756–7, this is indicated by a single asterisk; where the commencement date is 1758–9, a double asterisk appears. Neither form of notation carries any implication as to the length of time the relevant model continued to be manufactured (but see page 39). See also Appendix 1 for notes on references and measurements.

Romantics

A. 1. Pair of seated musicians, the youth playing the bagpipes, a dog at his feet, the girl playing a mandolin with a sheep lying beside her, 203 and 190mm (8 and $7\frac{1}{2}$in) or 212 and 200mm ($8\frac{3}{8}$ and $7\frac{7}{8}$in) respectively. *Col. Pl. J(a)* and *(c)*. *Mus.* British (large version of the youth with 'WDCo' incised—292mm ($11\frac{1}{2}$in) high); Cecil Higgins.

With bocage 190 and 184mm ($7\frac{1}{2}$ and $7\frac{1}{4}$in) respectively. S 20 Nov. 1979, L 110.

In trellised arbour, but without animals 305mm (12in). C 16 June 1975, L 17. B. & Th., Pl. 72 (with pagoda) (girl). *Mus.* Derby.

With double candlesticks 222 and 206mm ($8\frac{3}{4}$ and $8\frac{1}{8}$in) respectively. Herb. All. Col., Fig. 40, Pl. 9 (ascribed to Chelsea). *Mus.* V. & A.

With single candlesticks. Mus. Luton Hoo.

*2. Pair comprising standing boy and girl, the former playing a tambourine, the latter holding flowers, 146mm ($5\frac{3}{4}$in). C 28 Apr. 1975, L 10.

3. Candlestick figures of gardener and companion, each standing beside flowering branches holding flowers, 235, 247, 254, 269 or 311mm ($9\frac{1}{4}$, $9\frac{3}{4}$, 10, $10\frac{5}{8}$ or $12\frac{1}{4}$in). S 18 March 1969, L 80; 4 Feb. 1975, L 147; C 10 March 1975, L 129. Herb. All. Col., Fig. 42, Pl. 11 (ascribed to Chelsea); Binns, *First Century of English Porcelain*, Pl. XV (ascribed to Chelsea); B. & Th., Pl. 70 (girl). *Mus.* V. & A.

4. Pair of musicians seated before elaborate branches with applied flowers ending in single candlesticks, the boy playing a flute, the girl a mandolin, 311mm ($12\frac{1}{4}$in). C 10 March 1975, L 130.

**5. Shepherdess and companion, each standing before a tree-stump, the former holding flowers in her left hand, a sheep at her feet, the man holding in his outstretched right hand a fruit taken from a basket of fruit in his other hand, a dog lying beside him, 215, 241, 254, 260, 273 or 292mm ($8\frac{1}{2}$, $9\frac{1}{2}$, 10, $10\frac{1}{4}$, $10\frac{3}{4}$ or $11\frac{1}{2}$in). *Pl. 44* (shepherdess). C 19 Feb. 1973, L 124 (man); 7 Oct. 1974, L 87; S 13 Feb. 1979, L 123 (pair), L 125 (man); 3 July 1979, L 82. Lane, Pl. 63 (man); Twitchett, Pl. 90 (man). *Mus.* British (man); Derby (shepherdess); V. & A.

**6. Pair comprising a gallant, usually without a hat, holding a fruit in outstretched right hand, a basket of fruit in his left, and a lady (with a hat) covered with applied flowers and holding a posy in her left hand, 190 and 241mm ($7\frac{1}{2}$ and $9\frac{1}{2}$in), or 222 and 203mm ($8\frac{3}{4}$ and 8in) respectively. *Pl. 48*. Stonor, Pl. 52 (for man *without* the hat).

(Note: the gallant without the hat is also

recorded as paired with the shepherdess of 5. above.) *Mus.* Derby (lady).

**7. A man (hatless) seated on rock-work holding a basket (presumably a sweetmeat dish), whilst two lambs and a dog lie at his feet, and a companion wearing a hat and likewise holding a basket with two lambs recumbent beside her, 235 and 244mm (9¼ and 9⅝in) respectively (man also recorded, 247mm (9¾in)). *Pl. 45* (man). S 11 Nov. 1969, L 191; *Apollo*, Aug. 1933, p. 101, Fig. VII. *Mus.* British (lady); Royal Crown Derby (man).

8. Group of sportsman and companion, 152mm (6in) (the same model as in *Pl. 89(b)*, but instead of holding grapes the lady has game). *Mus.* British.

9. Pair comprising sportsman and companion, each with a dog at his or her feet, the man holding a gun, the lady in riding habit, 190, 209 or 222mm (7½, 8¼ or 8¾in). *Pl. 46.* (Based on Chelsea models.) *Mus.* V. & A.

10. (a) A group comprising a boy playing a hurdy-gurdy and a girl teaching a dog dressed as Harlequin to dance or sing, after Carl Van Loo, 260 or 279mm (10¼ or 11in). Schr. Col., No. 299, Pl. 36; Untermyer Col., Fig. 275, Pl. 101; Dixon, Pl. 36; Twitchett, Pl. 64. *Mus.* Metropolitan (Untermyer Col.); V. & A.
   (b) A companion group to the above, with the boy and girl differently positioned, the girl holding the dog by its forepaws, the boy pulling it by the ears, seemingly in an endeavour to teach it to dance or sing, after Carl Van Loo, 279mm (11in). C 19 Nov. 1973, L 186. Lane, Pl. 67. *Mus.* Metropolitan.

11. Pair of candlestick figures of a gardener and companion before flowering bocage, 318mm (12½in). C 19 Feb. 1973, L 136; S 25 Nov. 1980, L 97. Twitchett, Col. Fig. 12. *Mus.* Royal Crown Derby.

*12. Pair of sweetmeat figures of a hatless man and girl seated holding shell-shaped baskets, 165, 178 or 241mm (6½, 7 or 9½in). *Pl. 47.*

*13. Pair comprising a boy playing bagpipes and a dancing girl, lifting up her skirt slightly with her right hand and holding flowers in her left, each wearing small hats, 158 and 165mm (6¼ and 6½in) respectively. *Col. Pl. L(a)* and *(c)*.

14. Gallant and companion, the former holding a lamb and a basket of flowers, the latter with an apron of flowers and a basket of eggs, each standing before flowering tree-stumps, 222 or 247mm (8¾ or 9¾in). *Pl. 49.* *Mus.* V. & A.

15. As above, but with fruit replacing the eggs and the flowers. S 17 Oct. 1972, L 14. W.W., Pl. 59.

16. Shepherd and shepherdess, the former playing a flute with a dog at his side, the latter holding a posy of flowers in dancing attitude with a sheep at her feet, both standing before flowering trees, 203 and 215mm (8 and 8½in) respectively. S 2 April 1968, L 55. Bradshaw, Pl. 109.

17. A pair of figures portraying the same theme as above, 228mm (9in). C 11 Dec. 1978, L 243 (with elaborate bocage); Hurlbutt, Pl. 10 (as candlestick figures).

18. A group of lovers, the man seated on a stump playing the flute, his companion lying down beside him holding a score, with elaborate bocage, 190mm (7½in). *Pl. 50.*

*19. A pair of candlestick figures of a standing boy and girl, the former playing a flute, the latter holding a flower, 241, 247 or 254mm (9½, 9¾ or 10in). *Pl. 51.*

*20. Pair of dancers, the man with his left arm bent and raised, his right arm outstretched, left foot pointed, the lady holding in her right hand a corner of her apron, her left hand bent and raised, 165 or 171 or 178mm (6½ or 6¾ or 7in). *Pl. 17(b)* (lady). S 15 July 1969, L 93; 6 Dec. 1977, L 64 (man); 8 July 1980, L 110 (man). B. & Th., Pl. 51; W.W., Pl. 22 (man); Twitchett, Pl. 92; *Mus.* Derby.

*21. Pair comprising a boy with hat and a girl

without, each seated on a tree-stump and kicking, 152 and 146mm or 139 and 133mm (6 and 5¾in or 5½ and 5¼in) respectively. *Pl. 52* (boy). W.W., Pl. 24; Twitchett, Pls 80 and 81. *Mus.* British (girl); V. & A. (boy).

22. Pair of standing children, one dancing, one crying, 190 or 206mm (7½ or 8⅛in). S 22 Oct. 1968, L 106. *Mus.* Cecil Higgins (boy crying).

*23. Boy and girl, the former playing a tambourine, the girl with a garland of flowers on her head and another hanging from her shoulder, 146mm (5¾in). S 7 May 1968, L 178.

*24. Girl seated on a rock, her hat in her lap, with her right leg bent and her foot stretched in front of her, and companion wearing a hat, 133mm (5¼in). *Pl. 53(a)* (girl). Gil., Col. Pl. VII.

25. Shepherdess, standing with apron full of flowers, a posy in her left hand and a sheep at her feet, 203, 215 or 241mm (8, 8½ or 9½in). S 2 April 1968, L 56.

26. Sometimes the above model is paired with a man holding out a fruit (see No. 5). C 11 Dec. 1978, L 241; Gil., *CDP*, Fig. 143; Savage, *18th-Century English Porcelain*, Pl. 83(b). *Mus.* Cecil Higgins; V. & A.
A variant appears with left hand outstretched. S 23 Oct. 1979, L 196; 20 Nov. 1979, L 107.

27. Shepherdess as No. 25, but with a dog instead of a sheep, 215mm (8½in). S 12 July 1977, L 138.

28. Candlestick figures of a man and woman, probably gardeners, the former carrying a basket of fruit, his companion supporting a basket of flowers with her apron, 305mm (12in). S 2 Apr. 1968, L 57.

*29. Seated figure of a man with tricorn hat playing a violin, 133 or 139mm (5¼ or 5½in). S 27 Sept. 1977, L 75. Untermyer Col., Fig. 273, . 96 (with initials 'IG' painted in lavender, thought to stand for James Giles). *Mus.* Metropolitan; V. & A.

30. Sailor and lass, the former carrying a stick and displaying three gold coins in the palm of his left hand, the latter coyly beckoning, around her neck a ribbon with a pendant consisting of a heart pierced by an arrow, 247 and 241mm (9¾ and 9½in) or 273 and 260mm (10¾ and 10¼in) respectively. *Pl. 54. Mus.* British; V. & A. (lass).
(Note: it has been suggested that these figures represent Woodward and Nancy Dawson in character. It is possible they may be connected with Gay's ballad 'The Farewell of Sweet William to Black-eyed Susan', published in 1720.)

**31. Pair of pastoral figures, the man wearing a cocked hat and holding a struggling cockerel in his arms, a stick in his hand, the barefoot woman holding a hen, both on bocage scroll bases, 152, 203 or 209mm (6, 8 or 8¼in). *Pl. 55.* S 10 Dec. 1973, L 207 (woman *with* shoes). *Mus.* British (man); V. & A.

32. Flautist as a young boy standing bare-footed against a tree-stump, 139mm (5½in). S 17 July 1973, L 232; 6 Dec. 1977, L 37.

33. Pair of candlestick figures of putti, the chubby children seated on a flower-applied stump, wearing a garland of flowers in their hair and holding a posy in one hand and with the other supporting a foliate candle nozzle, 158mm (6¼in). S 17 July 1973, L 241.

**34. Pair of naked putti, each seated on a round rococo base, with garlands of vine twined about him, a wine-cup in his left hand, and his head supporting a foliate candle nozzle, 209, 228 or 235mm (8¼, 9 or 9¼in). S 4 Feb. 1975, L 145; 6 Dec. 1977, L 63; 18 May 1982, L 140 (single). Gil., Pl. 22; *ECC Exh.*, No. 309, Pl. 69; Herb. All. Col., No. 29, Pl. 4 (ascribed to Bow); Savage, *18th-Century English Porcelain*, Pl. 29(b) (single); Bradshaw, Pl. 107 (single). *Mus.* V. & A.
(Note: these figures may represent Autumn.)

35. Pair comprising a man standing with a small barrel strapped to his back and wearing a tricorn hat, the woman holding a sheaf of corn and with a flask hanging from her waist, both with

flowering bocage supports, 203 and 196mm (8 and 7¾in) respectively. S 3 Apr. 1973, L 78.

36. Pair of standing musicians, each supported by a flower-encrusted tree-stump, the man playing a pipe in his left hand, and with his right hand beating a tambourine slung over his other arm, and wearing a long cap with three plumes, the woman with plumes in her hair holding a triangle and a beater, a satchel slung over her shoulder, 222 or 247mm (8¾ or 9¾in). Herb. All. Col., No. 35, Pl. 8 (man) (ascribed to Chelsea); Honey, Pl. 54(B) (man); Savage *18th-Century English Porcelain*, Pl. 71(b) (man).

More frequently these figures appear post-1770.

S 17 Oct. 1972, L 11 (No. 311 incised); 1 July 1975, L 153 (No. 311 incised), *Mus.* British (man); Fitzwilliam; V. & A. (man).

*37. Young girl standing, 152mm (6in). S 8 July 1980, L 111.

Query, whether a Season.

*38. Young man in dancing pose, with stump support, 171mm (6¾in). S 20 Nov. 1979, L 117, Gil. Col. Pl. VII.

39. Putto standing against a tree-stump, a garland of flowers draped around his naked body and a wreath on his head, 120mm (4¾in). S 20 Nov. 1979, L 124.

Query, whether a Season.

40. Candlestick figure of a girl holding a pheasant, standing before a flowering tree, 295mm (11⅝in). No illustration.

*41. Pair of children dancing in pose reminiscent of the Bow so-called 'Dutch Dancers' or 'New Dancers', 120 and 114mm (4¾ and 4½in) respectively. W.W., Pls 20, 23 (girl); Twitchett, Col. Pl. 4.

*42. Shepherdess, holding up a flower-laden apron, whilst a sheep attempts to clamber up her skirt and a dog rests at her feet, 241mm (9½in). W.W., Pl. 11 (for the identical dry-edge model).

*43. A seated putto holding a vase of flowers, 76 or 114mm (3 or 4½in). W.W., Pl. 21; Gil., Pl. 57.

Query, whether Spring.

44. A standing putto with flowers in his hair and holding a basket of flowers, slight bocage, 152mm (6in). Gil., *CDP*, Fig. 146.

45. Pair of dancers, the lady holding her skirt in her left hand, with her right hand raised before her, the man lifting his cloak, both supported by tree-stumps, 241mm (9½in). Stonor, Pl. 55. *Mus.* British (lady).

46. Pair of musicians, the man playing a double bass, the woman a hurdy-gurdy, 158mm (6¼in). Stonor, Pl. 56. After the Bow (see Stonor, Pl. 86).

*47. Dancer with his left hand turned inwards on his hip, his right hand held out and bent. Gil., Col. Pl. VII.

*48. Candlestick group comprising boy and girl plucking flowers from a flowering tree supporting two candle nozzles and a nesting bird, a dog lying recumbent on the round pad base, 254mm (10in). B. & Th., Pl. 30 *Mus.* Derby.

*49. Boy with hat playing fife and drum, 139mm (5½in). B. & Th., Pl. 49. *Mus.* Derby.

50. Pair of minuet dancers, the man leaning backwards slightly, the lady holding out her skirt with both hands, 282 and 273mm (11⅛ and 10¾in) respectively. *Pl. 56. Mus.* V. & A.

51. Pair comprising a man with a dog holding out a card and a girl with a garlanded sheep leaping up, sometimes with, sometimes without, bocage, 139, 158 or 222mm (5½, 6¼ or 8¾in). Herb. All. Col., No. 39, Pl. 12 (ascribed to Chelsea); Twitchett, Pl. 60. *Mus.* V. & A.

52. Small bare-footed boy playing a flute with both hands, whilst his dog looks up. He wears a broad-brimmed hat, 165mm (6½in). Bradley, Pl. 12; Twitchett, Pl. 87.

Direct copy from a Meissen model by J. J. Kändler (R. Rückert, *Meissener Porzellan 1710–1810* (1966), No. 922, Pl. 225).

*53. Seated youth with tricorn hat playing a pipe, 178mm (7in). Honey, Pl. 53(B). *Mus.* V. & A.

*54. Boy standing with a basket of flowers held in his left hand, proffering a single flower with his right, 114mm (4½in). Twitchett, Pl. 89.

This model may possibly represent Spring.

55. Pair of candlestick figures of a fruit seller (male) and a flower seller (female), 292mm (11½in). Twitchett, Col. Pl. 12. *Mus.* Royal Crown Derby.

*56. A boy with plumed hat holding in his left hand a pot of flowers and in his outstretched right hand a single flower, 120mm (4¾in). Twitchett, Pl. 89.

*57. Putto, with head and shoulders covered with encrusted flowers, 127mm (5in). Twitchett, Pl. 86.

58. A man with plumed hat in dancing pose, both arms held out slightly, with bocage. *Apollo*, Aug. 1933, p. 101, Fig. XII.

Incised under the base 'George Holmes did this figer 1765'. (Formerly in Lord Leverhulme's Collection.)

59. Centrepiece modelled as a gallant and companion seated back to back, each holding an oval basket, on a circular scroll-moulded base, 235mm (9¼in). *Pl. 58.*

*60. A male flautist, 178mm (7in). Gil., Pl. 15; Bradshaw, Pl. 104.

61. A candlestick figure of a putto supporting on his head a tulip candle nozzle, 254mm (10in). *Pl. 57.*

62. A standing figure of a drummer, 152mm (6in). Twitchett, Pl. 52.

63. A seated boy in the form of a taper-stick, 152mm (6in). Twitchett, Pl. 57.

*64. A seated figure of Kuan-Yin, 114mm (4½in). (After the Chelsea.) Twitchett, Pl. 99.

65. A female dancer holding a mask in her left hand, 165mm (6½in). No illustration. *Mus.* V. & A.

Theatricals

B. 1. Pair of 'Ranelagh figures', the gallant and his companion in dancing attitude, each with one hand on hips and the other outstretched.

In the best examples the man holds a letter inscribed 'Dominae Lucretiae' and the lady a locket representing an admission ticket to the Ranelagh Gardens, 215, 247, 289, 292, 305, 314 or 318mm (8½, 9¾, 11⅜, 11½, 12, 12⅜ or 12½in). *Pl. 59. Mus.* British; Cecil Higgins; V. & A.

Variant pair of exaggeratedly slim proportions, 292mm (11½in). S 22 Oct. 1968, L 83 (man); *The Connoisseur* Aug. 1903, p. 197; C 2 June 1969, L 121 (lady).

2. Pair of candlestick figures of Ranelagh dancers (see above) standing before flower-encrusted branches supporting candle-nozzles, 260 to 279mm (10¼ to 11in). C 11 March 1974, L 107; S 23 Oct. 1979, L 201. *Mus.* British; Cecil Higgins; V. & A.

3. Pair of standing figures of Harlequin and Columbine holding slapsticks, 108mm (4¼in). S 22 Oct. 1968, L 101. Gil., *CDP*, Fig. 149.

As above, but standing before flowering branches, 101 or 120mm (4 or 4¾in). C 19 Feb. 1973, L 127. *Mus.* V. & A.

4. Harlequin, standing with his left foot forward, holding his slapstick in his left hand and dramatically clasping his breast with his right (from the Italian Commedia dell' Arte), 178mm (7in). S 12 March 1974, L 157. Twitchett, Pl. 58.

The model appears to have been taken from the Chelsea, which in turn owes its inspiration to continental figures adapted by Simon Feilner at Fürstenburg and Höchst from contemporary engravings.

*5. Pair of candlestick figures of Punch and Harlequin, from the Italian Commedia dell' Arte, Punch masquerading as a nightwatchman holding in his right hand a lantern and standing in a dancing attitude, Harlequin with his hands outstretched, 247mm (9¾in). *Pl. 60* (Punch). S 26 Nov. 1974, L 65 (nozzles of Bow porcelain). Gil., Pl. 25. *Mus.* V. & A. (Punch).

*6. Group of Harlequin and Columbine dancing, 152, 158, 165, 171 or 178mm (6, 6¼, 6½, 6¾ or 7in). *Pl. 61. Mus.* V. & A.

7. Group of lady, gallant and jester, the two lovers seated beneath a flowering tree embracing, whilst the jester stoops obsequiously to offer them a tray set with two cups.

(i) *Early version*, 139mm (5½in) or with tree at the back, 184 or 190mm (7¼ or 7½in). *Pl. 62. Mus.* Metropolitan (Untermyer Col.); V. & A.

(ii) *Later version*, 279, 292 or 311mm (11, 11½ or 12¼in). *Pl. 63. Mus.* Metropolitan (Untermyer Col.); Royal Crown Derby.

8. Duet singers, each with one hand on hip, the other outstretched in eloquent attitude, 203 and 196mm (8 and 7¾in) or 228 and 212mm (9 and 8⅜in) respectively. *Pl. 64. Mus.* British (man) (7⅛in); Derby; V. & A.

9. Group consisting of a pair of Tyrolean dancers, 178 or 187mm (7 or 7⅜in). Gil., *CDP*, Fig. 187; Stonor, Pl. 54.

After the Meissen. The same basic model was produced at Bow and Chelsea.

**10. James Quinn as Falstaff holding a sword and shield, 247, 260, 311, 330 or 375mm (9¾, 10¼, 12¼, 13 or 14¾in). *Pl. 65. Mus.* British; Cecil Higgins; Royal Crown Derby; V. & A.

11. David Garrick as Tancred, wearing a fur-lined cape, and Mrs Cibber in the character of a Vivandière with a basket of bottles and gourds in the crook of her arm, 225 and 219mm (8⅞ and 8⅝in) respectively. S 17 July 1973, L 239. Schr. Col., Nos 301, 301A, Pl. 34; Gil., *CDP*, Fig. 177 (Mrs Cibber); Gil., Pl. 156; Lane, Pl. 69(a) (Mrs Cibber); B. & Th., Pl. 63; Twitchett, Pls 47, 48. *Mus.* British; Derby; V. & A.

David Garrick (1717–99) first appeared in Thomson's *Tancred and Sigismunda* in 1744–5. Lane says that there is no evidence that the other figure is Mrs Cibber (1714–66), but the de-

scription is a convenient method of identification, even if erroneous.

12. Cupid in disguise as a lawyer before a tree-stump with tricorn hat under his arm, 127mm (5in). C 19 Feb. 1973, L 128.

*13. Group of Harlequin and Columbine around a flowering tree, the latter figure holding a child, 171mm (6¾in). B. & Th., Col. Pl. A.

(This model is, with the addition of the tree, directly based on a Kändler original—see p. 53 of Hugo Morley-Fletcher's *Meissen Porcelain in Colour*.)

Mus. Fitzwilliam.

14. Group comprising lady, gallant and jester seated in a circle, each holding a shell sweetmeat dish, 247mm (9¾in). Possibly taken from the Italian Commedia. Stonor, Pl. 59.

Personalities
C. **1. Shakespeare, standing beside a pedestal on which three books are resting together with a scroll with a passage from *The Tempest*; and Milton, standing against a pedestal moulded with Adam and Eve and the Angel from *Paradise Lost*, with three books resting on the top, 279 to 318mm (11 to 12½in).

S 8 Oct. 1968, L 212 (Milton); 28 Oct. 1969, L 57 (Shakespeare); C 15 Oct. 1973, L 162 (Shakespeare); 10 March 1975, L. 128; King, Figs 40 (Milton), 41 (Shakespeare); Lane, Pls 64, 65; W.W., Pl. 55; Twitchett, Pls 76 (Milton), 67 and 83 (Shakespeare). *Mus.* British; Royal Crown Derby (Shakespeare); V. & A.

2. John Wilkes standing beside a pillar holding a scroll inscribed 'Bill of Rights' and 'Magna Carta' with a putto at the base, and General Conway standing before martial trophies with a putto at his feet holding a shield painted with the head of a Negro, 228, 298, 305 or 318mm (9, 11¾, 12 or 12½in). C 16 Nov. 1970, L 211 and 212; Hobson, Pl. XII (11.44) (Wilkes), ascribed to Chelsea.

These models continued into the Bloor period. Examples 1770–5 are in the V. & A. (Schr. Col., Nos 362, 362a, Pl. 35). See also B. & Th., Col. Pl. D (post-1770).

In 1764 Conway was removed from his command and his position in the royal bedchamber for speaking on questions related to Wilkes's case. He became Lieut-General of the Ordnance in 1767. Wilkes became Lord Mayor of London in 1775.

Mus. British; V. & A.

*3. St Philip, standing gazing earnestly at the crucifix in his right hand, with long beard, a cloak over his tunic and a basket of stones at his feet, 241 or 266mm (9½ or 10½in). *Pl. 67.*

*4. St Thomas, King Lear or the Roman soldier, as a bearded long-haired man wearing a cloak and Roman-type sandals, with some trophies at the base including a sword hilt, 241 or 254mm (9½ or 10in). Gil., Pl. 55; W.W., Pl. 28, Twitchett, Pl. 78. *Mus.* Royal Crown Derby; V. & A.

5. Charles Pratt, Baron Camden, as Lord Chancellor (1766) in his wig and robes, holding a scroll in his left hand which rests on a large book upright on a pillar, 314mm (12⅜in). (Based on an engraving by Charles Simon Ravenet after Sir Joshua Reynolds.) Lane, Pl. 72. *Mus.* Of Fine Arts, Boston.

6. Lord Chatham, resting his right arm on a pedestal inscribed 'VISCOUNT PITT OF BURTON PYNSENT, EARL OF CHATm LORD KEEPER OF HIS MAJESTY'S PRIVY SEAL', whilst at his side are a kneeling Red Indian woman and an alligator, emblematic of America; on the pedestal and at its foot are books, 368mm (14½in). *Pl. 66. Mus.* British; V. & A.

(Note: the example in the V. & A. differs in detail from that in the British Museum.)

Birds
D. 1. 'Birds in branches' candlestick group, with two birds perching amongst flowering bocage beneath a single candle-sconce, the whole supported on a scroll-edge base, 222 or 241mm (8¾ or 9½in). S 14 May 1974, L 57. Twitchett, Pl. 63. *Mus.* Royal Crown Derby.

With ormolu foliate candle nozzles, 241mm (9½in). C 21 April 1969, L 145.

2. Bunting, perched upright on a flowering tree-stump, its head turned slightly to one side, 139mm (5½in). S 14 May 1974, L 58.

3. Pair of buntings, each perched on a tree-stump looking downwards at the ground, 95mm (3¾in). Untermyer Col., Fig. 281, Col. Pl. 110.

4. Pair of small finches, each perched on a tree-stump and looking upwards, 98 and 101mm (3⅞ and 4in) respectively. Untermyer Col., Fig. 284, Pl. 105.

5. Pair of warblers (?), with heads turned in opposite directions and wings partly unfurled, each perched on a tree-stump, 101 and 114mm (4 and 4½in). Untermyer Col., Fig. 287, Pl. 105.

6. Pair of goldfinches, each perched on a flowering tree-stump, its head turned slightly to one side, 63, 89, 98, 105, 120 or 127mm (2½, 3½, 3⅞, 4⅛, 4¾ or 5in). *Pl. 69* (single). *Mus.* Luton Hoo (single); V. & A.

7. Pair of chaffinches, each perched on a flowering tree-stump, 139 or 152mm (5½ or 6in). *Pl. 72.*

8. Pair of owls, each perched on a flower-encrusted tree-stump, 63 or 76mm (2½ or 3in). S 24 Oct. 1972, L 182, 183; 25 March 1974, L 183, 184. *Mus.* Cecil Higgins.

9. Pair of blue-tits, each perched on a tree-stump, 70, 117 or 127mm (2¾, 4⅝ or 5in). *Pl. 68. Mus.* British; Luton Hoo; Metropolitan (Untermyer Col.); V. & A.

10. Pair of canaries, each perched on a tree-stump, 63 and 73mm (2½ and 2⅞in) or 136 and 139mm (5⅜ and 5½in) respectively. *Pl. 73(b)* (single, 122mm (4¹³⁄₁₆in)). *Mus.* Luton Hoo (single); Metropolitan (Untermyer Col.).

11. Pair of woodpeckers, each perched on a high tree-stump, with its head turned back over its body, 127 or 133mm (5 or 5¼in). S 17 July 1973, L 69. Schreiber, *Journals*, Vol. II, Pl. facing p. 24; Untermyer Col., Fig. 288, Col.

Pl. 110. *Mus.* Luton Hoo; Metropolitan (Untermyer Col.); V. & A.

12. A variant model of woodpecker, perched on a tree-stump, 158mm (6¼in). *Pl. 70.*

13. Pair of doves, each standing on a round base amid ears of corn and flowers, 70mm (2¾in). B. & Th., Pl. 54. *Mus.* V. & A.

14. Pair of parrots, each perched on the stump of an apple tree with fruit and leaves, the base scrolled, 225mm (8⅞in). *Pl. 71. Mus.* V. & A.

15. Finch with outspreading wings, perched on a tree-stump, 120mm (4¾in). *Col. Pl. D(b).*

16. Songbird with perky tail and partly unfurled wings perched on a tree-stump, 127mm (5in). Untermyer Col., Fig. 286, Pl. 105.

17. Bird perched on a tree-stump, 100 mm (3 15/16in). *Pl. 74(b). Mus.* Luton Hoo.

18. Bird perched on a tree-stump, 135mm (5 5/16in). *Pl. 73(a). Mus.* Luton Hoo.

19. Group of two birds in branches, 193mm (7⅝in). No illustration. *Mus.* Luton Hoo.

20. Bird perched on a tree-stump, 114mm (4½in). *Pl. 74(a). Mus.* Luton Hoo.

Animals

E. *1. Pair of pug dogs, seated erect on rectangular mound bases, 89 or 82mm and 92mm (3½ or 3¼in and 3⅝in) respectively. *Pl. 77. Mus.* British (single dog); Cecil Higgins; V. & A.

(Note: a similar pug dog lying recumbent on a tasselled cushion, seemingly after the Chelsea, is also recorded. Savage, *18th-Century English Porcelain*, Pl. 89(b).)

*2. Pair of pug dogs, seated with front legs braced and heads erect and with short curled tails on oval slightly rococo bases, 50 and 63mm (2 and 2½in) respectively. S 7 Oct. 1968, L 211. Twitchett, Pl. 69.

3. Pair of stags with elaborate bocage, 196mm

(7¾in). C 28 June 1971, L 78; 17 June 1974, L 130.

*4. Pair comprising stag and hind at lodge without bocage, 203 and 114/120mm (8 and 4½/4¾in) respectively. C 23 Feb. 1970, L 92; S 25 March 1974, L 174; 6 Dec. 1977, L 38; 19 Dec. 1978, L 145. Twitchett, Pl. 71.

*5. Alternative version of stag and hind at lodge, 101mm (4in) long (a reissue of the dry-edge models of *Pl. 29*). W.W., Pl. 57.

6. A candlestick group with one sheep climbing a tree applied with flowers, whilst another lies recumbent at the bottom, 228 or 235mm (9 or 9¼in). *Pl. 75(b).*

**7. Candlestick group of two dogs barking at squirrels on branches of a flower-applied tree, 228mm (9in). C 27 March 1972, L 5 (sconces missing). B. & Th., Pl. 58. *Mus.* Derby.

8. Candlestick group of two rabbits, one nibbling elaborate bocage, the other lying recumbent at the base, 235mm (9¼in). C 27 March 1972, L 6.

9. Pair of candlestick groups, one of a seated hen and chickens, the other of two fighting cocks, each with elaborate bocage, 241mm (9½in). C 15 June 1970, L 105 (? post-1770).

10. Pair of candlestick groups of a fox attacking a chicken, with or without elaborate bocage, 260mm (10¼in). S 13 Oct. 1970, L 214 (with elaborate bocage).

(The group sometimes appears without the candlestick.)

The model is inspired by the Meissen—see a Meissen miniature S 15 Dec. 1972, L 258—or the Sèvres 'The Fox and the Bird' by Blondeau after a painting by Jean Baptiste Oudry (1686–1755)—see Paul J. Atterbury ed., *European Pottery and Porcelain*, opp. p. 89.

11. Lowing cow under an overhanging tree in flower, 76, 95 or 101mm (3, 3¾ or 4in) long. *Pl. 53(b).*

12. Monkey musician wearing a tricorn hat, his

right hand resting on his hip, his left hand holding a French horn, 178mm (7in). S 22 Oct. 1968, L 81.

Inspired by the Chelsea model—see the 1756 Catalogue, 'Monkies in different attitudes playing on musick'—in turn inspired by the *Affenkapelle* of Meissen.

13. Monkey musician playing the violin, stooping forward and wearing a tricorn hat, 101 or 190mm (4 or 7½in). S 22 Oct. 1968, L 82; 27 Sept. 1977, L 77. Gil., Pl. 148.

See note to No. 12 above.

*14. Recumbent ram and ewe, 110 and 101mm (4⅓ and 4in) or 133 and 127mm (5¼ and 5in) long respectively. S 7 Dec. 1976, L 2; 23 Oct. 1979, L 197.

Alternative version, with bocage, 108mm (4¼in). S 3 April 1973, L 79 (? post-1770).

15. Florentine boar seated on an oval base, its head turned to one side, with large nose and pricked ears, 63mm (2½in). S 25 March 1974, L 173.

*16. Pair of goats lying down, 95 and 108mm (3¾ and 4¼in) respectively. S. 25 March 1974, L 192. Savage, *18th-Century English Porcelain*, Pl. 68(a).

17. Pair of sheep groups, comprising ewe suckling a lamb, and a ram with lamb lying down, 127 and 120mm (5 and 4¾in). S 25 March 1974, L 190 (ram and lamb, 139mm (5½in)). W.W., Pl. 58.

18. Candlestick group of a young dog looking up at two birds perched on the branches of a flowering tree, 209mm (8¼in). *Pl. 75(a)*. *Mus.* V. & A.

*19. (a) Pair of leopards, each with one front paw raised, standing on a pad base applied with flowers, 89mm (3½in). *Pl. 76*. *Mus.* V. & A.

(b) A different model of a single leopard, 89mm (3½in). Twitchett, Pl. 91. *Mus.* Derby.

20. Extremely rare pair of sitting cats, one with a mouse or rat, 101mm (4in). Formerly in the possession of Winifred Williams, London. No illustration.

(Samson copies are sometimes encountered.)

21. Pair of cow and calf groups, 82mm (3¼in). Savage, *English Pottery and Porcelain*, Pl. 141. *Mus.* Hastings Museum and Art Gallery.

22. Figure of a bull, 63mm (2½in). Gil., Pl. 151.

23. Pair of squirrels, each nibbling a nut, 89mm (3½in). Twitchett, Pl. 72. *Mus.* V. & A.

24. Pair of candlestick groups of a dog leaping up and frenziedly barking at a cat perched with arched back in the branches, 222 and 228mm (8¾ and 9in) respectively. S 28 Oct. 1969, L 53 (no illustration).

25. Spaniel dog, standing barking, its head and body slightly turned to the right, 76mm (3in long). *Col Pl. L(b)*.

Classical mythology

F. 1. Leda and the Swan, the goddess seated on bulrushes stroking the swan, 266 or 292mm (10½ or 11½in). C 7 July 1975, L 32. B. & Th., Pl. 59; Hurlbutt, Pl. 7 (on a stand) (305mm (12in)) or with pedestal (387mm (15¼in)); Dixon, Pl. 39. *Mus.* Derby; Cecil Higgins.

2. Europa and the Bull, 279, 289 or 298mm (11, 11⅜ or 11¾in). *Pl. 78*. *Mus.* V. & A. Seemingly a companion to 1. above.

3. Pair of figures of Cupid and Psyche kneeling before flowering trees, Cupid fitting an arrow to his bow, and Psyche holding a heart, 209mm (8¼in). C 1 April 1974, L 165.

4. Jupiter with an eagle at his side, holding a thunderbolt in his raised right arm, 282, 438 or 483mm (11⅛, 17¼ or 19in). C 10 Dec. 1973, L 108. King, Fig. 46; Twitchett, Col. Pl. 7. *Mus.* British; Derby; Royal Crown Derby; V. & A.

5. Juno holding the neck of a peacock standing beside her, 381mm (15in). King, Fig. 45. *Mus.* British.

Seemingly a companion to 4. above, perhaps symbolic of Air. Smaller versions are known.

**6. Pair of figures of Jupiter and Juno, the god and goddess finely modelled and shown seated in chariots among swirling clouds, 279 and 266mm (11 and 10½in) respectively. S 19 May 1970, L 132. Twitchett, Pl. 70. *Mus.* Cecil Higgins.

7. Venus, virtually naked, a dolphin with tail fin entwined around her legs, 171 or 266mm (6¾ or 10½in). S 12 July 1977, L 141. Stonor, Pl. 53.

8. Neptune, the crowned sea-god striding forward clasping his windswept cloak, a torrent of water issuing from the mouth of the dolphin at his feet, all on a rocky base encrusted with shells and aquatic weeds, 203, 241 or 406mm (8, 9½ or 16in). S 9 Nov. 1976, L 135; S 16 Mar. 1982, L 106. B. & Th., Pl. 96. *Mus.* British; Derby; Cecil Higgins.

9. Venus and Cupid on a dolphin resting on a coral and shell base, 222 or 381mm (8¾ or 15in). B. & Th., Pl. 60. *Mus.* Derby. Seemingly a companion to No. 8. above.

10. Pluto and Cerberus, 178mm (7in). B. & Th., Pl. 47; Bradshaw, Pl. 117. *Mus.* Derby.
    This model was produced in the dry-edge period (*Pl. 15*).

11. Pair of candlestick figures of Mars and Venus, the former in full armour with shield and banners at his side, the latter accompanied by Cupid, 247, 254 or 266mm (9¾, 10 or 10½in). S 3 Feb. 1970, L 63; 13 Feb. 1979, L 120. Bradley, Pl. 18 (Mars); Twitchett, Pl. 79 (Mars). *Mus.* British; Luton Hoo; Royal Crown Derby (Mars); V. & A. (Mars).
    As above, but with sconce to the side of, instead of above, the figure and with elaborate bocage, 203mm (8in). S 26 Feb. 1980, L 211.
    *Without candlestick or bocage, 171, 190, 196, 343 or 356mm (6¾, 7½, 7¾, 13½ or 14in). S 26 Feb. 1980, L 208 (Mars); 16 Mar. 1982, L 118 (Mars). Gil., *CDP*, Fig. 141 (Venus); Bradley, Pls 9, 17 (Mars). *Mus.* V. & A. (Mars).

**12. Minerva, standing with right hand raised, her left hand resting on a shield, with a plumed hat and with an owl resting on three books at her feet, 305, 337 or 387mm (12, 13¼ or 15¼in). S 15 July 1969, L 97; 16 Mar. 1982, L 121.
    Alternative form, with no owl or books, 305 or 343mm (12 or 13½in). C 9 Feb. 1981, L 213. Bradley, Pl. 10. *Mus.* British; V. & A.
    Said to be related to the lead garden statues of John Cheere (1709–87). M. Whinney, *Sculpture in Britain 1530–1830* (1964), Pl. 107(b).
    (Note: a variant form of Minerva represents Britannia, with a recumbent lion, a flag and martial trophies at her feet.)

**13. Diana as the huntress with both hands raised and a quiver of arrows on her back, a greyhound at her feet, 254, 260, 266, 285 or 311mm (10, 10¼, 10½, 11¼ or 12¼in). S 18 March 1969, L 81; 12 July 1977, L 142; 25 April 1978, L 81; C 9 Feb. 1981, L 212; S 16 Mar. 1982, L 109. Dixon, Pl. 38; Twitchett, Pl. 53. *Mus.* British; Cecil Higgins; Royal Crown Derby; V. & A.

14. Vulcan, with a flame arising out of a brazier standing on a pedestal, a swan at his feet, 381mm (15in). King, Fig. 44. Perhaps symbolic of Fire.

15. Pair of standing figures of Minerva and Venus, the latter somewhat muscular, the former wearing a helmet and holding a shield in her left hand, both supported by flowering tree-stumps, 254mm (10in). C 27 Nov. 1978, L 295.

16. Pair of figures of Minerva and Mars, each wearing plumed hat and cuirass, the former leaning on a shield moulded with Medusa's head, 190mm or 356 and 337mm (7½ or 14 and 13¼in) respectively. S 14 May 1974, L 121. Schr. Col., No. 303, Pl. 34. *Mus.* V. & A.

*17. Cybele or Earth, wearing a coronet and with a lion and cornucopia at her feet, 215 or 228mm (8½ or 9in). *Pl. 79*. *Mus.* Royal Crown Derby; V. & A.

18. The Muse Clio reclining with her lyre, accompanied by a cherub, 228mm (9in). Lane, Pl. 68. *Mus.* British.

19. The Muse Erato reclining with her tambourine, accompanied by a cherub, 228mm (9in). *Pl. 80. Mus.* British.

This model is the companion to No. 18. above and both models are based on engravings by J. Daullé after Boucher.

20. Time clipping the wings of Cupid, in the form of the bearded god Chronos with drapery round his waist, Cupid on his knee; at his feet are scythe, hour-glass, crown, sceptre, terrestrial globe and skull, and Cupid's quiver, 311mm (12¼in). *Pl. 81.*

After a painting by Sir Anthony Vandyke, formerly in the collection of the Duke of Marlborough at Blenheim, of which a mezzotint by Charles Phillips dated 1772 accompanies the Schreiber Collection. The model appears prior to 1770 and must have been based on an earlier engraving.

Mus. V. & A. (post-1770 example).

Street vendors

G. 1. Jewish pedlar, supported by a tree-stump, wearing a fur cap and fur-lined coat, with a basket of bottles slung in front of him, and companion, likewise supported by a tree-stump, holding a rectangular box of trinkets, 190mm or 260 and 254mm (7½in or 10¼ and 10in) respectively. *Pl. 82.*

Based on the Chelsea (see Untermyer Col., Fig. 43, Pl. 27 (man)).

Mus. Luton Hoo; Metropolitan (Untermyer Col.); V. & A.

2. Mapseller, holding an open map in one hand and a rolled one in the other, with his wares in a case on his back, and companion holding a two-drawered tray and wearing a broad-brimmed hat, 158mm (6¼in). *Pl. 83. Mus.* British (man); Derby; V. & A.

The man is after the Meissen (either directly or via the red anchor Chelsea model) being virtually, apart from the map's not being of part of Germany, an exact copy of the figure by Kändler of about 1745. For examples of the Chelsea model see Untermyer Col., Fig. 42, Pl. 24, and G. Savage, *English Pottery and Porcelain*, Pl. 110. The Meissen is based on a drawing by Bouchardon, engraved by Caylus—see

Sale Catalogue of the Salz Collection, Pl. XVI, No. 110, and S 27 March 1973, L 14.

Rustics

H. 1. 'Tithe pig group'
(a) As a composite group comprising the rector, the farmer (holding a pig) and his wife (holding a baby), 152, 165 or 178mm (6, 6½ or 7in). *Pl. 84. Mus.* Derby; V. & A.

(b) As separate individuals, 152, 171, 184 or 279mm (6, 6¾, 7¼ or 11in). *Pl. 85. Mus.* British.
(Note: the parson was modelled separately in earthenware by Ralph Wood and bears the inscription 'I will have no child tho' the y pig'.)

2. Pair of groups of Welsh tailor and his wife, both riding on goats, the husband with two kids in a hod on his back and a pistol slung over the goat's neck, the wife nursing one child and with two others in a basket on her back, 254mm (10in). S 15 July 1969, L 98. Bradley, Pls 15, 16.

These groups are more frequently found post-1770. Gil., *CDP*, Fig. 151, 152mm (6in); Gil., Pl. 146, 241mm (9½in).

They are after the Meissen, modelled in 1740 by Kändler (the husband) and Eberlein (the wife). They are supposed to have been made in mockery of Von Bruhl's tailor who wished to be present at a court banquet. He appeared as a porcelain table decoration. The description 'Welsh' arises from a mis-translation of the Meissen title 'Schneider, welcher auf einem Ziegenbock reutet'.

Representational

I. *1. Senses*
*'Hearing', as a woman in a pannier skirt seated playing a lute, 133, 139 or 152mm (5¼, 5½ or 6in). *Pl. 8(a).* This model may be a reissue of the dry-edge version of 'Hearing'. *Mus.* Derby; Fitzwilliam; V. & A.

2. Continents
(a) Africa, represented by a Negro boy with elephant head-dress, kneeling on a lion and holding a cornucopia and a lobster, 139, 178, 215 or 228mm (5½, 7, 8½ or 9in).
(b) Europe, represented by a crowned child holding a globe, 139, 178, 215 or 305mm (5½, 7, 8½ or 12in).

(c) Asia, represented by a child standing before a camel, 139, 178, 215, 244 or 298mm (5½, 7, 8½, 9⅝, or 11¾in).

(d) America, represented by a Red Indian standing beside an alligator, 139, 178 or 215mm (5½, 7 or 8½in). *Pl. 86. Mus.* Derby; Cecil Higgins; V. & A. (Asia).

(Note: examples of a single composite model where all four continents are placed around an obelisk seem invariably to be post-1770.)

3. Seasons
*(i) Represented by scantily attired putti, respectively holding a basket of flowers (Spring), a sheaf of corn (Summer), grapes (Autumn) and a brazier (Winter), 89, 127, 139, 165 or 178mm (3½, 5, 5½, 6½ or 7in).

S 22 Oct. 1968, L 87; 11 Nov. 1969, L 192 (Winter); 19 May 1970, L 131; 3 Oct. 1972, L 190; C 7 July 1975, L 34 (may be post-1770). Gil., Pl. 56; Twitchett, Pl. 122.

**(ii) Represented by standing adults, Spring as a girl with a putto at her side supporting a basket of flowers, Summer as a girl with a putto at her side holding a sheaf of corn, Autumn as Bacchus with a drinking putto sitting on a barrel, and Winter as an old man wearing a fur-lined coat, a brazier at his feet and a putto chopping wood, 215 to 254mm (8½ to 10in). *Pl. 87.*

This version of the seasons is virtually an exact copy of the Meissen (Gil., Pls 19, 20).

Mus. V. & A. (Summer, Autumn and Winter.)

(iii) Represented by seated children
(a) *Without hats* *Spring as a boy and a girl, each seated on a tree-stump, their hair garlanded with flowers, 95, 108 or 114mm (3¾, 4¼ or 4½in). *Pl. 88.* Gil., *CDP,* Figs 147, 148 (boy with elaborate bocage). *Mus.* Derby; V. & A.

*As above, but each figure on a gilt four-footed base, from the back of which issues a tall bocage with painted green leaves and gilt metal stalks, set with a variety of porcelain flowers with one branch terminating in two white porcelain nozzles, 425mm (16¾in). S 28 Oct. 1969, L 51.

Autumn as a boy seated on a tree-stump, holding a basket of grapes, with a wreath of grapes on his head, bunches of grapes in his hands and grapes at his feet, 162mm (6⅜in). Schr. Col., No. 292, Pl. 14.

(b) *With hats* *Pair of figures of Spring and Autumn, the former as a seated girl holding a basket of flowers on her lap, the latter as a seated boy likewise holding a basket of fruit, 120 and 130mm (4¾ and 5⅛in) or 127 and 133mm (5 and 5¼in) respectively, or each 127 or 139mm (5 or 5½in). *Pl. 89(a)* and *(c).*

*Autumn, represented by the girl above, who this time holds fruit, 127mm (5in). S 22 Oct. 1968, L 78.

(iv) Represented by standing children
(a) *Without hats* *Spring and Autumn, the former as a girl whose hair is garlanded with flowers, the latter as a boy with a basket of grapes on his back and grapes in his hands, 127 and 139mm (5 and 5½in) or 152 and 165mm (6 and 6½) respectively. *Pl. 90.*

(b) *With hats* *Spring and Autumn, the former as a girl holding a single flower in her outstretched left hand, the boy holding a bunch of grapes in his outstretched right hand and a basket of fruit in his left, 152mm (6in). *Pl. 91.*

(v) Represented by standing adult figures, with hats
*Summer and Autumn, the former as a girl with wheat in her apron, the latter as a man holding a basket of fruit in his left hand and proffering a fruit with his right, 120mm (4¾in). B. & Th., Pl. 52 (the man incised 'New D' which probably stands for 'New Dresden'). *Mus.* Derby.

*Winter as a peasant woman wrapped in an ermine coat and hood, warming her hands over a flaming brazier, supported on a circular mound base, 114 or 120mm (4½ or 4¾in). S 6 Dec. 1977, L 35; 20 November 1979, L 111.

(vi) Represented by a group of two figures for each season
*Summer as a candlestick group of a girl leaning against a tree with a seated boy on the other side holding a sheaf of corn, 292mm (11½in) *Pl. 92.* Untermyer Col., Fig. 274, Pl. 96 (without the top of the tree or the sconce). *Mus.* Metropolitan.

*Autumn as a group of a man and woman

walking side by side, the former with his arm around his companion who carries in her apron bunches of grapes, 158mm (6¼in). *Pl. 89(b)*. *Mus*. Royal Crown Derby.

For the Bow equivalent see Honey, Pl. 45(b).

(vii) Spring as a woman holding a large vase of flowers resting on a base, a loose garment coiled round her body, 241mm (9½in). B. & Th., Pl. 56. *Mus*. Fitzwilliam.

(viii) **Autumn in the form of a large putto as Bacchus, with a vine trailing around his body and with a bunch of grapes in his right hand; he stands beside a cornucopia of fruit, 394mm (15½in). No illustration.

4. Britannia, as a young girl wearing a helmet and holding a sword, with a lion at her side and martial trophies at her feet, 254, 318, 324 or 368mm (10, 12½, 12¾ or 14½in). C 17 June 1974, L 131; S 16 Mar. 1982, L 115. Twitchett, Pl. 59; Bradshaw, Pl. 118. *Mus*. V. & A.

5. As No. 4. above, but Britannia is a mature woman, 311mm (12¼in). S 3 July 1979, L 81.

6. Pair of candlestick figures emblematic of 'Liberty', and 'Matrimony', the former as a boy standing before a flowering arbour (with branches supporting two sconces) and holding a bird's nest, 'Matrimony' as a girl standing before a similar arbour and holding an open bird cage, 279 or 311mm (11 or 12¼in). C 21 April 1969, L 176. Twitchett, Pl. 62. *Mus*. Royal Crown Derby.

7. Pair of standing figures of 'Liberty' and 'Matrimony', the former as a man holding a bird's nest, the latter as a girl holding a cage, 222 or 228mm (8¾ or 9 in). *Col. Pl. K. Mus*. Cecil Higgins (girl).

8. Pair of candlestick figures of 'Liberty' and 'Matrimony', both seated against a wall and flowering trees, flanked by two candle nozzles, the man holding a bird cage, a large dog at his feet, the lady holding a bird, a large sheep at her feet, 212, 241 or 266mm (8⅜, 9½ or 10½in).

(Note: as for the holding of the cage and bird, the usual roles are reversed.)

S 17 Oct. 1972, L 12. Hobson, Fig. 40 (11.51) (man) (attributed to Chelsea); Stonor, Pl. 62 (attributed to 1770–5). (Here the man holds the bird, the lady the cage.) *Mus*. British (man).

9. A young god, symbolic of the Arts, wearing a laurel wreath over his flowing hair, whilst emblems of the arts lie at his feet, including a palette, a violin and several large books, on scroll-edged base, 196mm (7¾in). S 17 July 1973, L 230.

This model, in slightly smaller form, appears in the dry-edge period. *Pl. 18*.

10. Blind woman as Justice standing with a sword in her left hand and scales in her right, 241, 263 or 292mm (9½, 10⅜ or 11½in). C 9 Feb. 1981, L 214; Schr. Col., No. 300, Pl. 35; Herb. All. Col., No. 34, Pl. 8 (ascribed to Chelsea). *Mus*. V. & A.

11. Young man representing War, holding a dagger in his right hand, a cannon at his feet, 215mm (8½in). B. & Th., Pl. 61. *Mus*. Cecil Higgins.

Elements
'Water', represented by a standing figure of a woman wearing a loosely draped robe and holding a fish in her right hand, whilst a basket of fish rests at her feet, 235mm (9¼in). S 16 Mar. 1982, L 128 (after the Meissen).

Miscellaneous
J. 1. Virgin with St John and Mary Magdalene gathered round the Cross (missing—at the back is a socket for the insertion of a wooden cross). The Virgin stands with clasped hands, St John standing behind her with right arm outstretched as a support to the Cross, whilst the Magdalene is seated mourning at her side, 266mm (10½in). *Pl. 93. Mus*. V. & A.

*2. Pair of Turkish children in turbans, 98, 114, 203 or 206mm (3⅞, 4½, 8 or 8⅛in). S 2 April 1968, L 53; 22 Oct. 1968, L 104 (boy); 31 July 1979, L 84 (boy); C 18 Nov. 1974, L 174 (boy). Stonor, Pl. 51. *Mus*. Cecil Higgins; Royal Crown Derby; V. & A. These models are after the Meissen.

3. Oriental boy climbing the branches of gnarled tree supported on a circular mound base, 212 or 228mm (8⅜ or 9in). S 23 Oct. 1979, L 195. B. & Th., Pl. 25. *Mus.* Fitzwilliam.

*4. A rococo candlestick with two Chinese boys, one on either side of it, 260 or 266mm (10¼ or 10½in). Stonor, Pl. 49; Untermyer Col., Fig. 289, Pl. 107. *Mus.* Metropolitan (Untermyer Col.).

5. Abyssinian archer and companion, the former holding a bunch of arrows in his right hand and clasping with his left a low-slung belt, from which protrudes a dagger, a quiver of arrows slung across his shoulder, the companion holding an apple in her raised left hand, 318mm (12½in). (Note: sometimes the faces are white.) *Pl. 94. Mus.* Luton Hoo; V. & A.

6. Pair of standing blackamoors, 209mm (8¼in). B. & Th., Pls 65, 66. *Mus.* Royal Crown Derby.

7. Pair of blackamoors, each kneeling on one knee and supporting a shell with the other, 196mm (7¾in). Schr. Col., No. 302, Pl. 34. *Mus.* V. & A.

8. Group of four kneeling blackamoors holding shells around a central pillar, surmounted by a shell, 235mm (9¼in).

(Note: the two kneeling blackamoors of No. 7. are included in this group.) Pl. 95.

9. Pair of fable candlesticks of the Cock and the Jewel and the Vain Jackdaw, with flowering bocage, 235mm (9¼in). C 7 July 1975, L 33. *Mus.* V. & A.

*10. Pair of Turkish dancers, the man 136mm (5⅜in), the lady 171mm (6¾in) (possibly taken from an actor and actress appearing in contemporary drama). Honey, Pl. 53 A and C. *Mus.* V. & A.

APPENDIX 3—USEFUL WARE 1756–70

This appendix contains a list (not exhaustive) of useful ware produced during the period from 1756 to 1770. See also Appendix 1 for notes on references and measurements.

Teapots and covers

1. Lobed
With lobed body and scroll handle, the slightly domed cover surmounted by an acorn finial, 139mm (5½in). B. & Th., Pl. 36; Bradley, Pls 47–49. *Mus.* Castle, Norwich; Derby; Cecil Higgins.

2. Ribbed
With globular ribbed body, flat scroll handle and a slightly domed cover, similarly ribbed, surmounted by an acorn, conical or flower finial, 139mm (5½in). *Col. Pl. J(b)*. *Mus.* Castle, Norwich; National, of Wales.

3. Smooth with fluted spout
With smooth globular body, fluted spout and scrolled handle, the domed cover surmounted by a 'mushroom' finial, 127mm (5in). *Col. Pl. I*.

4. Smooth all over
With smooth globular body, smooth spout and loop handle, the slightly domed cover surmounted by a conical or onion-shape finial, 89, 127, 146 or 158mm (3½, 5, 5¾ or 6¼in). S 17 July 1973, L 146. Bradley, Pls 52, 53 and 135. *Mus.* Castle, Norwich; V. & A.

Coffee pots and covers

1. Ribbed
With baluster-shape body, wide neck, low-curved spout and scrolled loop handle (sometimes with a turned-up thumb terminal) together with domed cover surmounted by a 'spinning top' finial, both the body and the cover ribbed, 222, 241 or 254mm (8¾, 9½ or 10in). *Pls 97* and *98*. *Mus.* Derby; Royal Crown Derby; V. & A.

2. Plain (after the silver)
With smooth pear-shape body, standing on a pedestal foot, and scrolled loop handle, the curved spout moulded at the top and the base with leaf decoration, the domed cover surmounted by an acorn or conical finial, 209, 215 or 228mm (8¼, 8½ or 9in). *Pl. 99(a)*. *Mus.* Derby; National, of Wales; V. & A.

3. Straight-sided conical (after the silver)
Of straight-sided conical or pyramidic form, with scrolled loop handle with turned-up thumbpiece terminal, the domed cover with conical or other shape finial, 203, 209, 215, 228 or 235mm (8, 8¼, 8½, 9 or 9¼in). *Pl. 96(a)*. *Mus.* City of Birmingham; Derby; National, of Wales; Royal Crown Derby.

Cups and saucers

1. Fluted
(i) Tea bowl and saucer, fluted. S 3 April 1973, L 55.

(ii) Coffee cup with loop handle, and saucer, fluted; cup 50 or 76mm (2 or 3in). *Pl. 100(b)*. *Mus.* Derby.

2. Octagonal
(i) Tea bowl and saucer, of octagonal form. S 26 Feb. 1980, L 203.

(ii) Coffee cup with wish-bone handle and saucer, of octagonal form; cup 60mm (2⅜in).

Gil., *CDP* Fig. 7 (cup only); Bradley, Pl. 69 (cup only).

3. *Quatrefoil*

(i) Tea bowl and saucer of quatrefoil shape; cup 57mm (2¼in) high, saucer 127mm (5in) in diameter. Gil., Pl. 53.

(ii) Coffee cup with wish-bone handle and saucer, of quatrefoil shape; cup 60mm (2⅜in). S 20 April 1982, L 97 (no saucer). Gil., *CDP*, Fig. 7 (no saucer); Bradley, Pls 65–68 (no saucer). *Mus.* V. & A. (without saucer).

4. *Ovoid*

Coffee cup of ovoid form with wish-bone handle and saucer; cup 76mm (3in). Gil., Col. Pl. VI, Pl. 37 (cup only).

5. *Cylindrical*

(i) Coffee cup, of cylindrical form, with flat base and wish-bone handle; 63mm (2½in). Gil., *CDP*, Fig. 6.

(ii) Coffee cup of cylindrical form with slightly raised base and loop handle, 38mm (1½in). Bradley, Pl. 73. *Mus.* V. & A.

6. *Circular with moulded decoration*

Coffee cup, circular in form, on slightly raised base, with wish-bone handle, moulded around the sides with sprigs, 60mm (2⅜in). Bradley, Pl. 71. *Mus.* V. & A.

7. *Circular without moulded decoration*

Tea bowl, circular in form, on slightly raised base, and saucer; cup 44mm (1¾in) high, saucer 120mm (4¾in) in diameter. W.W., Pl. 75.

8. *Circular with slightly everted rim*

Tea bowl, circular in form, but with slightly everted rim, on raised base, and saucer; cup 44mm (1¾in) high, saucer 127mm (5in) in diameter. W.W., Pl. 67.

9. *Circular with 'spurs' and scroll handle*

Coffee cup, circular in form, with scroll handle and spurs, 63mm (2½in). Bradley, Pl. 146. *Mus.* V. & A.

10. *Bell-shaped*

Bell-shaped coffee cup with serrated rim, the flat ear-shaped handle with four irregularly pierced

holes, together with saucer; cup 70 or 76mm (2¾ or 3in) high, saucer 127mm (5in) in diameter. S 12 July 1977, L 130. W.W., Pl. 74; Bradley, Pl. 70 (cup only).

(These cups and saucers invariably seem to be decorated after a *famille verte* Chinese original.) *Mus.* Ashmolean; British; V. & A.

11. *'Trembleuse'*

Two-handled 'trembleuse' cup, together with a stand with open-work gallery to receive the cup; cup 44 or 50mm (1¾ or 2in) high, saucer 133 or 139mm (5¼ or 5½in) in diameter. *Pl. 101. Mus.* Derby; V. & A.

Sugar basins and covers

Smooth deep bowl, with low-domed cover surmounted by a flower and leaf knop, 95mm (3¾in). Bradley, Pl. 168.

Cream ewers

(i) *Ribbed* With pear-shaped ribbed body, sparrow beak spout and scroll handle, 86mm (3⅜in). No illustration.

(ii) *Smooth* With pear-shaped smooth body, sparrow beak spout and loop or scrolled handle, 76 or 82mm (3 or 3¼in). Gil., Col. Pl. VI; Bradley, Pl. 140. *Mus.* V. & A.

Tea poys

Ovoid shaped with flared foot and short narrow cylindrical neck, 146mm (5¾in). Bradley, Pls 165, 166. *Mus.* National, of Wales; V. & A.

Spoon trays

Hexagonal in shape with fluted sides, 139mm (5½in) long. Bradley, Pl. 167. *Mus.* V. & A.

Butter dishes, covers and stands

1. *Square with fluted corners*

Of square form with fluted corners, the high-domed cover surmounted by a floral finial, together with a stand of corresponding shape; dish 67, 95 or 114mm (2⅝, 3¾ or 4½in). S 3 Apr. 1973, L 57 (without cover or stand). W.W., Pl. 76; B. & Th., Pl. 2 (without cover or stand). *Mus.* Derby.

2. *Rectangular with canted corners*

Of rectangular form with canted corners, the

domed cover surmounted by a fruit, 127 or 165mm (5 or 6½in) long. S 18 May 1982, L 170 (without cover). Gil., Pls 33 and 34 (without cover); B. & Th., Pl. 83; Bradley, Pl. 81 (without cover). No example is recorded with the stand. *Mus.* Royal Crown Derby; V. & A.

3. *Cylindrical*
Cylindrical in form with double upright handles, sometimes standing on three legs, sometimes with a flat base, together with low-domed cover and a stand with everted serrated rim; dish 101mm (4in) high, stand 152mm (6in) in diameter. Hobson, Pl. V (1.59) (ascribed to Bow); Gil., *CDP*, Fig. 5; Twitchett, Col. Pl. 14. *Mus.* British; V. & A.

Punch pots, covers and stands
Of nearly globular form, with scrolled handle, the cover surmounted by a knop in the shape of a lemon with leaves, the stand with everted serrated rim, 203 or 215mm (8 or 8½in). *Pl. 102* (without stand). *Mus.* National, of Wales; V. & A.

Punch kettle and cover
Of nearly globular form, with ormolu handle, the cover surmounted by a knop in the shape of a lemon with leaves, 260mm (10¼in), *Col. Pl. H.*

Punch bowls
Circular, standing on a pedestal foot (with lumps of irregular clay applied to the exterior of the foot before glazing), 254mm (10in) in diameter. *Pl. 103. Mus.* V. & A.

Jugs
1. *Ovoid*
(i) Ovoid in form, with pointed lip and scrolled handle, 171, 178, 190 or 228mm (6¾, 7, 7½ or 9in). Schr. Col., No. 319, Pl. 25; Gil., Pl. 49; W.W., front page; Bradley, Pl. 112; Twitchett, Pl. 98. *Mus.* V. & A.

(ii) Ovoid in form, with mask spout and scrolled handle, 152, 158, 165, 171 or 184mm (6, 6¼, 6½, 6¾, or 7¼in). Schr. Col., Nos 328, 333, Pl. 25; W.W., Pl. 72; B. & Th., Pl. 81; Bradley, Pl. 114. *Mus.* Derby; V. & A.

2. *Pear-shaped*
(i) Pear-shaped in form, with pointed lip and

scrolled handle, 146, 158, 215 or 228mm (5¾, 6¼, 8½ or 9in). *Pl. 104. Mus.* V. & A.

(ii) Pear-shaped in form, with mask spout and scrolled handle, 165mm (6½in). *Pl. 105.*

(iii) Pear-shaped in form, with unusually shaped spout and scrolled handle, 228mm (9in). *Col. Pl. G.*

Tankards or mugs
1. *Barrel-shape*
Of barrel-shape form, with raised moulded straps around the body, the loop handle sometimes scrolled, sometimes not, 89, 111, 120, 127, 146 or 171mm (3½, 4⅜, 4¾, 5, 5¾ or 6¾in). *Pl. 96(b). Mus.* City of Manchester Art Galleries; V. & A.

2. *Ovoid-shape*
Of ovoid form, the loop handle sometimes scrolled, sometimes not, 101, 114, 127 or 152mm (4, 4½, 5 or 6in). *Pl. 106. Mus.* V. & A.

3. *Inverted bell-shape*
(i) *Normal version* Of inverted bell-shape, the loop handle sometimes scrolled, sometimes not, 101, 139, 146, 152, 158, 165 or 171mm (4, 5½, 5¾, 6, 6¼, 6½ or 6¾in). *Pl. 99(b). Mus.* British; V. & A.

(ii) *Truncated version* As above but truncated, 82 or 117mm (3¼ or 4⅝in). *Pl. 107.*

4. *Straight-sided*
Straight-sided with scrolled handle, 101 or 127mm (4 or 5in). *Col. Pl. E(b).*

Goblets
Of ovoid form, standing on a small foot, 133mm (5¼in). No illustration. *Mus.* V. & A. (Schr. Col., No. 334).

Dessert plates
1. *'Spectacle'*
The outer rim in the form of a chain of discs or circles linked one to another by a bridge, giving the overall appearance of a series of spectacles.

(i) *Centre with overlapping leaves* Centre moulded with three overlapping leaves, the rim pierced and applied with one or three rows of florettes, 184 or 193mm (7¼ or 7⅝in). *Col. Pl. D(a). Mus.* British; Derby.

(ii) *Smooth centre* (a) *Pierced* Centre smooth,

the rim pierced and applied with one or three rows of florettes, 184 or 190mm (7¼ or 7½in). S 20 Dec. 1972, L 108; S 18 May 1982, L 117.

(b) *Unpierced* Centre smooth, the rim unpierced but applied with three rows of florettes, 184mm (7¼in). W.W., Pl. 39; B. & Th., Pl. 32, Bradley, Pl. 95. *Mus.* Derby.

2. Overlapping leaves and wicker work
(i) *Unpierced* Centre moulded with overlapping leaves extending into a shaped border moulded with a wicker-work pattern, 209mm (8¼in). *Col. Pl. C(a)*.

(ii) *Pierced* Shaped as above, but with pierced border and one/two rows of applied florettes, 203mm (8in). Gil., Pl. 36.

3. Rim with raised scrolling and diagonal wicker-work moulding
(i) *Unpierced* Smooth centre, the rim with raised scrolling (to take painted vignettes) interspersed between diagonal wicker-work moulding applied with florettes, 209mm (8¼in). S 20 Dec. 1972, L 110. Dixon, Pls 32(b), 33(b); *Gil., CDP*, Fig. 13; Gil., Pl. 39; W.W., Pl. 45; *ECC Exh.*, No. 291.

(ii) *Pierced* Shaped as above, but with pierced border, 203 or 219mm (8 or 8⅝in). Gil., Pl. 137; Honey, Pl. 55C; Bradley, Pl. 209. *Mus.* Leeds Art Galleries; V. & A.

4. Twelve-sided
Smooth centre, with shaped twelve-sided rim, 228mm (9in). W.W., Pl. 52.

5. Ten-sided
Smooth centre, with shaped ten-sided rim, 206mm (8⅛in). *Pl. 108(a)*.

6. Feather-moulded border
Smooth centre, with feather-moulded border, 203 or 209mm (8 or 8¼in). *Col. Pl. E(a)* and *Pls 109* and *113(a)*. *Mus.* V. & A.

Dishes
1. Silver-patterned
Modelled, after the silver, with fluted rim and moulded with shells, 203mm (8in) long. W.W., Pl. 41.

2. Diamond-shaped
Diamond-shaped, the border moulded with four shells and panels of four-petalled flowers divided by hoops, 266mm (10½in) long. W.W., Pl. 51.

3. Lobed oval
Oval in form and lobed, 209 or 215mm (8¼ or 8½in) long. S 19 May 1970, L 61. Gil., Pl. 46.

4. Leaf-shaped with wicker-work border
Leaf-shaped with a border moulded with a wicker-work pattern, 254mm (10in) long. *Pl. 110*.

5. Leaf-shaped with five overlapping leaves
Leaf-shaped, modelled as five overlapping leaves with the stalk as the handle, 203mm (8in) long. S 3 Apr. 1973, L 52. Bradley, Pl. 97.

6. Sunflower
In the form of a sunflower, 165mm (6½in) long. *Pl. 111. Mus.* Derby.

7. Peony
In the form of a peony overlaid by a serrated leaf, the rustic handle with bud terminals, 209mm (8¼in) long. *Pl. 112*.

8. Oval with wavy edge
Oval with wavy edge and moulded with floral and other motifs, 152mm (6in) long. Gil., *CDP*, Fig. 14a; Gil., Pl. 35.

9. Oval with elaborately moulded rim
Oval, with the edge of the rim elaborately moulded with a swirling motif, 241mm (9½in) long. B. & Th., Pl. 79; Bradley, Pl. 99. *Mus.* Derby.

10. Oval with vine-moulded rim
(i) Oval, the wavy rim moulded in relief with vine branches bearing grapes and leaves, 178, 209 or 222mm (7, 8¼ or 8¾in) long. *Col. Pl. F. Mus.* Derby; V. & A.

(ii) Shaped essentially as above, but with the crinkled effect of the rim less pronounced, 279mm (11in) long. Honey, Pl. 55A. *Mus.* British; V. & A.

Baskets and stands

1. *Shallow oval*

Shallow oval in form, with wavy rim and twin single- or double-rope handles, the exterior moulded with a diagonal wicker-work pattern applied with florettes at the intersections. Matching stand.

(i) *With solid sides* 139, 228, 244, 279 or 292mm (5½, 9, 9⅝, 11 or 11½in) long. S 3 Apr. 1973, L 56; 17 July 1973, L 143. Gil., Pl. 45; Bradley, Pl. 102. *Mus*. V. & A.

(ii) *With pierced sides* 241, 266, 273, 279 or 292mm (9½, 10½, 10¾, 11 or 11½in) long. C 22 Feb. 1971, L 61 and 62; S 14 May 1974, L 43; 24 Oct. 1978, L 47; 8 July 1980, L 118; 16 Feb. 1982, L 91, 93. Bradley, Pl. 107; Twitchett, Pl. 100. *Mus*. National, of Wales; V. & A.

2. *Shallow oval, variant form*

Shallow oval in shape, with wavy rim, twin single- or double-rope handles and a single row of applied florettes at the top of the rim, the unpierced external moulding taking the form of a basket-weave pattern, 95, 139 or 152mm (3¾, 5½ or 6in) long. *Pl. 114* (pair of baskets with stands). *Mus*. V. & A.

3. *Deep circular*

Deep circular in form, with everted wavy rim, the pierced exterior moulded with a diagonal wicker-work pattern applied with florettes at the intersections, the twin handles with single or double ropes. Matching stand. Basket 152, 155, 165, 171, 178 or 184mm (6, 6⅛, 6½, 6¾, 7 or 7¼in) in diameter. *Pl. 115*. *Mus*. Derby; V. & A.

4. *'Spectacle'*

(i) *Shallow oval* As No. 1 (ii) above restricted to double-rope handles, except that the edge of the rim consists of a chain of pierced circles or discs linked one to another by a bridge, giving the appearance of a row of spectacles. Matching stand. Basket 152, 196, 203 or 215mm (6, 7¾, 8 or 8½in) long. *Pl. 113(b)*. *Mus*. V. & A.

(ii) *Deep circular* As No. 3 above restricted to single-rope handles, except that the rim consists of a chain of pierced circles or discs linked one to another by a bridge, giving the appearance of a row of spectacles; 120 or 184mm (4¾ or 7¼in) in diameter. *Pl. 116*. *Mus*. V. & A.

5. *Oval with everted rim*

Oval in shape with wavy everted rim and twin double-rope handles, the exterior moulded with a diagonal wicker-work pattern. Matching stand. 247mm (9¾in) long. *Pl. 117*. *Mus*. V. & A.

6. *Chestnut*

(i) *Circular* Circular in shape, moulded in relief with flowers and leaves against a wicker-work moulded background, the domed cover pierced and surmounted by a loop finial. Matching stand. Basket 165, 178 or 193mm (6½, 7 or 7⅝in) in diameter. *Pl. 118* (without stand). *Mus*. Derby; V. & A.

(ii) *Oval* Oval in shape, with twin twig handles terminating in flowering branches, the exterior moulded with flower-heads, together with domed pierced cover surmounted by a twig finial, and matching lozenge-shaped stand, 260mm (10¼in) long. *Pl. 119* (a pair).

7. *Fluted*

Oval in form, with twin single-rope handles and with fluted sides, and applied at the rim with one row of florettes, 89mm (3½in) long. Bradley, Pl. 103.

8. *Deep oval with central handle*

Deep oval, with single central handle, encrusted with flowers at the top of the rim, the sides moulded with a basket-weave pattern, 152mm (6in) long. *Pl. 120* (a pair).

9. *Eel*

Oviform and moulded with wicker work, the sleeve and flared neck pierced, the handles modelled as bulrushes and the rock-work base applied with two ducks, 215 or 241mm (8½ or 9½in). *Pl. 121* (set of three).

10. *Deep circular with a cover surmounted by a bird*

Deep circular, with florettes applied on the outside at the points of intersection of the moulded diagonal wicker-work pattern, supported on a rococo scrolled base, the cover surmounted by a bird among flowers and leaves, 127mm (5in). *Pl. 122* (a pair). *Mus*. V. & A.

Tureens and covers

1. Pigeon

In the form of a pigeon with a ruff seated on an oval-shaped nest, the lower half of which is moulded and applied with simulated straw and leaves, 184, 209, 215 or 222mm (7¼, 8¼, 8½ or 8¾in) long. *Pl. 123* (a pair).

(For an example without a ruff see S 16 Feb. 1982, L 92.)

Mus. Cecil Higgins.

2. Partridge

In the form of a partridge, head turned and seated on an oval-shaped nest edged with corn, mosses and twigs, 120, 127, 152 or 165mm (4¾, 5, 6 or 6½in) long. *Pl. 124* (a pair). *Mus.* V. & A.

3. Quatrefoil

Of quatrefoil shape with domed cover surmounted by a cherry resting on leaves, together with matching stand and ladle; tureen 127mm (5in) high. *Pl. 125* (without stand). *Mus.* V. & A. (without stand).

4. Grape

In the form of a bunch of grapes resting on and partially covered by vine leaves, 120mm (4¾in) long. *Pl. 126*.

Sauceboats

1. Plaice

In the form of a plaice with the tail curled round to form the handle of the boat, the cover with a handle modelled as acanthus foliage, 241mm (9½in) long. *Pl. 127* (a pair).

2. Leaf-shaped

In the form of overlapping leaves, with curled twig handle, one side ornamented with a moulded fruit and applied leaves, 89, 127, 165 or 184mm (3½, 5, 6½ or 7¼in) long. *Pl. 128*. *Mus.* British; Cecil Higgins; V. & A.

3. Lobed with elaborate scroll handle

Lobed in form, with a double line moulding around the rim and an elaborate scroll handle, 228mm (9in) long. Bradley, Pl. 197. *Mus.* V. & A.

4. Lobed with looped handle

Lobed, with scalloped rim and looped handle, 127, 178 or 203mm (5, 7 or 8in) long.

(i) *On pedestal foot Pl. 100(a). Mus.* Royal Crown Derby.

(ii) *On almost flat base* W.W., Pl. 77.

5. Decoratively moulded

Moulded on the outside with decorative ornament, the handle being of scrolled shape, 178, 196, 203, 209 or 222mm (7, 7¾, 8, 8¼ or 8¾in) long. S 18 May 1982, L 112, 167. Gil., *CDP*, Figs 117, 124; Gil., Pl. 45; Bradley, Pl. 85; Twitchett, Pl. 29. *Mus.* British; V. & A.

6. Helmet-shaped (after the silver)

Helmet-shaped, with shell-moulded sides, on a pedestal foot with high scroll handle, 89 or 139mm (3½ or 5½in) long. S 18 May 1982, L 169. Gil., *CDP*, Figs 122, 123; Bradley, Pls 196, 198. *Mus.* British; Derby; V. & A.

7. Branch-handled

V-shaped with branch handle, 165mm (6½in) long. B. & Th., Pl. 34. *Mus.* Derby.

Centrepieces

1. Shell

Modelled with two or three tiers of scallop-shell containers, standing on a mound of rock-work and weeds encrusted with smaller shells, and generally surmounted by a kingfisher or human figure, in the latter case sometimes holding a shell over his head, 158, 175, 228, 247, 266, 375, 413 or 460mm (6¼, 6⅞, 9, 9¾, 10½, 14¾, 16¼ or 18⅛in). *Pl. 129*. *Mus.* Derby; Cecil Higgins; V. & A.

2. Pillar

In the form of a shaped round pillar or column with square holes from which extend metallic supports holding porcelain flowers, 330mm (13in). Gil., *CDP*, Fig. 8 (without supports or porcelain flowers).

Ice pails

Of four-lobed shape with two scroll handles immediately below the circular rim, 120mm

(4¾in). Bradley, Col. Pl. at p. 46, and Pl. 108. *Mus*. City of Manchester Art Galleries; V. & A.

Cruet pieces

1. *Complete set* consisting of vinegar bottle, oil bottle, sugar sifter, pepper pot and mustard pot, each with silver top, 108 to 158mm (4¼ to 6¼in). *Pl. 130. Mus*. Derby (sugar sifter only); V. & A.

2. *Mustard pot*
Cylindrical in form with reeded exterior and smooth sleeve, the cover (likewise reeded) surmounted by a floral finial and with a cut-out to take a spoon, 89mm (3½in). Bradley, Pl. 84.

Salts

1. Scallop shells
In the form of three deep scallop shells resting on a coral- and shell-encrusted base and surmounted by a conch shell, 101mm (4in). Twitchett, Col. Pl. 11. *Mus*. V. & A.

2. Satyr's mask handles
Of depressed globular form, with twin satyr's mask handles, standing on a high-domed foot, the moulded cover surmounted by a flower finial, 76, 89, 92 or 95mm (3, 3½, 3⅝ or 3¾in). *Pl. 131. Mus*. V. & A.

3. Lion paw feet
In the shape of a shallow cup with applied mayflowers ('schneeballen') standing on three lion paw feet, 50mm (2in). Bradley, Pl. 80. *Mus*. V. & A.

4. Wish-bone handle
In the form of a depressed globular bowl with wish-bone-shape handle, standing on a circular pedestal foot 44mm (1¾in). Bradley, Pl. 75.

Broth bowl and cover

Circular, with double scroll handles, the slightly domed cover surmounted by a flower finial, 215mm (8½in) in diameter. Bradley, Pl. 92, Col. Pl. at p. 45.

Pickle/oyster/sweetmeat dish/winetaster

Small shallow circular dish of lobed form with cut-out or shaped handle, 76mm (3in) long. Gil., Pl. 139; Bradley, Pls 221, 222.

Pickle dish

Moulded as overlapping geranium leaves with rustic loop handle, 82mm (3¼in) in diameter. Bradley, Pl. 186.

Asparagus butter boat

Moulded as a leaf with rustic handle, 70mm (2¾in) long. Bradley, Pls 187, 188.

A variant marked with a script 'N' painted in red is illustrated in Hurlbutt, Pl. 4.

APPENDIX 4—ORNAMENTAL WARE

This appendix contains a cross-section of ornamental ware produced during the period from 1756 to 1770. See also Appendix 1 for notes on references and measurements.

Vases

1. Mazarine blue Garniture comprising:

(i) a centre vase of ovoid shape, with short straight neck and double scrolled handles applied with floral terminals; and

(ii) two flanking vases of similar shape, but with flared neck, the covers of each vase encrusted with flowers, 292mm ($11\frac{1}{2}$in) (centre vase) and 266mm ($10\frac{1}{2}$in) (flanking vases).

(A somewhat larger version was also produced where the centre vase is 324mm ($12\frac{3}{4}$in).)

(Note: these vases seem invariably to be decorated with a mazarine blue ground.)

Pl. 132. Mus. British; Derby; Luton Hoo; V. & A. (centre vase).

2. Eight-lobed
Of eight-lobed form, with generously splayed foot and with leaf moulding towards the base, the top of the body applied with a variety of large and small flowers, 222mm ($8\frac{3}{4}$in). *Pl. 133(b).*

3. 'Parfum' burner
Of bulbous shape (the sides with pierced scrollwork) on a raised splayed foot, the tall domed cover surmounted by a floral cluster knop, 241mm ($9\frac{1}{2}$in). *Pl. 133(a)* and *(c)* (a pair).

(Note: the same vase with moulded scrollwork unpierced—and accordingly not a potpourri vase—and with encrusted flowers was also produced.)

B. & Th., Pl. 29 (without cover); Bradley, Pl. 117 (without cover).

4. Pear-shaped with domed cover
(i) *Long-necked* Pear-shaped with long neck, standing on a circular base, both the vase and the domed cover encrusted with flowers, 190 or 203mm ($7\frac{1}{2}$ or 8in). *Pl. 108(b).*

(ii) *Short-necked* Pear-shaped with high waist and short neck, standing on a circular base, both the vase and the domed cover encrusted with flowers, 215 or 228mm ($8\frac{1}{2}$ or 9in). B. & Th., Pl. 28; *The Connoisseur*, Jan. 1933, Pl. V, p. 17. *Mus.* Royal Crown Derby.

5. Frill
(i) *Baluster-shape* Garniture comprising:

(a) centre vase of baluster-shape with pierced rounded shoulders and galleried neck, sometimes with, sometimes without, twin female masks, the pierced high-domed cover surmounted by a bird; and

(b) two flanking vases, each of beaker shape with pierced flared top, the low-domed cover encrusted with flowers and surmounted by a bird.

All the vases applied with flowers and characterised by a frill of shell-shaped leaves towards the base. The centre vase 215, 292 or 349mm ($8\frac{1}{2}$, $11\frac{1}{2}$ or $13\frac{3}{4}$in), the flanking vases, when accompanying a 292mm ($11\frac{1}{2}$in) centre vase, 241mm ($9\frac{1}{2}$in). *Pl. 135. Mus.* British (centre vase); Derby (centre vase); Luton Hoo; Royal Crown Derby (centre vase); V. & A. (centre vase).

(ii) *Asymmetrical* Garniture consisting of:

(a) centre vase, asymmetrical in form, with

elaborate rococo moulding, the flower-encrusted high-domed cover surmounted by a shaped finial; and

(b) two flanking vases, each with shaped pierced tops and with twin scrolled handles.

All the vases applied with flowers and characterised by a swirling frill towards the base. Centre vase 305mm (12in), flanking vases 190mm ($7\frac{1}{2}$in). *Pl. 136* (flanking vase only). Gil., *CDP*, Fig. 3; Savage, *18th-Century English Porcelain*, Pl. 69(a) (centre vase only).

(Note: the flanking vases probably had covers now lost. For a vase of this shape with a lid appears in an advertisement of Law Foulsham & Cole on the inside front cover of *The Connoisseur*, May 1924.)

6. Asymmetrical with rococo moulding

(i) Asymmetrical with elaborate rococo moulding, standing on a circular pedestal foot and filled at the top with a cluster of applied flowers, 89 or 117mm ($3\frac{1}{2}$ or $4\frac{5}{8}$in). *Pl. 137* (a pair). *Mus.* British; V. & A.

(ii) Asymmetrical with elaborate rococo fluting and moulding and with twin scroll handles, standing on a shaped foot and filled at the top with a cluster of applied flowers. C 15 June 1970, L 236 (on an ormolu base—222mm ($8\frac{3}{4}$in)).

(iii) As (i) above, except that the top of the neck is shaped and the cluster of applied flowers is absent, 171mm ($6\frac{3}{4}$in). *Pl. 138. Mus.* British; V. & A.

(iv) Substantially as (iii) above, except that the top of the neck is flat, suggesting that this type of vase was supplied with a cover, 228mm (9in). B. & Th., Pl. 75; W.W., Pl. 32. *Mus.* British; Derby.

(v) Asymmetrical with elaborate rococo fluting and moulding without handles, 196mm ($7\frac{3}{4}$in). *Pl. 143*.

7. Figure-applied

Large vase of elaborate rococo form, standing on a widely spreading shaped base, with the figure of Venus on one side and Cupid on the other, 305mm (12in). *Pl. 139*.

8. Dolphin-handled

Large rococo style vase with twin handles in the form of dolphins and with moulded masks at the front and rear, 260mm ($10\frac{1}{4}$in). *Pl. 140. Mus.* V. & A.

9. Urn-shaped

Urn-shaped with fluted neck and foot, the twin shell-shaped scroll handles festooned with applied flowers, the pierced cover surmounted by a fruit knop, 318mm ($12\frac{1}{2}$in). *Pl. 141*.

10. Sugar-caster shaped

Similar to a sugar-caster in shape and filled at the top with a cluster of flowers, 171mm ($6\frac{3}{4}$in). *Pl. 142. Mus.* V. & A.

11. Rectangular-panelled

Tall with four rectangular-panelled sides flaring outwards, shoulder panels and flared neck ending in a square rim, after the Chinese, 254mm (10in). Bradley, Pl. 119. *Mus.* City Art Gallery, Bristol; V. & A.

12. Mayflower

(i) Cone-shaped, encrusted all over with mayflowers ('schneeballen'), the cover surmounted by a cluster of berries and leaves, 178mm (7in). W.W., Pl. 80.

(Note: a variant without applied mayflowers, but with a single-stemmed branch rising spirally around the vase, albeit without the cover, is shown in Bradley, Pl. 82.)

(ii) Of square baluster form encrusted all over with mayflowers ('schneeballen'), the domed cover surmounted by berries, the body of the vase sporadically applied with holly sprays, 228 or 279mm (9 or 11in). *The Connoisseur*, Jan. 1933, Pl. VI, p. 17; Hobson, Fig. 28 (II 23) (without cover) (ascribed to Chelsea). *Mus.* British (without cover).

13. Scroll-handled

Tall, ovoid in form, with flared neck and base, the distinctive twin handles intricately scrolled, 305mm (12in). Godden, *Illustrated Encyclopaedia of British Pottery and Porcelain*, Pl. 214.

(Note: presumably this type of vase had a cover but no example is recorded.)

14. Ovoid with flared neck

Ovoid in form with flared neck, standing on a

round splayed foot, 127 or 139mm (5 or 5½in). S 17 July 1973, L 185. Bradley, Col. Pl. at p. 99. Slight variant—Bradley, Pl. 224.

15. Ovoid with looped handles and cover
Ovoid in shape, with slightly flared neck, twin loop handles and domed cover surmounted by a finial, 292mm (11½in). Savage, *English Pottery and Porcelain*, Pl. 139. *Mus.* Hastings Museum and Art Gallery.

Inkstands
1. The shaped and scroll-moulded rectangular stand (supported on five scroll feet) holding a pen-tray and cover (the finial of which is composed of two Bacchic boys, a goat and bunches of grapes), an inkwell and cover, a pounce pot and cover and a small candlestick, 260 or 247mm (10¼ or 9¾in) long. *Pl. 144. Mus.* V. & A. (without the inkwell and cover, the pounce pot and cover and the small candlestick).

2. Substantially as above, but without the five scroll feet supports, 190 or 203mm (7½ or 8in) long. S 24 Oct. 1978, L 53. B. & Th., Pl. 80; Twitchett, Pl. 32. *Mus.* British; Derby.

Guglets and basins
The guglet or bottle bulbous in shape with long neck, projecting ring near the top and slightly flared mouth, the basin circular in form; bottle 228 or 235mm (9 or 9¼in). *Pl. 145* (pair without the basins); Bradley, Pl. 228 (basin, 228mm (9in) in diameter). *Mus.* (without basin) British; Derby; Leeds Arts Galleries; V. & A.

Toilet boxes and covers
(i) *Rose*
In the form of a rose, the handle of the cover composed of a prickly twig and bud and leaves, 76mm (3in). *Pl. 146.*

(ii) *Apple*
In the form of an apple, with loop handle, the cover surmounted by a floral knop, 76mm (3in). Gil., Pl. 30.

(iii) *Peach*
In the form of a peach, with loop handle, the cover applied with leaves and a flower, 76mm (3in). *Pl. 147. Mus.* Derby; V. & A.

(iv) *Lemon*
In the form of a lemon with naturalistic surface, the cover surmounted by a floral spray with buds and leaves, 89mm (3½in). S 16 July 1982, L 7.

(v) *Cylindrical*
Cylindrical in form, with low-domed cover surmounted by a flower finial with moulded leaves, 76mm (3in). Gil., *CDP*, Fig. 14; Bradley, Pl. 126.
    Sometimes encrusted with mayflowers. *The Connoisseur*, Jan. 1933, Pl. VI, p. 17.

Flower pots
(i) Of slightly flaring form, moulded with horizontal bands, containing bouquets of flowers in full relief, 178mm (7in). *Pl. 148* (a pair). *Mus.* V. & A.

(ii) As (i) above, but with flowers arranged in pyramidic form, 127 or 203mm (5 or 8in). Gil., Pl. 150; Bradley, Pl. 123.

(iii) Flared, with twin shaped handles, containing flowers in full relief arranged in pyramidic form. No illustration. *Mus.* V. & A.

(iv) Flared, without handles or moulded decoration or flowers, together with stand, 101 or 114mm (4 or 4½in). C 15 Feb. 1982, L 62; 19 Apr. 1982, L 77.

Dovecotes
In the form of a flower-encrusted 'perfume pot', the necessary perforations representing nests which applied doves are seen to be entering or leaving; a dog at the base sniffs the steps leading to the door of the building; the domed cover is surmounted by a bird with outstretched wings, 546mm (21½in). B. & Th., Col. Pl. B.

Cornucopia or wall pockets
Horn-shaped, with elaborate scrollwork moulding, the top pierced to hold flowers, 254mm (10in). B. & Th., Pl. 78; W.W., Col. Pl. 61.

Chamber candlesticks
(i) The base of circular quarter-lobe form with a

raised centre surmounted by a shaped candle nozzle, the twig handle twisted in shape with an applied flower thumb rest, 63, 76 or 82mm (2½, 3 or 3¼in). S 26 Nov. 1974, L 74; 7 Nov. 1978, L 110; C 9 Feb. 1981, L 161. Bradley, Pls 127, 128 and 230.

(ii) The base of lozenge-shape with a wavy upturned edge, the candle nozzle in the centre, the handle shaped, 127mm (5in) long. Bradley, Pl. 229.

(iii) The base shaped as a leaf, the domed centre surmounted by a shaped candle nozzle, the handle scrolled, 158mm (6¼in) long. *Pl. 149.*

Pastille-burners
In the form of a cone decorated with applied mayflowers, except on four small spaces near the top which are perforated, the top surmounted by a rose, 149mm (5⅞in). No illustration. *Mus. V. & A.*

CHRONOLOGICAL
BIBLIOGRAPHY

Francis Barlow, *Aesop's Fables*, 1665

——, *Royal Society's Journal Book*, February 1742–3

Rouquet, *Present State of the Arts*, 1755

Letters of Josiah Wedgwood 1762–95

Anonymous, *A Short Tour in the Midland Counties of England Performed in the Summer of 1772*, 1775

Notice in *British Magazine & Review*, October 1782

Pilkington, *View of the Present State of Derbyshire*, 1789

William Hutton, *History of Derby*, 1791

——, *Gentleman's Magazine*, 1799

Cecil, *Memoirs of Bacon*, 1801

Lysons', *Derbyshire of 1817*

—, *Manchester Commercial Directories* for 1818, 1819 and 1820

Cunningham, *Lives of the Most Eminent British Sculptors and Artists*, 1830

Various notices in *Public Advertiser, Derby Mercury, Aris's Birmingham Gazette*

A. Wallis and W. Bemrose, *The Pottery and Porcelain of Derbyshire*, 1870

Hugh Owen, *Two Centuries of Ceramic Art in Bristol*, 1873

William Chaffers, *Marks and Monograms on Pottery and Porcelain*, 4th edn 1874, 8th edn 1897

J. Haslem, *The Old Derby China Factory*, 1876

L. Jewitt, *Ceramic Art in Great Britain* (two vols), 1878

J. E. Nightingale, *Contributions towards the History of Early English Porcelain*, 1881

William Bemrose, *Bow, Chelsea and Derby Porcelain*, 1898

R. L. Hobson, *Catalogue of the Collection of English Porcelain in the British Museum*, 1905

W. Moore Binns, *The First Century of English Porcelain*, 1906

William Bemrose, *Longton Hall Porcelain*, 1906

R. L. Hobson, *Worcester Porcelain*, 1910

Lady Charlotte Schreiber, *Journals* (two vols), 1911

Bernard Rackham, *Catalogue of the Herbert Allen Collection of English Porcelain*, 1923

Reginald Blunt (ed.), *The Cheyne Book of Chelsea China and Pottery*, 1924

F. Hurlbutt, *Old Derby Porcelain*, 1925

William King, *English Porcelain Figures of the Eighteenth Century*, 1925

Edward Hyam, *The Early Period of Derby Porcelain*, 1926

W. B. Honey, *Old English Porcelain*, 1928, 3rd edn 1977

Bernard Rackham, *Catalogue of the Schreiber Collection of English Porcelain*, revised 1928

Mrs Donald MacAlister, *William Duesbury: London Account Book 1751–53*, 1931

Frank Hurlbutt, *Chelsea China*, 1937

——, *English Ceramic Circle, Commemorative Catalogue of an Exhibition held at the Victoria & Albert Museum, May 5–June 20 1948*, 1949

F. Brayshaw Gilhespie, *Crown Derby Porcelain* 1951

George Savage, *18th-Century English Porcelain*, 1952

J. L. Dixon, *English Porcelain of the Eighteenth Century*, 1952

Reginald G. Haggar, *Staffordshire Chimney Ornaments*, 1955

Frank Stonor, *Chelsea, Bow and Derby Porcelain Figures*, 1955

Yvonne Hackenbroch, *Chelsea and Other English Porcelain, Pottery and Enamel in the Untermyer Collection*, 1957

Bernard Watney, *Longton Hall Porcelain*, 1957

Wolf Mankowitz and Reginald L. Haggar, *The Concise Encyclopaedia of English Pottery and Porcelain*, 1957

Arthur Lane, *English Porcelain Figures of the Eighteenth Century*, 1961

George Savage, *English Pottery and Porcelain*, 1961

F. Brayshaw Gilhespie, *Derby Porcelain*, 1961

M. Whinney, *Sculpture in Britain 1530–1830*, 1964

Geoffrey Wills, *The Country Life Book of English China*, 1964

G. A. Godden, *Illustrated Encyclopaedia of British Pottery and Porcelain*, 1966

Franklin A. Barrett and Arthur L. Thorpe, *Derby Porcelain*, 1971

Hugo Morley-Fletcher, *Meissen Porcelain in Colour*, 1971 (republished 1979)

Winifred Williams, Catalogue of *Early Derby Porcelain 1750–70*, 1973

John Cushion, *Continental Porcelain*, 1974

S. Ducret, *The Colour Treasury of Eighteenth Century Porcelain*, 1976

H. G. Bradley (ed.), *Ceramics of Derbyshire*, 1978

Paul J. Atterbury (ed.), *European Pottery and Porcelain*, 1979

John Twitchett, *Derby Porcelain*, 1980

Robin Reilly and George Savage, *The Dictionary of Wedgwood*, 1980

Peter Bradshaw, *18th-Century English Porcelain Figures 1745–1795*, 1981

Various articles from *The Connoisseur*, *Apollo*, *Burlington Magazine*, *English Porcelain Circle ('EPC') Transactions*, *English Ceramic Circle ('ECC') Transactions*, *Journal of the Royal Society of Arts*.

ACKNOWLEDGEMENTS

I am deeply indebted to Christie Manson & Woods Ltd and Sotheby Parke Bernet & Co. for their generous provision of photographs of pieces which have over the years passed through their sale-rooms, and for their permission to reproduce them here. I am similarly indebted to the Victoria and Albert Museum, whose staff have been most painstaking in dealing with my enquiries, to the Trustees of the British Museum, to the Trustees of the Werner Collection at Luton Hoo, to Albert Amor Ltd, to Delomosne & Son Ltd, to Klaber & Klaber and to Winifred Williams, London, for photographs and consent to reproduce.

I would like to express my special gratitude to Mr Anton Gabszewicz, of Christie Manson & Woods Ltd, for his assistance with the supply of photographs and for his encouragement generally. I am similarly grateful for the various conversations about early Derby porcelain which I have enjoyed with Mr Robert Williams, of Winifred Williams, London. Mr Hugh Tait of the British Museum went to a great deal of trouble to show me the collection of early Derby porcelain in his charge and to make available suitable photographs. Mr Urwick Smith rendered a like service with regard to the Werner Collection at Luton Hoo, of which he is the curator. I am indebted to them both. I must also record my thanks to Miss J. E. Poole, assistant keeper of applied art at the Fitzwilliam Museum, and to Miss Halina Grubert, curator of the Cecil Higgins Art Gallery, for their help in answering queries relating to the collections in their charge. The colour photography was skilfully undertaken by Messrs Richard P. Miller and Alan G. Tabor. My acknowledgements would not, however, be complete if I did not record the help that I have received from my wife, whose keen powers of observation and remarkably retentive visual memory have resolved questions which would otherwise have gone unanswered.

INDEX